Practical Pig Keeping

PRACTICAL PIG KEEPING

Paul Smith

The Crowood Press

First published in 2001 by
The Crowood Press Ltd
Ramsbury, Marlborough
Wiltshire SN8 2HR

British Library Cataloguing-in-Publication Data
A catalogue record for this book is available from the British
Library.

ISBN 1 86126 388 0

Dedication
To Mavis, the girl I met in Primary School who became my wife.
She has not only tolerated my 'pig brain', but has positively
encouraged me throughout my career.

Acknowledgements
Having grown, and sometimes withered, on the 'pig vine' for over a
quarter of a century, it is inevitable that I lent on it for support
when approaching unchartered territory.

I am grateful to fellow-consultant Bernard Peet for his encour-
agement, and for much help from the Meat & Livestock
Commission. Helpful comments are appreciated from Keith
Poulson and his colleagues at Rattlerow Farms Ltd; Paul Penny at
JSR Healthbred Ltd; and Kevin Stickney of Farm Nutrition.
Thanks are also due to Roger Jones of BOCM-Pauls Ltd; David
Wilby of Tuckbox Ltd; Suffolk vet Alastair Douglas; and Nick
Manderfield of Breckland Farms Ltd.

Special thanks go to my ex-ADAS colleagues Sandra Edwards
and Jonathan Green. I am also most grateful to Sarah Wiltshire,
who started typing for me in 1989 and hasn't stopped since.

Line illustrations by David Fisher

Typeset by Carreg Limited, Ross-on-Wye, Herefordshire

Printed and bound in Great Britain by Antony Rowe, Chippenham

Contents

Introduction

We share our world with around 800 million pigs, about half of which live in the People's Republic of China. In the UK, people outnumber pigs by a factor of around 7:1, whereas in Holland pig numbers almost equate with the human headcount. In Denmark pigs have the upper hand, since there are more than twice as many pigs as people.

Modern sows are highly prolific and their offspring have the potential for rapid growth, hence the pig industry can quickly expand to compensate for, and will invariably exceed, any temporary shortfall in production. The notorious 'pig cycle' reflects fluctuations in prices both within the EU and increasingly on a global scale. This is all not such good news for those who would like subsidies, because an industry which can be rapidly expanded – and moreover one which has the potential to pollute the environment – understandably fails to attract government subsidies. Economists acknowledge that the pig job survives and succumbs in the 'perfect marketplace' in that it ultimately becomes self-regulating because of supply and demand.

Temporary production gluts in some countries tend to obscure the overall picture. Global consumption of pigmeat looks set for growth, particularly as inhabitants of the Asian Pacific Region strive to add meat to their diet, and this increase might be as much as 2 to 4 per cent per annum for the foreseeable future. This should provide opportunities for countries with the capability of trading pigmeat of a defined specification on world markets. Environmental constraints suggest that countries with a sustainable balance between pigs, land and people are most likely to have a long-term future in pig production.

Pigmeat consumption levels are to some extent influenced by the vagaries of the pig cycle, though in general within Europe these levels increased during the 1970s and 1980s, but flattened out in the 1990s.

However, the vast fluctuations recorded between the individual European countries reflect their diversity in climate, culinary habits and social factors. Within the EU, consumers in the United Kingdom and Greece apparently eat pigmeat with a wooden spoon. In 1998, average UK consumption was a lowly 25.1kg (55.3lb) per person as compared to an EU

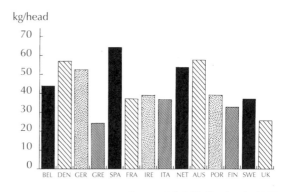

Source: MLC Pig Yearbook, 1999

EU per capita pig meat consumption in 1998.

average of 44.1kg (97.2lb). Since the UK bacon market is only 49 per cent self-sufficient, and the pork market does no better than hover around self-sufficiency, the figures indicate a potential for increased consumption. In 1997, overall UK self-sufficiency in pigmeat production was 79 per cent, but it plummeted thereafter as a result of the strong pound and a huge influx of cheap imports from systems of production rated illegal in the UK.

Market researchers Taylor Nelson Sofres continually monitor household consumption of all meats within the UK: a cross-section of 10,000 households are equipped with bar scanners which record their in-home meat consumption, and for example in 1998, 24 per cent of total household meat consumption comprised pigmeat.

In particular this market research has highlighted the success of the UK poultry industry, which has made an impressive step forward by marketing poultry as a convenience food, and by creating value-added products. In the same way, consumption of pigmeat in UK homes is likely to increase if pigmeat processors can bring lean, novel food products to the market place. Thus pig farmers must recognize the importance of working along-side abattoirs and processors, and striving to develop new markets in the pig-meat product industry.

Home consumption of meat products only tells part of the story. Forecasts suggest that by the year 2010 between 30 and 40 per cent of all meat sales will go through catering outlets – around three times higher than the level of a decade earlier. Furthermore, as UK consumers increasingly travel abroad, there is every likelihood that their eating habits will reflect more closely those of mainland Europe, and these shifts in consumer demand will in particular become apparent on the menus of catering establishments. However, the UK pig industry should benefit from these forecasted changes, particularly if UK consumers are encouraged to recognize the advantages of good animal welfare, and of product traceability.

Within Europe, the UK pig industry is unique in its commitment to both indoor intensive pig production as well as indoor straw-based production, and also extensive outdoor systems. Intensive pig farming facilitates large-scale production and labour efficiency, but it bears the disadvantage of not being sufficiently differentiated from mainstream European pig production, and also it is perceived as being less pig-friendly than more extensive systems. Whereas many UK consumers claim to prefer pigmeat from extensive systems, relatively few are prepared to pay premium prices to reward the farmer for the hassle involved. Some systems are a hybrid between indoor and outdoor production policies, their aim being to maximize the advantages of both systems. This situation does little for product differentiation and, along with 'foggy labelling' at the point of sale, tends to confuse consumers who would really like to know where their purchases came from, and struggle to do so.

The June 1998 pig census indicated

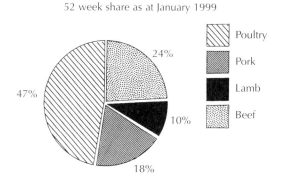

52 week share as at January 1999

Poultry
Pork
Lamb
Beef

24%
47%
10%
18%

Source: Taylor Nelson Sofres

Percentage volume share of total UK meat market.

marked polarization in herd size within the UK. There were 9,896 holdings with sows, 50 per cent of these being hobby farmers with between one and ten sows, and 29 per cent with more than 100 sows. These larger producers between them owned 83 per cent of the UK herd, and would be the focus of supermarket buyers. Indeed, as vertical integration continues, so will the trend towards larger herd sizes – though this in turn should provide opportunities for small-scale producers dedicated to differentiated outlets.

A marked production feature from the mid-eighties has been a swing towards outdoor pig farming; current estimates suggest that around 30 per cent of the UK herd was outdoors in the year 2000. The availability of suitable land is a limiting factor, but otherwise – in view of high building costs, planning constraints and electricity charges associated with indoor units, along with anticipated increased consumer preference for pig-friendly systems – this sector looks set for growth. Lower labour costs are also a feature of outdoor production.

On the other hand, despite the marketeer's obsession with the perception of improved pig welfare, pig farmers have to confront the reality of production, fifty-two weeks of the year. Thus those charged with carting straw bales in storm conditions to replenish wet bedded areas under sometimes airborne ark units do not see enhanced welfare as such a clear-cut issue in the great outdoors. Indeed, in the wrong environment, outdoor production can be a disaster: the system demands light, free-draining soils overlying sand, chalk or gravel, and annual rainfall should not exceed 30in (76cm) – and this upper limit is governed by factors such as shelter and soil type.

The shift outdoors, coupled with a trend to increased slaughterweights, has led to the emergence of a new market for robust weaners. Traditionally weaners were sold at 30kg (66lb) liveweight aged ten to eleven weeks, but increasingly weaners from large outdoor units are sold direct from the field at twenty-four to thirty-one days of age when weighing around 7kg (15lb) liveweight; however, disease can be a problem. This market is driven by vertical integrators, and realization prices are particularly sensitive to the extremes of supply and demand. On many breeding-only units, weaners are still sold at 30kg (66lb); however, this market looks set to decline with the move towards three-site production – finishers are reluctant to pay the extra costs associated with small loads of weaners.

Information from the Meat and Livestock Commission (MLC) indicates three main deadweight bandings for slaughter pigs. Improved genetics have resulted in less backfat in pig carcases and a higher lean meat content; consequently pig slaughter weights tend to be on the increase. By 1998, carcase weights of 60kg (132lb) and above represented 91 per cent of all slaughterings, and the trend to produce carcases in the 75kg–80kg (165–176lb) deadweight range (100 to 106kg (220–234lb) liveweight) looks set to continue as British producers exploit genetic improvements, and strive to reduce fixed costs to those of producers in mainland Europe.

Pigmeat is now recognized as an important component of a healthy diet. It has less saturated fat content than other red meats, and in the future pig diets are likely to be manipulated to benefit the health of the consumer: for instance, higher rates of omega-3 fatty acids such as those found in fish oils could be fed in the late finishing stages, resulting in a healthier and value-added pork product. Pigmeat is also a good source of protein; it is rich in minerals, especially iron, copper and zinc which in particular are known to be vital in the diets of infants and adolescent females; and it is a prime source of vitamin B12, which if in deficit, can cause pernicious anaemia.

Data from the Royal Society of Chemistry, and the Ministry of Agriculture, Fisheries and Food, suggested that food tables published in the 1970s failed to take account of the lower fat content of modern pigmeat. Since then the tables have been revised, and have been used to re-analyse research undertaken in 1996 at Liverpool University on the diet and growth of vegetarian children: this indicated that the fat intake of meat-eating children is now below that of vegetarians.

Vertical integration of the poultry industry has enabled close relationships to be moulded between its farmers, processors and retailers; this has led to product differentiation, and increasingly

pig farmers are expected to follow this route. Meat products created from pigs of known genetics, produced on specified feeds, and raised on a particular system, will become more widespread, and such a management policy offers opportunities to both small, specialist producers and those involved in large-scale production supplying volume sales. In particular, smaller producers could benefit from farm gate sales as consumers demand a closer link with their suppliers. Internet shopping also provides an opportunity to bring the pig producer and consumer closer together.

Globally, pork is the most important single source of meat, providing nearly twice as many calories as cattle, four times as many as poultry, and ten times as many as sheep. Despite this, only in

---

Percentages of Pig Carcases in Three Weight Ranges with Average Carcase Weights and P2 Fat Depths, 1994–1998

	Weight Range	1994	1995	1996	1997	1998
<60kg	% of total	20.0	16.6	11.1	9.2	8.9
	Av. carcase weight (kg)	53.9	54.1	54.4	54.6	54.5
	P2 (mm)	9.6	9.4	9.4	9.4	9.5
60–80kg	% of total	74.1	78.5	83.1	83.3	82.5
	Av. carcase weight (kg)	69.4	69.4	69.9	70.2	70.4
	P2 (mm)	11.3	11.2	11.1	11.2	11.2
>80kg	% of total	5.9	4.9	5.8	7.6	8.6
	Av. carcase weight (kg)	83.7	83.6	83.4	83.7	83.7
	P2 (mm)	13.5	13.53	13.1	13.2	13.1
All carcases	Av. carcase weight (kg)	67.1	67.6	68.9	69.8	70.1
	P2 (mm)	11.1	11.0	11.0	11.2	11.2
Av. lean meat %*		57.8	58.0	58.1	57.9	58.0

*An average of predicted lean meat percentage based on the equation:
Lean meat % = 65.5 - 1.15 × P2 (mm) + 0.076 × cold carcase weight (kg)

Source: MLC Pig Yearbook, 1999

9

Europe and South-East Asia is pigmeat the leading source of meat. In Europe, much of the pig industry depends on modern technology, whereas in South-East Asia – as yet – most pigs are scavengers living on kitchen waste and foraging in forests. Africa offers pig producers the greatest long-term potential, because although Europeans brought pig keeping to Africa some long time ago, pigs still do not form an important part of the farming system or diet.

Millions of people enjoy eating pigmeat. Pig producers throughout the world compete vigorously with each other in the market place, but all enjoy a common bond and exude a readiness to share information: pig enthusiasm knows no geographical boundaries. The pig industry has witnessed amazing increases in productivity in recent years, driven onwards by the furious pace of technical development, tempered by the ability of stock people to adjust to changing circumstances and help ensure the welfare of pigs in their care.

Pigs fascinate people, and people fascinate pigs. They offer *Homo sapiens* the challenge of engaging in a demanding contest of intellectual gymnastics which the pig always seems to win. At the same time pigs offer great opportunities to those who still appreciate the nobility of manual labour: whether one is engaged in hobby farming, or at the mercy of the global pig industry, the basic challenges remain the same. Pig keepers the world over have an insatiable thirst for technical knowledge, and a feeling of awesome responsibility for the welfare of the pigs entrusted to them.

> The hog never looks up to him that threshes
> down the acorns.   (English proverb)

Practical Pig Keeping does not claim to provide all the answers to pig-keeping questions. However, it unashamedly aims to fuel the enthusiasm of pig people and potential pig people, and to help them think about some of the questions.

1 Getting Started ———

ANIMAL WELFARE

Whatever the scale of a pig keeper's enterprise, all share the same responsibilities regarding the well-being of the stock in their care. To start with, they must familiarize themselves with the Code of Recommendations for the Welfare of Pigs – pigs should never be subjected to an unacceptable degree of discomfort or distress by denying them their basic needs. In fact, the anatomy and physiology of the species closely resembles that of human beings, hence they are likely to share a broadly similar requirement for comfort. Besides, consumers are becoming more vigilant and vociferous about the welfare of pigs, particularly in well fed, affluent societies: it therefore behoves every pig keeper to safeguard the well-being of the animals in their care.

A casual approach to pig keeping has no place in modern society. Profit margins are such that the labour force is hard stretched on most existing pig units, and owners are often glad to take on temporary labour for holiday cover and suchlike. This also provides an opportunity for would-be pig keepers to discover if they are suited to running their own pig keeping venture; those who are not, tend to be confronted with reality at a very early stage in their involvement.

TRAINING OPPORTUNITIES

In the UK many people live within an hour's drive of a pig discussion group. Established pig keepers can therefore keep up-to-date regarding technicalities, and can share their enthusiasm with like-minded people; these groups also give newcomers the chance to meet other 'pig people', and help them to attune to the technical wavelength that responsible pig keeping undoubtedly demands. Pig discussion groups are usually well supported by the 'trade' and allied industries. Another useful source of information and

---

Pig Welfare Priorities

- Comfort and shelter;
- Readily accessible fresh water and a diet to maintain the pigs in full health and vigour;
- Freedom of movement;
- Company of other pigs;
- The opportunity to undertake most normal behaviour patterns;
- Light during the hours of daylight and readily available inspection lighting at all times;
- Flooring which neither harms the pigs, nor causes undue strain;
- Prevention, or rapid diagnosis and treatment of vice, injury, parasitic infestation and disease;
- Avoidance of unnecessary mutilation, e.g. tail docking, ear notching;
- Emergency arrangements to deal with outbreaks of fire, essential equipment breakdown and disruption of supplies.

---

contact for newcomers to the pig scene would be sales representatives of local pig feed companies or breeding companies.

The technical side of the industry experiences such rapid development that local colleges of agriculture will often arrange relevant short-duration courses: some of these comprise one-day sessions concentrating on specialist aspects, others might run on one day a week for several weeks and be more general in nature. These courses are usually linked to the National Vocational Qualification scheme, whose first requirement is to ensure a basic standard of competence as expected by the pig industry. Training is progressive, which means that in the long run it is the most suitable students who will acquire specialist skills, together with a sound working knowledge of the more complex issues of running a pig business, embracing the technical requirements as well as people management skills.

National Vocational Qualifications Competence Levels

Level 1   AWARENESS
  Wide ranging, varied and routine
    activities

Level 2   VARIED
  Work activities
  Different contexts
  Complex – one-off jobs
  Team work

Level 3   BROAD RANGE
  Complex/one-off jobs
  Responsibility – autonomy
  Supervision

Level 4   BROAD RANGE
  Complex
  Technical/professional
  Personal responsibility/
    people centred
  Resource management

Approaches to training are changing, however. In the year 2000 the MLC, the University of Aberdeen, and Garth Veterinary Group obtained funding for a training initiative within the MAFF Agricultural Development Scheme (1999): this aimed to use modern multimedia technology to help improve productivity within the British pig industry. Bank managers tend to back new entrepreneurs with a good track record, and it was hoped that a more focused approach to training in pig keeping would help achieve this objective.

Before embarking on your own pig enterprise, you would be well advised to do the following:

- read the Pig Welfare Code;
- start subscribing to specialist pig magazines;
- join a pig discussion group, or contact those who would help you become more informed;
- identify your training needs, and do something about it;
- arrange some sort of work experience for yourself before you risk any substantial capital or commitment;
- establish an enviable track record.

POLLUTION AND PLANNING ISSUES

The need to provide consumers with wholesome pigmeat must be balanced against environmental and amenity issues. Pig units have no place in an urban environment, and equally some country dwellers may complain bitterly if they happen to live near to a pig unit or learn that one might be established near them. However, it must be said that those who choose to move out of town in order to enjoy the benefits of rural life must also appreciate that they are locating themselves on the edge of a food-factory floor –

In-pig sows making the most of good welfare. (PIGSPEC)

and like any production system, farming has its downside. Not all that goes on in the countryside is necessarily pleasant to look at, kind on the ear, or sweet-smelling, and both indigenous country dwellers and the nouveau rural must expect *some* degree of impairment of their amenity: it is part and parcel of country life.

From the farmer's point of view, rural natives are generally more tolerant of long-established pig farms – nevertheless, *all* residents are potential consumers, and so pig farmers must endeavour to respect the sensitivities of their neighbours, in particular those of 'urban invaders': they should give these incomers every assistance to ascend what is bound to be for them a formidably steep learning curve. And on the other side of the fence, consumers and newcomers must appreciate that unless hard-working, caring pig farmers are allowed to get on with their job, the UK countryside will become a rural wilderness, and the pork eaters of the future will become increasingly dependent on imported pigmeat, some of which could well be of doubtful origin.

He that loves noise must buy a pig.

(English proverb)

Good Agricultural Practice

- If possible, collect slurry on a daily basis and transfer it to a suitable store.

- Do the same with dung from non-bedded concreted areas.

- Concreted areas around buildings should be kept clean and free from any build-up of slurry or manure.

- Dead pigs and foetal remains must be removed from the site for effective disposal.

- Drains should be maintained; broken or badly laid concrete should be repaired to stop the accumulation of effluent on its surface.

- Bedding should be stored in a dry area and be used to help reduce odours by keeping pigs clean.

- Drinking water should be managed such that spillage and overflow is minimised.

A large group of well-bedded finishers. (ABN Ltd)

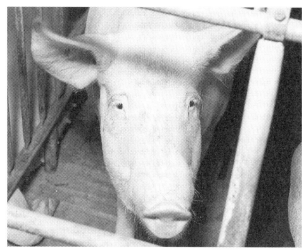

Sow stalls eliminated bullying and provided individual feeding. (ABN Ltd)

Sow stall houses are now banned in the UK but are widespread throughout Europe. (ABN Ltd)

Group-housed dry sows on 'trickle-feed' system. (Newsham Hybrid Pigs Ltd)

An uncovered dung passage allows dirty water to mix with clean roof water. (PIGSPEC)

Pig farmers and potential pig farmers must face the reality that pigs are a major source of dispute between neighbours. Environmental health officers consistently report that almost half of all justified farm smell nuisance complaints relate to pigs – and unfortunately, the beleaguered pig is sometimes ruthlessly used as a vehicle to kick-start rural hostilities. Planners and environmental health officers are well aware of these issues, and they frequently have to tread a difficult path, and one which rarely leads to an outright victory for either party. Under Part III, Section 79 of The Environment Protection Act 1990, health officers have a duty to inspect their areas to detect any statutory nuisances, and are also required to investigate all complaints of such nuisance. If a resident persists in complaining, the officer will then give him a log sheet on which to record the incidence of smell, and any other alleged nuisance from the offending pig unit. Human

Seepage of dirty water can become a big problem if it is not contained. (PIGSPEC)

Pollution of water courses can lead to hefty fines. (PIGSPEC)

nature is such that log sheets are usually completed with zeal, so that eventually the officer must take follow-up action. Needless to say, frequent statutory visits from health officers are expensive for local authorities; however, they now have the power to serve an 'Abatement Notice' under Part III, Section 80 of The Environment Protection Act. This effectively curtails any further expenditure from the departmental budget, since it requires the farmer to bring about:

• the abatement of the nuisance;
• the execution of such works or any steps necessary to put matters right.

Further forces of law can be brought to bear on a pig farmer who fails to comply with an Abatement Notice without reasonable excuse; indeed, continued violation is regarded as a criminal offence, and fines of up to £20,000 can be imposed in a Magistrates' Court. Abatement Notices are therefore best avoided.

Those involved in the pig industry should familiarize themselves with the

Planning appeals generate a lot of paperwork: the author studying an 'urgent' fax from a solicitor. (PIGSPEC)

Ministry's 'Code of Good Agricultural Practice for the Protection of Air', and its 'Code of Good Agricultural Practice for the Protection of Water'. In short, it would be good policy to abide by the following management practices:

• Familiarize yourself with the 'Codes of Good Agricultural Practice'.
• Avoid sites near watercourses and dwellings.
• Formulate a strategy for pig waste collection, storage and distribution.
• Ignore dirty water at your peril: it usually goes away, but it could cost you up to £20,000 in fines.
• If in doubt, ask.

Lawyers and painters can soon change black to white.   (Danish proverb)

Places to Avoid when Applying Pig Waste to Land

• Fields prone to flooding.

• Hard, frozen fields.

• Land near to watercourses, springs or boreholes, especially if the soil surface is severely compacted.

• Water-logged fields and steep fields near to springs, watercourses or boreholes.

• Recently drained fields, particularly if the soil above the drains is cracked.

• Where fissured rock is covered with cracked soil less than 12in (30cm) deep.

From the outset, pig units should be planned with expansion options in mind. (SEGHERS genetics)

The easiest means of obtaining planning permission for a pig enterprise is at the first attempt: planning disputes are both financially and emotionally expensive, and are best avoided. The Town and Country Planning Act of 1947 preceded the days of intensive livestock production and allowed a casual approach to agriculture – but this situation has radically changed, and what was permissible in a country recovering from a devastating world war is usually unacceptable these days. Local planning authorities (LPAs) are now constrained by a very important document called 'Planning Policy Guidance 7, The Countryside – Environment Quality and Economic and Social Development'. Otherwise known as PPG7, this document is the 'bible' of the LPA, and is used to formulate their development plans.

When contemplating setting up a pig unit, it is essential to familiarize yourself with PPG7 at an early stage. Planners are charged with encouraging a sustainable rural economy without impairment of the countryside and environment: thus they are not keen on large pig units near to residential areas, nor on the type of hobby unit which does little for the rural economy yet manages to attract complaints from neighbours and to damage the reputation of established farmers.

Pollution prevention has become a glob-

Thoughtful siting should help eliminate complaints from neighbours. (SEGHERS genetics)

al issue, and the pig industry is faced with this reality. At the Rio Earth Summit Conference in 1992, world governments took stock of the current situation and pledged to improve the global environment, and this thinking was reinforced at the 1997 Kyoto Conference. The European Union response has been the 'Integrated Pollution Prevention and Control (IPPC) Directive 96/61' (1996): this aims to prevent or reduce pollution in order to achieve a high level of protection of the environment. When implemented it is likely to affect large pig units, such as those with over 750 sows, or those with 2,000 finishing pigs over 30kg (66lb) liveweight.

New installations above the agreed threshold will need a permit to operate; existing installations already above the threshold have until the year 2007 to com-

ply. Under this directive, pig farmers must practise 'best available techniques' (BAT) to prevent pollution. It is also likely that the application of organic manures will be limited to no more than 250kg (550lb)/ha/yr of total nitrogen averaged over the farm area in crops and grassland. This legislation could affect both indoor and outdoor units, and large and small units where insufficient land is available to take the muck from the pig unit; some farmers already have to live with the constraints imposed by 'nitrate vulnerable zones' (NVZs). So for those contemplating establishing a pig unit, those already running one, and those intending to expand, the key message is that they must first ensure they have a sufficient waste disposal area available to prevent poisoning the land.

Getting planning permission for pig

Understanding and Negotiating the Planning Process

Informal advice	Talk to your planning officer and local councillor, and inform yourself by reading literature from the Development Directive. 'Sound' your neighbour about your proposal.
Submit	Complete application forms, take them in to your local authority and get them checked before parting with the planning fee. Personally deliver a copy to your councillor.
Validation	Await written confirmation that your paperwork is in order. Remember, the clock does not start until you reach this stage.
Publication	Expect to see a notice placed on site for twenty-one days. Be aware that your neighbours will get written notification of your intentions and be given twenty-one days to comment. An advertisement might be placed in the local press.
Consultation	The Parish Council, County Council and Environmental Health Department will be invited to comment.
Site Inspection	The case officer will visit the site and make an assessment. His recommendations will have to conform to local planning policies and other material considerations.
Amendments	If some aspects of your application are deemed to be unacceptable, try to be flexible. Don't try to beat the planners, but work with them.
Decision Time	Some decisions are made by the Director of Development. Otherwise a detailed report is sent to the Planning Application Sub-Committee (Councillors). If a proposal contravenes local policy it can only be approved by the Development Committee.
Notification	The application or agent is sent a decision notice. All people who have made representations will be informed of the outcome at this stage.

The consumer has positive welfare perceptions about outdoor production. (PIGSPEC)

buildings can be a difficult process. Professional help is usually enlisted, and whoever is charged with obtaining approval is required to 'box clever'. Nowadays planning permission regulations for pig units increasingly look like a 'catch-all' process. The erection of new pig units, or the extension of existing ones, is legally defined as 'development', of which there are three categories:

- permitted development which can be carried out without informing the local planning authority (LPA);
- permitted development which requires prior notification to the LPA before building work starts;

- development which requires planning permission.

The regulations are complex, and any detailed study is beyond the scope of this book. A short synopsis might, however, be useful: thus, 'permitted development' relates to minor extensions to existing buildings, and the discretion varies according to the size of the farm. New pig buildings generally need planning permission, however, and alarm bells will start ringing if they are located within 400m (1,300ft) of a dwelling, or within 25m (85ft) of a classified road. Thus before embarking on any pig building project, a scheduled visit to the LPA is strong-

Sows in their natural environment. (ABN Ltd)

Baby pigs retained within a fender. (ABN Ltd)

ly recommended so that preliminary 'soundings' can be made.

Temporary structures are not constrained by planning legislation. Provided they are of 'limited size', are easily portable, do not have foundations, and are not linked to the ground by facilities such as piped water or electricity cables, they are generally exempt. Ark units and tents used by outdoor producers fall into this category. Even so, difficulties can arise in designated areas such as National Parks and 'Areas of Outstanding Natural Beauty'.

A Plan to Succeed

- Assume planning permission is required until you know otherwise.
- Talk to your neighbours, and if possible build beyond sight, smell and earshot of residents.
- Make an appointment to see your LPA and seek an informal opinion.
- Keep your councillor well informed.
- Don't part with your planning fee until you know the paperwork is in order.
- Be aware that your first chance is your best chance – give it time and effort,

During winter outdoor pig keeping can pose problems for both pigs and people. (ABN Ltd)

Well sheltered outdoor pigs thriving in the depths of winter. (PIGSPEC)

and be prepared to engage professional help.

OUTDOORS OR INSIDE

Outdoor pig keeping is only an option where the criteria for soil type, drainage, rainfall and the levelness of the land can be met. Generally feed represents over 70 per cent of the total costs of a pig-keeping enterprise – and it will be seen that low-cost pig keeping does not exist. However, outdoor production is a system that is considerably cheaper to set up.

Often outdoor pig keeping takes place on rented land comprising part of the rotation on an arable farm, and is therefore one way for young people and newcomers to enter the industry without being landowners. In quite recent times when returns for cereal growing were low, land that was poor for cropping but good for pigs was available at a comparatively low rent; however, this situation has been tempered by the payment of grants to landowners in schemes such as 'set-aside', and various projects for environmental enhancement, and this has tended to increase land rents. Typically one acre of land would be required for every six to ten sows (fifteen to twenty-five per hectare), and ideally around one and a half acres (0.6ha) of 'clean' ground would be required for every ten sows every year, though many producers successfully run systems based on a two-year cycle.

Traditionally outdoor sows were provided with shelter in the form of low-cost ark units made out of curved and corrugated galvanized metal sheets; however, more-sophisticated insulated farrowing arks have emerged as a result of the upsurge in outdoor systems. Insulated arks help retain the sow's body heat during winter, and in summer they help to reduce any extreme rise in temperature inside the ark, thus encouraging the sow to remain in the ark with her litter. Hence insulation provides year-round comfort benefits for the sow – and inevitably this helps to improve feed utilization. There are also

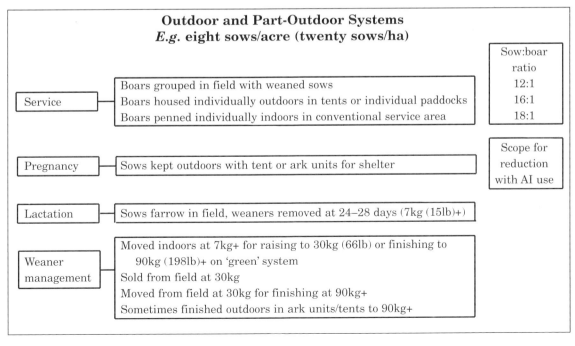

Outdoor and Part-Outdoor Systems
E.g. **eight sows/acre (twenty sows/ha)**

		Sow:boar ratio
Service	Boars grouped in field with weaned sows	12:1
	Boars housed individually outdoors in tents or individual paddocks	16:1
	Boars penned individually indoors in conventional service area	18:1
Pregnancy	Sows kept outdoors with tent or ark units for shelter	Scope for reduction with AI use
Lactation	Sows farrow in field, weaners removed at 24–28 days (7kg (15lb)+)	
Weaner management	Moved indoors at 7kg+ for raising to 30kg (66lb) or finishing to 90kg (198lb)+ on 'green' system	
	Sold from field at 30kg	
	Moved from field at 30kg for finishing at 90kg+	
	Sometimes finished outdoors in ark units/tents to 90kg+	

Indoor pigs oblivious of the weather. (ABN Ltd)

double-skin insulated ark units, though these are disadvantageously heavy and are best suited to enterprises that have some sort of heavy machinery to move

them. If only a limited number of insulated arks are available on a particular unit, priority should be given to first litter gilts.

Low-cost tents with side walls made of big straw bales are now a feature of many outdoor pig units; they are used mainly to house newly weaned sows in close proximity to boars, and for in-pig sows. Some pig farmers use them for weaner shelters, and occasionally for outdoor finishing systems. Compared to ark units they offer more scope for accommodating larger groups, and it is easier to control ventilation rates.

Outdoor-born pigs offer the opportunity to produce a finished commodity that is different to that produced from mainstream pigs as they are reared throughout Europe. If, however, young pigs are brought indoors at weaning for rearing and finishing within intensive set-ups,

Provision of shade should be the first line of attack against summer sunshine. (PIGSPEC)

Wallows provide a cooling effect and help create a sun barrier. (ABN Ltd)

the 'green' benefit is sacrificed. In view of this, there has been a shift towards developing more pig-friendly follow-on systems for outdoor-born pigs, spear-headed by the field-rearing of weaners. Practical experience has shown that hardy outdoor-born pigs thrive outdoors, as long as they are given a dry, draught-free bed and access to fresh air. Moreover the system is not burdened with heating costs, and any losses in feed conversion efficiency because of extremes of weather seem to be offset by improved respiratory health, and less susceptibility to the enteric diseases associated with intensively reared pigs.

On the very best drained land, good

Outdoor weaning accommodation with kennel and run. (Cosikennels)

Skid-mounted weaner kennel on the move. (PIGSPEC)

results have been obtained with weaners reared in the field. Pigs weaned at twenty-four to thirty-one days of age – i.e. 7kg (15lb)+ – are size-batched into groups of up to sixty in a portable, floorless, insulated kennel or ark unit. These weaners have free access to an open run surrounded by fully sheeted hurdles. The system depends on an abundance of straw bedding to provide thermal comfort, and a draught-free lying area; the dunging area is within the hurdled run, where straw is scattered to minimize puddling and to help keep the pigs clean. The system has the advantages of low cost, and effective containment of the pigs, and it provides

Tents are now widely used for sows on outdoor units. (J. Harvey Engineering)

24

'Duraweave' novel pig housing under construction. (Coverall UK Ltd)

reasonable scope for observing the weaners. It can, however, be problematic on unsuitable, poorly drained land, particularly during periods of prolonged wet weather. When pigs reach 30kg (66lb) at around ten to eleven weeks of age they are usually moved to a follow-on stage, when they are kept indoors, although on some pioneering units weaners are now left outdoors until they weigh around 40kg (88lb) liveweight; thus they will have spent half their anticipated life outdoors.

The next stage often comprises indoor housing on a neighbouring farm, or it might involve transport to a distant specialist finishing unit. After each batch of weaners, the ark units or kennels should be moved to clean land using a tractor and fore-end loader. A mini-dungstead remains, and ideally this should be given early attention so as to discourage flies, minimize pollution from run-off, and prevent poisoning the land. Pig farmers using this system in rented fields are generally required to restore the land to a reasonable state after use.

Typically, outdoor-reared weaners are finished indoors on 'pig-friendly', straw-based systems which enable pigs to be marketed on a 'green contract', thereby hopefully realizing a premium price. As yet, finishing pigs outdoors has had little impact on the UK farming scene, the main difficulty being that of transporting large tonnages of feed to pigs kept outdoors in all weathers. In particular the period from December to February can bring all sorts of problems, and many pioneers – including vastly experienced pig keepers and hauliers – have concluded that the system is best avoided during the depths of winter.

There has, however, been some success in finishing pigs outdoors in low-cost tent units, particularly on sheltered, well-drained land serviced by an adjacent all-weather road. An interesting development from Canada involves housing finishing pigs under a Duraweave fabric cover supported by tubular steel truss arches. Trials at the University of Manitoba involving more than 1,000 finishing pigs indicated that as long as they were well bedded, finishing pigs could be cost effectively produced on this system. Furthermore, farm trials involving more

Typical Pig Output for Various Herd Sizes				
Sows in herd	Farrowings/ week	Weaned pigs/ week	Finished pigs/ week	Finished pigs/ year
22	1	10.2	10	520
44	2	20.4	20	1040
66	3	30.6	30	1560
88	4	40.8	40	2080
110	5	51.0	50	2600
132	6	61.2	60	3120
154	7	71.4	70	3640
176	8	81.6	80	4160
198	9	91.8	90	4680
220	10	102.0	100	5200

2.36 litters/sow/year

than 8,000 pigs have supported the researchers' findings, and good results have also been obtained in Canada during extremes of weather (regarded as normal by the inhabitants!). These novel Duraweave structures are light and airy, with scope for varying the ventilation rates. Since they can be moved and re-sited with relative ease, they are readily leased, and could well offer new market-orientated opportunities for forward-thinking producers.

By way of summary, it is generally good policy to make the most of your assets; so:

• Don't operate inside if you could be out-side.
• Never operate outside if you don't have keen staff and if the conditions are basi-cally unsuitable.
• Safeguard 'green' bonuses by keeping intensive and outdoor production sepa-rate.
• Look at the facilities available, and use the best that are offered by both indoor and outdoor systems.
• Consider an outdoor breeding unit with split-site production of weaners, and finishers in hired buildings.

SETTING UP SHOP

The fortunes of all pig producers are dic-tated by the vagaries of the pig cycle, and the success of an enterprise depends to a great extent on whether it was a propi-tious moment, or not, to establish a pig unit, given the market forces at the time. The problem is, nobody can ever really tell *how* propitious a time it is to set up shop until ten months afterwards.

A hog upon trust grunts till he's paid.
(English proverb)

Despite the complexity and industrializa-tion of the modern pig industry, in the UK nearly half of the producers are part-timers or hobby farmers. Small producers are likely to encounter fewer pig health problems as compared to larger operators, but have to live with higher fixed costs per pig, and the burden of organizational inefficiencies. On large units, batch man-agement makes it easier to establish a predictable weekly work routine; whereas on small units, since there are fewer sows farrowing, most jobs have to be undertak-en as 'one-off' events. Batch-farrowing

Tubular steel truss arches supporting a 'Duraweave' structure. (Coverall UK Ltd)

management – such as only weaning every third week – can help small producers improve the predictability of events, but since a boar's work rate would be irregular, artificial insemination is a key element of the system.

The scale of operation on productive pig units of different sizes has a marked impact on the management strategies employed. Thus a smallholder with just twenty-two sows producing ten finished pigs per week would necessarily have a different approach to building layout, labour and marketing strategy as compared to a 220 sow herd owner turning out 100 pigs every week. Furthermore, abattoirs are reluctant to offer slaughter contracts to smaller producers, and hauliers prefer customers who have enough pigs to make up one load. However, Section Three of the Pig Welfare Code states: 'Although very large herds can be managed successfully, in general the larger the size of the unit, the greater the degree of skill and conscientiousness needed to safeguard welfare.' This would appear to argue in favour of the smaller concern, in that able, well-informed hobby farmers can offer more individual attention to their stock – indeed their survival as pig people depends in some measure on their unstinting provision of uncosted

Who Does What on Pig Schemes?

Contractor	Contractee	
Pig supply	Accommodation:	building
		field
		ark unit, etc.
Feed specification and delivery	Labour	
Limited management supervision	Straw bedding	
Veterinary input	Water	
Pig transport and marketing	Electricity	
	Insurance	
	Waste collection/disposal	
	£ pig place/headage payments and bonuses	

Types of Pig Schemes/Contracts			
		Location	
Pig	Stage	Inside	Outside
Breeding sows	7kg+ weaners	√	√
	30kg weaners	√	√
	90kg+ cutters/baconers	√	Rarely
Nursery pigs	7+–18kg weaners	√	√
	7+–30-kg weaners	√	√
Finished pigs	7+–90kg+ cutters/baconers	√	Rarely
	30–90kg+ cutters/baconers	√	Rarely

labour. It also depends on their being able to realize premium prices for their pigmeat. This can be achieved by supplying added-value products through specific outlets dedicated to offering consumers goods that can be easily traced, and that are guaranteed 100 per cent wholesome. On the down side, if the hobby farmer

Good results have been recorded in Canada for finished pigs housed in draught-free temporary structures. (Coverall UK Ltd)

fails to attract a premium, then the extra costs of the smaller producer will almost certainly offset any profits.

So how does a hobby farmer or aspirant commercial pig farmer get a foot on the farming ladder? 'Scheme pigs' are a well tested route. As the industry becomes more vertically integrated, some feed companies and abattoirs, in a bid to secure tonnage and throughput, offer schemes which help share the cost of capitalizing a pig unit. In recent years, some schemes have been disbanded as operators elect to inject capital into their core businesses but others have thrived and become sizeable concerns, and it seems likely, therefore, that schemes such as these will continue to provide a helpful inroad for newcomers, and will have a major impact on production in the UK.

A characteristic of many successful large-scale business operations is their reluctance to become saddled with inflexible long-term contracts. Pig keepers have to live with this reality, and agreements tend to be made on a batch-to-batch basis, particularly on contracts for finishing pigs. Contractors supply pigs, feed, veteri-nary input and market the slaughter pigs; contractee farmers supply accommodation, labour (usually their own), straw bedding, water and electricity. They are paid on a pig place or 'headage' basis, and receive bonuses for quality production. Such schemes are most attractive where appropriate buildings are available that have fallen out of use. However, those tempted to borrow money for these schemes must question the medium- to long-term financial implications. For instance, inefficient contractees who consistently fail to produce quality pigs not only miss out on bonuses, but will also discover the consequences of fair-weather friendships.

In summary:

- Bad timing saps morale, strains the purse and creates debts.
- Pig keeping demands enthusiasm: if you can't give it commitment, then don't bother.
- Do it different: try to add value to your pigs.
- Consider scheme pigs to get yourself in business – but beware of the pitfalls.

Notes for Novices

- Familiarize yourself with the Pig Welfare Code.
- Do not take the risk of falling foul of planning laws.
- Keep on the right side of environment laws.
- Do not give your neighbours cause for complaint.
- If someone tries to sell you an existing pig unit – take expert advice.
- Avoid erecting expensive pig buildings and laying concrete.
- If you acquire existing general purpose buildings and concreted areas, consider modifying them for pigs.
- Take advice and try to build a simple system round these existing facilities.
- Low cost pig keeping does not exist, since feed generally accounts for over 70 per cent of production costs.
- Pig feed still has to be purchased for pigs, even when pig prices are low.
- Most hobbies cost money – pig keeping is no exception.
- Adding value and shrewd marketing is the key to generating profit.
- Make sure you like pigs before launching a new venture.

2 Breeding for Future Generations

'Geneticists make pigs, but vets make them better': this is a maxim that every pig breeder must heed. The close relationship between sophisticated genetic research and well-respected pig-breeding companies has resulted in amazing increases in productivity. Indeed, pig breeding has become an international business, with some companies listed on the stock exchanges of the world. But despite all this science, at commercial level pig producers still fail to exploit 20 to 30 per cent of the genetic potential for improved sow productivity and growth rates, which is within the make-up of their pigs. Disease challenge is a major reason for this shortfall, particularly on larger pig units and in regions where pig density is high. Furthermore, inadequate housing, inappropriate management and a dearth of knowledge about the finer points of feeding modern pigs also conspire to limit the ultimate realization of genetic progress on commercial farms. And when selecting replacement breedingstock, maintaining herd health in a specific commercial environment is a priority issue.

Headquarters of a globally active pig breeding company. (SEGHERS genetics)

Sometimes pigs do fly.
(SEGHERS genetics)

Traditional breeding protocols are well understood by pig farmers, and generations of consumers have been comfortable with the science behind them. However, recent advances in biotechnology have rapidly changed this situation. The trend towards globalization of agriculture increases the need for genetic advances as the breedingstock market and pigmeat market become increasingly competitive and technically demanding. New technologies not only provide opportunities to reduce the cost of producing pigmeat, but also provide scope for actually enhancing the health of consumers and improving perceptions of animal welfare. On the downside, this relentless revolution in biotechnology has tended to take the 'fun' out of pig breeding since farmers have a declining influence on the genetic make-up of the breedingstock in their care. Nevertheless, improved pig genetics are increasingly seen as a key component within the human food chain, a vital link in the cost-effective production of wholesome lean meat.

Genetically improved pigs are exported throughout the world. (SEGHERS genetics)

31

Little knoweth the fat sow what the lean doth
mean.   (English proverb)

These days even trained scientists struggle to grasp the know-how behind the latest genetic advances, since powerful computer programs assist today's pig breeder.
It would be unrealistic therefore to
attempt to unravel modern genetic theory
– or even for the reader to expect it – in
this book. Instead it will provide a recap
of traditional genetics, along with hopefully lucid explanations of the basics of
some of the techniques commonly
employed in modern pig genetics. It will
also attempt to provide an insight into the
potential and possible pitfalls encom-
passed within the genetics of the pig of
the future.

DIPPING INTO THE GENE POOL

Large White

These pigs are the cornerstone of many
breeding programmes throughout the
world. They are renowned for their large
litters, their milkiness, and their mothering ability. They are lean and active, with
sound feet and legs; they also make good
terminal sires, and perform well both
indoors and outside. The adoption of the
EU Pig Carcase Grading Scheme, based
on lean meat content, has led to the selection of high conformation Large White
boars. These have been selected specifically for their more muscular conformation as compared to traditional lines.
Characteristically they have low backfat
levels, and help boost the yield of rib muscle and lean meat percentage in the carcases of their offspring, which have good
meat quality and are not stress-susceptible.

British Landrace

The British Landrace and its national
variants are widespread throughout the
UK and Europe, and pig breeders export
it throughout the world. Like the Large
White, it remains a popular pig both with
traditional breeders and breeding companies. It is long and muscular, and well
known for its prolificacy and docility as
well as for its pigmeat production.
Landrace boars were traditionally used to
produce crossbred pigs for bacon production. Synthetic sire lines have been developed for both pork and bacon markets,
and Landrace boars are frequently used
as dam-line grandparent stock for the production of commercial parent gilts.
Backfat levels are low, and the breed is
halothane negative (*see later*).

Duroc

The Duroc is both genetically and geo-
graphically diverse. It is red in colour,
varying from a light gold to a dark red.
Farmers in the US corn belt popularized

*Large White boar. (Rattlerow
Farms Ltd)*

the breed and saw its colour as a brand mark, though processors tasked with de-hairing the carcases were less enthusiastic. It was also adopted by the UK, where geneticists struggled until the mid-eighties to find a third breed to blend with the two established white breeds. Work at the former Animal Breeding Research Organization in Edinburgh identified the Duroc as a potential sire-line pig, and follow-up trials pinpointed its ability to perform well in a female cross. Stimulated by criticisms about the dryness of lean meat from genetically improved pigs and the demand for hardiness in the outdoor herd, Durocs have become popular in the UK. Importations from Denmark have helped exploit the Duroc's contribution to hybrid vigour. Carcases from Duroc-cross pigs characteristically have increased levels of marbling fat: how much is needed to improve succulence remains a moot point,

but the presence of this visible interstitial fat certainly gives consumers a perception of better eating quality. The Duroc is halothane negative (*see later*), and gives a higher percentage of heterosis when crossed with a white breed.

Pietrain

This breed takes its name from a Belgian village. It is a medium-sized pig with characteristic black spots and a rough coat, with an amazingly broad back, short legs and a stocky conformation. The hams are bulbous and muscular, and the carcase carries a high proportion of lean to fat. Particularly in Belgium and Germany, Pietrain boars have been used on Landrace females to boost meat yield. Pietrain sows are highly strung and not very milky, and so the breed is more commonplace as a sire. Geneticists often

Grandparent Large White gilts. (Rattlerow Farms Ltd)

make use of some Pietrain blood in synthetic breeding lines.

The Pietrain breed is closely associated with the halothane gene, and meat quality can be a problem. When used in a synthetic line it can help boost meat yield, but it tends to increase carcase variability.

Meishan

In 1987 five UK breeding companies, in conjunction with the Department of Trade and Industry, funded the importation of Meishan pigs from China; they also financed some follow-up research. On its home territory this hyper-prolific breed has been noted for its ability to utilize waste food and produce very large litters. It is very early-maturing, and exhibits improved embryo survival rates as compared to traditional breeds. Meishans are short, stocky pigs with a wrinkled skin that gives them a gruesome appearance.

Their contribution to pig genetics in Western Europe has involved the development of synthetic Meishan lines which have been crossed with lean white breeds. Their prolificacy is such that thirty pigs per sow per year becomes a realistic target in Meishan-cross sows. Slaughter pigs should have no more than around one-eighth Meishan genes, otherwise excessive carcase fat will be a problem.

F1 Hybrid

This is the name given to the first-cross parent gilt of two pure breeds sold by both traditional breeders and breeding companies. Particularly during the 1970s it became the cornerstone of success for the UK pig industry. Typically this hybrid comprises a cross of Large White and

Selection of grandparent Large White gilts. (Rattlerow Farms Ltd)

High conformation Large White boar. (Rattlerow Farms Ltd)

Landrace lines. It is a hardy female with good mothering ability and a high milk yield. When served with a meaty sire-line boar, the F1 Hybrid produces slaughter pigs with excellent growth rate and carcase composition.

Grandparent Stock

These are the seed-stock for breeding companies or for commercial pig farmers, and are made up of either dam-line pure-bred or crossbred lines. When used on

Duroc boar. (Newsham Hybrid Pigs Limited)

commercial farms they comprise up to 10 per cent of the total sows in that herd. Ideally they are artificially inseminated using semen from the best dam-line boars available, and selected gilt offspring are then used to provide replacement females in the commercial herd. By operating a grandparent system, farmers may be able to reduce their capital outlay on breedingstock and uniquely acclimatize the resultant replacement gilts to the health status of their commercial pig unit. Since it is more convenient to introduce replacement gilts in manageable groups, a grandparent system is best suited to larger herds. It provides farmers with the opportunity to take a greater degree of control over their replacement breedingstock management.

High Conformation (HC) Boars

These are mainly terminal sires that are robust and renowned for their libido. They are selected for their ability to sire offspring with a carcase with high lean meat content and extreme conformation. They confer good eating quality on the pigmeat, and produce pigs with a higher killing-out percentage. HC boars sometimes result from intensive selection within traditional white breeds; alternatively they could be hybrid boars incorporating a blend of genes specially selected to enhance pigmeat yield and quality. These boars are particularly suitable for siring slaughter pigs on ad lib feeding systems.

TRADITIONAL BREEDING

Traditional animal breeders have striven to upgrade the genetic profile of their stock by identifying the best parents or potential parents and selecting from these. The 'selection differential' is a term used to quantify the degree of superiority of a specified characteristic that selected parents have over the mean – i.e. how much better certain characteristics of pigs are, as compared to the rest of the population. This approach demands reliable record keeping and a good eye for the visual appraisal of the selected stock. More sophisticated versions involve a performance test, whereby the progress of

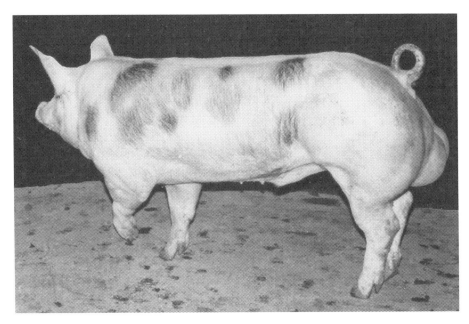

A Pietram boar. (SEGHERS genetics)

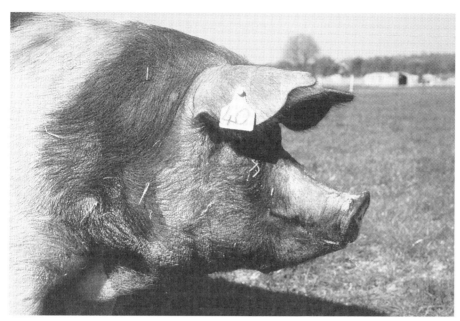

A British Saddleback sow. (Eastbrook Farms)

the potential parent is measured in terms of growth rate, feed intake, feed conversion efficiency, fat depth or lean percentage. Furthermore, progeny tests can be used to assess the suitability of their offspring. Pedigree pig breeders with a penchant for meticulous record keeping and a good eye built the foundation stock for the modern pig industry. Many of them remain in business to this day, and are seen as a traceable but unsophisticated source of replacement stock.

A pretty pig makes an ugly old sow.

(English proverb)

Heritability (h^2) is the scientific term used to measure the proportion of genetic variation within a population. If 100 per cent of the selected qualities pass the generation gap, the heritability (h2) would be 1.0. Hence a heritability of 0.1 for litter size indicates that if a sow has large litters, only 10 per cent of this benefit can be exploited by a simple selection programme. Generally, characteristics closely aligned with reproduction and survivability have low heritabilities.

Characteristics associated with growth and carcase composition have a higher heritability, and pedigree breeders have exploited these for the benefit of the pig industry.

Without massive gene populations and the aid of complex computer programs, the traditional breeder has been unable to make great advances into viability traits such as litter size. However, when sows are crossed with genetically diverse boars their offspring exhibit hybrid vigour, or heterosis. The resultant gene combination

Examples of Heritability Values for Selected Traits in Pig Breeding Programmes

	h^2
Litter size	0.10
Birth weight	0.15
Mature weight	0.25
Growth rate	0.2–0.4
Feed conversion efficiency	0.2–0.4
Backfat thickness	0.55
Lean content	0.60

is responsible for a pig performance which is better than the average of the two parents: it enhances the viability of the piglets. This phenomenon led to the widespread use of so-called F1 hybrid sows on commercial farms, and accelerated the growth of pig-breeding companies in the 1970s.

A French nobleman, Sebastien Le Prestre (1633–1707) – who, needless to say, did not have the benefit of a 'lap-top' – posed the question, 'How many pigs would a pregnant sow parent, grandparent and great-grandparent produce in a ten-year period?' His calculated answer was 6,434,338. He concluded that if you could buy one animal with which to make your fortune, it should be a pig. Apparently not all bank managers agree with his recommendation.

Small pedigree breeders eventually run out of new genes. Prolonged dependence on selection without the introduction of new blood results in inbreeding. A lifeline for these breeders has been the widespread availability of semen from, for

Evaluating the Boar Contribution from Improved Feed Conversion Efficiency

30–90kg (66–198lb) liveweight

FCE	2.8:1	2.7:1	2.6:1
Feed per pig (kg)	168	162	156
Feed cost per pig @ £150/tonne	25.20	24.30	23.40
Feed saved per pig (p)	–	90	90

example, Large White or Landrace boars through artificial insemination (AI) – they have been able to import superior genes on the male side in this way. This is attractive to smaller producers since the disease risk is reduced, and there is no need to outlay capital on spacious boar pens and inevitably under-worked boars.

A good boar can have a marked impact

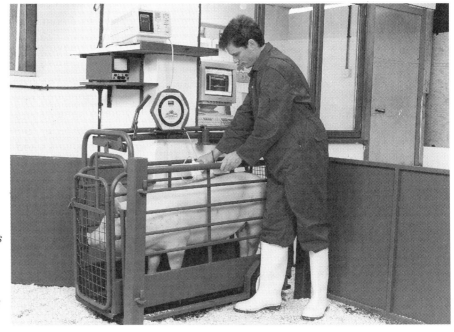

Real time scanning provides the link between the live pig and the carcase. (Rattlerow Farms Ltd)

on overall feed conversion efficiency (FCE). In the absence of AI, indoor units traditionally operated on a sow:boar ratio of 20:1; in outdoor units, a sow:boar ratio of 12:1 or 14:1 is typical, though in high-output indoor units, sow:boar ratios of 18:1 are more commonplace. Although the boar might numerically comprise a mere 5 per cent of the herd, its genes comprise half of the genetic make-up of the slaughter generation. However, the boar has a massive influence on the profitability of the herd, particularly in view of its impact on feed conversion efficiency. For example, a boar in a herd operating with a sow:boar ratio of 20:1 and producing twenty-two pigs/sow/year, and with just a 1.5-year breeding life, would sire around 660 slaughter pigs. Hence there is great potential to save feed if superior genetics can improve feed conversion efficiency. So if feed is costed at £150 per tonne, a 0.1 improvement in feed conversion efficiency saves 90p on the feed bill for a bacon pig. This equates with a feed saving of £594 (660 pigs × 90p) over the lifetime of the boar. Considering that the boar can also help realize benefits from improved growth rate and better grading, the importance of maximizing the genetic potential of the sire is paramount.

The following may therefore be summarized as the tools of the traditional breeder:

- Selection, performance tests and progeny tests have made in-roads into genetic progress.
- Growth, feed efficiency and carcase characteristics can be improved via selection.
- Viability traits are not readily passed to subsequent generations.
- Crossbreeding produces hybrid vigour, and is a route to increased prolificacy and viability.
- AI helps broaden the gene pool and upgrades the genetic status of stock.

Sire and Dam Lines

Pig breeders have exploited different selection objectives for males and females. Sire lines comprise specially selected strains of boar which aim to maximize genetic improvements in the growth rate, feed conversion and carcase characteristics of slaughter pigs. Traditionally, separate Large White and Landrace boar lines were used to achieve these objectives. These days, sire lines often comprise crossbred boars and so have an improved viability compared to purebreds, and some of this hybrid vigour is passed on to their offspring. Sire-line boars are often developed from a two- or three-breed cross often incorporating 'imported' genes, namely Hampshire, Pietrain and Duroc.

Certain breeds from Europe – notably Dutch, German and Belgian Landrace, as well as Belgian and Dutch Pietrain – are muscle-bound pigs renowned for their higher lean meat content. They carry the halothane gene that is associated with stress susceptibility, and pale soft exudative (PSE) muscle which causes drip loss in meat. Sudden death is common in stress-susceptible pigs.

Halothane-sensitive pigs respond unusually to the anaesthetic halothane, in that after limited inspiration of the gas there is a characteristic stiffening of their muscles. This is known as 'porcine stress syndrome' (PSS), and these pigs are said to be 'halothane positive'. Exposure to halothane gas is used as a screening technique for the gene.

Halothane-positive pigs usually have a double dose of the halothane gene on their chromosomes: geneticists refer to this as the homozygous state (hh). Halothane-negative pigs are also homozygous, but these pigs have no traces of halothane genes (HH). However, pigs with just a single dose of the gene are said to be heterozygous (Hh) but these pigs are stress negative, and their genetic status is such

Genetic Terminology Unravelled

Chromosomes	These comprise two strands of DNA. The number of chromosomes depends on the species; pigs have eighteen pairs of chromosomes.
Gene	A particular gene always occurs at the same location on its chromosome. Since there are two strands of DNA, there are two copies of the gene. These copies are known as the gene pair and may have different forms.
Allele	Each gene in the pair is known as an allele.
Genotype	The genetic make-up of an animal.
Phenotype	What an animal actually looks like; for example, a white pig may carry some black genes, yet appear white.
Genome	The genetic information in an animal.
Genetic Marker	A whole segment of a chromosome which carries specific genes that can be traced from parents to offspring viz Marker Assisted Selection.
QTL	'Quantitative trace loci': a group of several genes which together contribute to quantitative variation between animals, e.g. commercial characteristics such as growth rate and litter size.
Selection Index Value	This is the economic value (£) of the genetic merit of an animal.
BLUP	'Best linear unbiased prediction': a statistical method used to increase the effectiveness of selection by making use of information from close relatives.

that they have the advantages of extra lean meat content without the disadvantages. Sire-line breeding exploits this by identifying halothane-positive boars (hh) and mating these with sows without the halothane gene (HH). This technique is widely used to introduce a dash of Pietrain into slaughter pigs. More recently, identification of HAL-1843 – a selection of genes associated with halothane sensitivity – has made use of 'marker assisted selection' (MAS) to help minimize the incidence of PSE.

Specialized dam lines are one route to increased prolificacy, but the journey is beset with difficulties. Since these traits have low heritability, little progress can be made from selection on an individual basis: it would take too long, and if viability traits became the prime focus, carcase composition would suffer. Another problem is low repeatability. Just because a gilt's first litter might be small, the likelihood of this unwanted characteristic reappearing in the next generation is not very great. Similarly, if a gilt litter happens to

Advantageous use of the Halothane Gene

Boar	×	Sow	=	Progeny
Halothane **Positive**		Halothane **Negative**		Halothane **Negative**
hh		HH		Hh
Homozygous		Homozygous		Heterozygous
Double source of halothane gene		Total absence of halothane gene		Single source of halothane gene

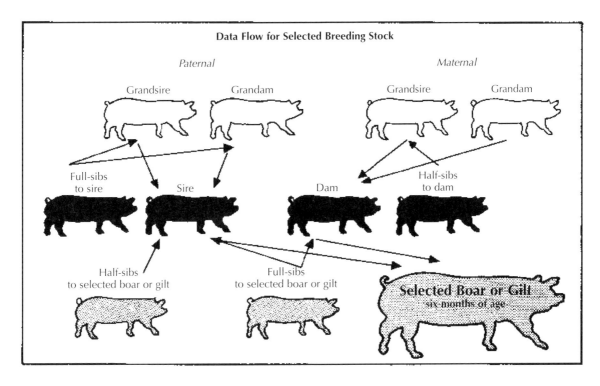

Best Linear Unbiased Prediction (BLUP).

be large, it does not necessarily follow that subsequent litters will also be large. The male side offers few opportunities for measuring litter size. Progeny from prolific males could be tested as breedingstock, but again this would take too long, and would slow down the rate of genetic progress.

A statistical technique known as 'best linear unbiased prediction' (BLUP) has largely replaced individual selection as a means of maximizing prolificacy. BLUP increases the validity of information from an individual animal by taking into account information from its near relatives. Thus a sow producing large litters is considered more likely to pass this trait on to the next generation if its parents and close relatives were also associated with large litters. This statistical initiative also facilitates comparison between pigs in different environments and during different time periods, provided they are genetically linked.

To summarize this policy of breeding with science:

- Sire lines and dam lines are used to exploit different genetic objectives.
- Sire lines help to boost growth rate and the efficient production of lean meat.
- Dam lines strive to increase prolificacy.
- BLUP accelerates progress with prolificacy using data from close relatives.

THE BREEDING COMPANY APPROACH

Spurred on by the success of the poultry industry, during the 1970s several pig-breeding companies emerged into the pig market intent on applying science to provide farmers with genetically superior

41

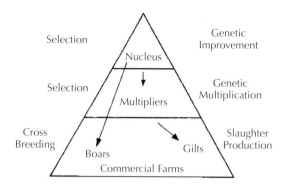

A simple breeding pyramid.

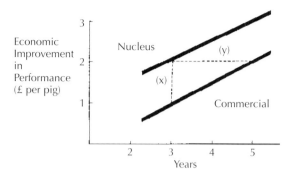

The concept of genetic lag.

breeding stock of a known health status. Their success was such that they rapidly had a national impact within the UK which spread across Europe and eventually became globally recognized. However, rationalization of the pig sector has resulted in only a handful remaining in business, though these all employ state-of-the-art expertise to bring their products to the marketplace. Breeding companies enjoyed an upsurge for various reasons:

- The need for home-produced pigmeat with consistent quality.
- Greater professionalism within farming, with pigs becoming a specialist enterprise.

- The need to improve the efficiency of feed utilization.
- Rationalization within the pig sector, leading to fewer herds but larger units.
- The need for stable health status and bio-security.

Breeding companies exploit selection and hybridization using a system of production that minimizes the risk of disease spread via a pyramid system. There are variations on this basic theme involving AI use, but the essentials remain relevant to the modern industry. Thus, superior genes are identified in a relatively small number of nucleus sows. After selection these progress to a multiplier site where the F1 hybrid is produced by crossing two

Different Breeding Systems Exploit Different Components of Heterosis (Hybrid Vigour)			
	Individual	*Maternal*	*Paternal*
Pure Mating			
A boar × A gilt	0	0	0
2 Breeds			
B boar × A gilt	100%	0	0
Terminal Programmes			
C boar × (A × B) gilt	100%	100%	0
D boar × (C × (A × B)) gilt	100%	100%	0
			Source: Rattlerow Farms Ltd.

distinct breeds. Genetically diverse boars and sows are then sold on to commercial breeding units which produce slaughter pigs. Many companies operate two or more of these pyramids to spread risk and lessen the likelihood and the impact of disease breakdown. Genetic traffic is one way: pigs only move down the pyramid, they never ascend it, and never cross it. This helps reduce the likelihood of disease transference. At nucleus level, new genes are usually cautiously introduced by AI, embryo transfer or hysterectomy. Various breeding systems can be used to exploit hybrid vigour (heterosis).

Just as new computers and associated software take time to emerge from the science park to the high street, the full benefits of progress at nucleus level take time to reach the commercial farm. This delayed 'pay day' is known as genetic lag. Commercial pig farmers can reduce its impact by:

- using AI;
- purchasing highly pointed boars directly from a nucleus herd;
- culling unproductive sows before they get old, and replacing them with genetically superior gilts.

The delay in conveying genes from nucleus to commercial level has a hidden financial cost: The figure opposite outlines the principles of genetic lag. The bold lines show the rate of genetic improvement of a commercial herd and the nucleus herd supplying it, and it can be seen that although the performance of these two herds runs parallel, the commercial herd lags behind the nucleus herd. Ultimately there is a financial penalty associated with this lag time because of the genetic progress not yet available. If the lag time were costing £1 per pig (x), this genetic improvement (y) would have been made over a two-year (5 - 3) period.

In order to increase the impact of selec-tion programmes, breeding companies are increasingly making use of computer tomography (CT) scanning, a technique first developed in human medicine. It involves an x-ray cross-section of the body and informs geneticists about body composition since different tissues show up as having characteristic but different densities. CT scanning is undertaken on the live pig, and so body composition can be determined several times during its lifetime, monitoring the deposition of fat and lean. It helps improve the present genetic assessment of fat and lean, and it also allows identification of intramuscular fat, and it records factors such as conformation and muscularity. The technique helps to ensure that the commercial farmer is providing the optimum carcase for a particular market.

Viewing the inside from the outside: Real Time Scanning. (Newsham Hybrid Pigs Limited)

The breeding company route can perhaps be summarized as follows:

- Several UK breeding companies have achieved global success.
- Breed companies make the most of selection, cross-breeding and AI using complex statistical techniques.
- Judicious use of the breeding pyramid should enable commercial farmers to make early use of healthy and superior genes.
- CT scanning can be a major boost to selection for carcase quality.

NOVEL BREEDING OBJECTIVES

The need to house dry sows in groups rather than individually has emphasized the importance of sow temperament. Although group housing systems provide freedom of movement, shyer and therefore more vulnerable sows are likely to be disadvantaged in these more competitive systems. Geneticists and breeding companies have responded by making more effort to suit the temperament of selected sows to the social environment likely to be encountered at commercial farm level. Robust sows are likely to produce more pigs per sow per year, and are also likely to remain productive in the herd for a longer time.

The degree of robustness in a pig depends on how much its performance is independent of favourable, well controlled conditions – in other words, the pigs must, *in themselves*, 'have what it takes'. Although this is difficult to measure in individual animals, it is an inheritable characteristic, and can be improved by selection. The way geneticists can stop sows and boars from becoming 'soft' – or can maybe even help them to become more robust – is to keep pig populations under a range of production systems and to select across environments. Otherwise, if pigs are just selected from a strictly standardized environment, only genotypes which are highly sensitive to their

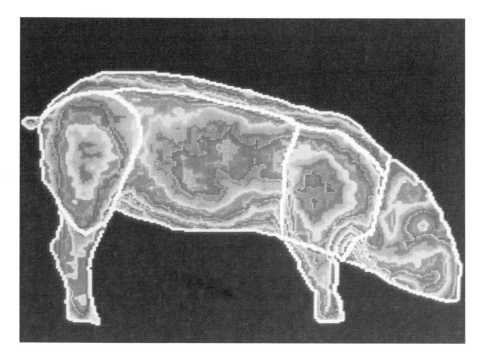

Computer tomograph scanning will accelerate progress. (SEGHERS genetics/ University of Leuven, Belgium)

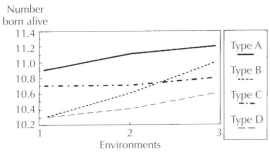

(Source: Falconer & Mackay, 1996)

Performance of four genotypes present in a population in a range of environments.

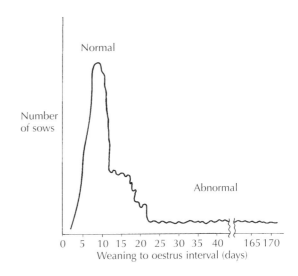

Variations in days to oestrus.

environments tend to be selected. There is little point in selecting replacement stock from a pampered indoor environment and expecting them to thrive on a demanding outdoor system. Thus if pigs were selected from environment 3 only (*see figure above*), then populations type A and type B would be favoured, and types C and D would be rejected. However, if all three environments were taken into account, C would be the best to take since it performs reasonably over them all, and would therefore ensure that robustness were maintained in the population.

Supermarket buyers demand that processed pigmeat must look attractive when presented at the point-of-sale. If bacon rashers look fairly uniform, consumers feel reassured as to the consistency of the product and there will be more likelihood of repeat purchases. Unfortunately, uniformity is difficult to achieve via genetic selection. Whilst it is true that unimproved populations will show more variation than improved populations, the latter still show substantial variation between individuals – indeed, it is this variation that geneticists seek to exploit in their selection programmes. However, commercial reality is such that processors demand uniform pigmeat in

terms of weight, fat content, lean distribution and meat quality, and this requirement is in fact generally met in the way the pigs themselves are managed, rather than via their genetics. Uniformity is improved by standardizing delivery and lairage arrangements, and avoiding aggressive behaviour on the farm, during transport and at the abattoir. Good loading and unloading facilities encourage uniformity, and the chilling regime and

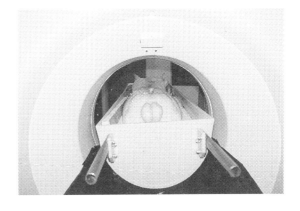

Computer tomography (CT) scanning on a live boar. (Newsham Hybrid Pigs Limited)

ageing procedures also have an important influence in pigmeat eating quality.

The interval from weaning to service

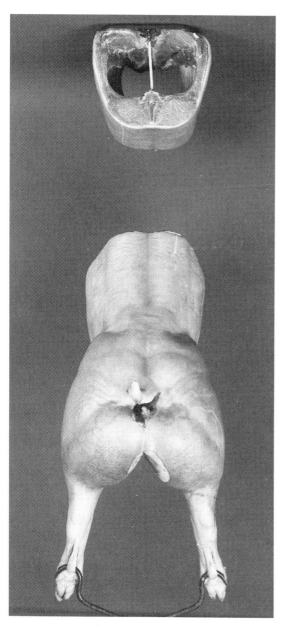

Computer tomography helps geneticists assess lean and fat distribution in selection programmes. (Newsham Hybrid Pigs Limited)

can be an expensive time if it is unproductive, costing a total of around £2.50 per sow for every lost day. Much of this inconsistency in 'empty days' is attributable to inadequate nutrition, particularly concerning first-litter gilts which are still growing. However, could some of this variation be genetic in origin? Trials conducted in ID-DLO, a research institute in Lelystad, Holland, have provided some answers. Over eight generations of sow were selected for the shortness of the interval from weaning to oestrus. After four generations, when compared to a control line, there was evidence that selection was proving effective, inheritability being estimated at 0.36.

Whereas it is helpful to reduce abnormally long intervals between weaning and oestrus, eliminating the incidence of *all* such prolonged breeding intervals would be even more preferable. Computer simulation exercises which have selected sows with empty days of seven or less show promise for the future.

Sow productivity would also be boosted if embryonic death could be reduced by genetic selection. Several breeds native to the People's Republic of China are amazingly prolific: these include the Fenjing, the Jaixing-Black, the Erhualian and the Meishan. Trials in Europe and the USA have highlighted the Meishan's ability to reach puberty three months earlier than conventional breeds, and to produce an average of four more live pigs per litter. Furthermore, crossbreeding has indicated that this large litter trait is inherited from the mother's side, and that the genes of the sire have no influence on litter size. Thus, at a given ovulation rate, it seems that Meishan sows have a higher embryo survival rate than conventional white breeds. Some UK breeding companies are therefore producing crossbred replacement gilts which carry a trace of Meishan genes. Increasingly in more conventional breeds, DNA testing of piglets is being used to facilitate the early identification of potential prolific breeding stock.

Potential opportunities for improvement might therefore be summarized thus:

- Group housing systems increase the need to select for robustness.
- The way pigs are managed influences the consistency of the pigmeat produced.
- The number of empty days from weaning to oestrus can be controlled genetically.
- Certain breeds confer advantageous embryo survival rates.
- Minimizing genetic lag time facilitates the early use of superior genes on commercial farms.

THE CHALLENGE OF BIOTECHNOLOGY

Genetic research departments and pig breeding companies survive and prosper because their key decision makers are good at predicting the needs of both farmers and consumers of pigmeat. Inevitably their research programmes operate on a planning horizon of five to ten years. Many European consumers have been raised in an era of choice, and enjoy a certain degree of affluence and an associated full stomach – yet some of these people are now assertively telling food retailers, processors, farmers and scientists that they find some aspects of biotechnology socially unacceptable.

'The time has come,' the Walrus said,
'To talk of many things;
Of shoes – of ships – and sealing wax
Of cabbages – and kings –
And why the sea is boiling hot –
And whether pigs have wings.'

Lewis Carroll *Through the Looking Glass*
(1871)

This situation has largely arisen because of insensitive non-labelling of genetically modified imported soya beans from the USA where there is less concern over these issues. Furthermore, as globalization continues, European pig markets could be subjected to fierce competition resulting from the use of biotechnology in more 'bottom line' motivated societies where ethics are not particularly a problem. Especially in the UK, there are sensitivities on such issues in view of consumers having had to live with the real and perceived consequences of bovine spongiform encephalopathy (BSE).

The human race has been involved in the genetic modification of animals since they were first domesticated some 12,000 years ago. Thus animals most suited to producing human food have been selected for centuries. This process somewhat accelerated in the eighteenth century when a human population explosion increased the need to feed hungry people. Scientists necessarily became involved, and accelerated genetic change by placing greater emphasis on selective breeding. Present biotechnology can achieve the remarkable: for example, the myostatin gene which is responsible for double muscling in Belgian Blue cattle can already be incorporated into the genes of laboratory mice. This gene confers the capacity to double the growth rate in the mice, and to treble their ham weight. Imagine what this might do for the prolific, but as yet fat-laden, Meishan sows! Are the consumers of today ready for patented genes?

Go-ahead breeding companies find themselves on the horns of a dilemma. Do they become early adopters of new biotechnology, and forge ahead genetically to safeguard their global impact? Or do they stand by and wait for other countries and rival food producers to show them the way ahead? And if they *do* proceed at a pace, might they not be running the risk

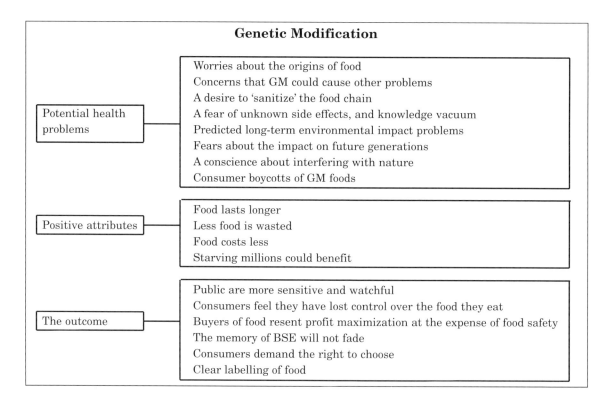

Genetic Modification

Potential health problems
- Worries about the origins of food
- Concerns that GM could cause other problems
- A desire to 'sanitize' the food chain
- A fear of unknown side effects, and knowledge vacuum
- Predicted long-term environmental impact problems
- Fears about the impact on future generations
- A conscience about interfering with nature
- Consumer boycotts of GM foods

Positive attributes
- Food lasts longer
- Less food is wasted
- Food costs less
- Starving millions could benefit

The outcome
- Public are more sensitive and watchful
- Consumers feel they have lost control over the food they eat
- Buyers of food resent profit maximization at the expense of food safety
- The memory of BSE will not fade
- Consumers demand the right to choose
- Clear labelling of food

of upsetting consumers who do not yet feel ready for this technology? Could they alienate those faced with financing the pig industry who might be reluctant to risk investing in consumer-sensitive new technology in a fickle, volatile market place?

Nutritionists understood the basics of amino acid synthesis in ruminants, and exploited it by making cannibals of cows by feeding them meat and bone meal – a source of quality protein. Unfortunately, not all aspects of the associated biology – and in particular the epidemiology, and the impact of lowering drying temperature – were fully understood, and the result was BSE. In view of this recent disaster, pig geneticists are likely to err on the side of caution when approving new technology.

Several UK pig breeding companies seem to be taking a 'wait and see' strategy, but meanwhile have elected to co-operate in the science of biotechnology. They

have decided to invest in fundamental research so that they gain information and experience of these new technologies. By working closely with biotechnologists they will be able to keep abreast of new developments. Fundamental researchers need a source of good genetic material, and breeding companies need information. This liaison should enable sound commercial decisions to be made from a position of strength, whilst still taking heed of the demands and concerns of consumers.

Consumers demand wholesome pig-meat produced under conditions providing pigs with good welfare. It seems likely, therefore, that most consumers would have no objections to biotechnology being used to prevent disease in pigs. Scientists at Edinburgh's Roslin Institute are pioneering this approach. The poultry, sheep and dairy industries are already realizing commercial benefits from disease-resistance selection programmes. Genotyping

Selecting for Disease Resistance

Specific disease – basic requirements:
Widespread and harmful to pigs
A major source of commercial loss
A zoonosis i.e. a source of human infection
A strong genetic component associated
with resistance

Disease in general – some fundamentals:
Not very heritable
Involves identifying pigs better able to
cope with disease resistance
Can be measured under normal commer-
cial conditions

of commercial pigs has indicated that almost 10 per cent of pigs are resistant to *E. coli* infections which cause post-weaning diarrhoea. Hence there seems to be considerable scope for using genetics to improve resistance to this particular pig disease.

Pathogenic *E. coli* which attach themselves to the gut wall do so by means of surface antigens called pili or fimbriae. Much neonatal diarrhoea arises because of infections with *E. coli* which have so-called F4 (K88)-type fimbriae; post-weaning diarrhoea, on the other hand, occurs because of *E. coli* with fimbriae known as type 18. Some pigs, however, are known to carry genetic resistance to the 'bug glues' F4 and F18. The receptor areas for these disease-bearing fimbriae are thought to contain complex carbohydrates which allow the disease to develop. DNA testing will enable scientists to identify the genotype of the individual pig and so allow selection against the traits which allow *E. coli* infections to proliferate.

As yet there is no evidence that disease resistance to bacteria causing salmonella infection in both pigs and humans has a genetic component. Scientists are, however, encouraged by the fact that in both mice and poultry, resistance has a genetic component. It is hoped that gene mapping will eventually identify a 'quantitative trait locus' (QTL) in pigs, and that this will confer resistance to salmonellosis. It seems that resistance to salmonella infection in mice is linked to anti-microbial activity of disease-causing cells known as macrophages. In mice this resistance is specifically linked to the *Nramp 1* gene. Already this gene has been identified in the pig, but as yet the link with resistance or susceptibility to salmonella infection has not been established.

Generalized immunity will be tackled after researchers ascertain whether pigs differ generally and genetically in their resistance to disease. Such selection processes must not, however, impair selection for more obvious characteristics. Even so, the use of genetic epidemiological modelling is likely to make great inroads into getting the best out of disease resistance in pigs of the future.

At the University of Guelph in Ontario, Ridley Inc., Cotswold Pig Development Company's Canadian parent have invested one million Canadian dollars in Gensel Biotechnologies Ltd. Their goal is to commercialize the technology already developed for the pre-selection of male and female sperm, in which case the inefficiencies associated with differences in performance between gilts and boars could be eliminated at one stroke. This process does not involve any genetic manipulation: it simply requires the addition of natural antibodies to collected

Collect X and Y sperm   X sperm clump together

Courtesy of Cotswold Pig Development Co. Ltd.

GENSEL semen sexing breakthrough.

49

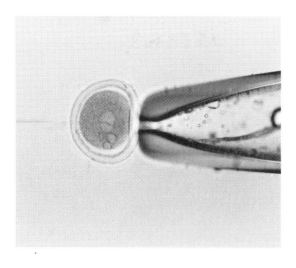

Biotechnology will accelerate progress. (SEGHERS genetics)

semen, after which the unwanted X or Y sperms clump together and are filtered off.

The technique will offer great opportunities to breeding-company multipliers who are in business to produce replacement gilts, because it would rid them of the burden of unwanted boars. This breakthrough would also provide an opportunity for UK producers to use pre-selected AI to increase slaughterweights of pigs. Current practice in the UK is to leave most male pigs entire, and this tends to put a ceiling on slaughterweights and hinders penetration of EU markets.

Pig breeding companies keeping a watching brief on biotechnology developments will certainly have plenty to monitor. The anatomical and physiological similarity of pigs to humans has resulted in substantial investment in medical research. This not only involves the use of genetics to control diseases in people, but also focuses on the potential for tissue and organ transplants from pigs to people. Given this degree of well funded and high-powered research for the benefit of mankind, ultimately the pig industry will

be the beneficiary – but it will take time for the consumer to accept this windfall.

Balancing biotechnology with consumer requirements may perhaps be summarized thus:

- Globally, all food processing industries will be under increased pressure to make use of biotechnological advances.
- Since many consumers are uneasy about biotechnology, scientists will have to adopt a cautious approach.
- Semen sexing is likely to have a major impact on production efficiency.
- Globalization will increase the need for clear labelling, and for easy traceability of biotechnologically driven meat products.
- Medical research on the pig for the benefit of mankind will give the pig industry opportunities to adopt these new findings.

Notes for Novices

- Every time new pigs are introduced to your unit there is a disease risk – take appropriate precautions.
- Think of modern pigs as a complex blend of finely tuned genes developed for specific markets.
- Traditional and rare breeds have 'eye appeal' in the farmyard, but this is not necessarily so in the market place.
- Don't get lumbered with a 'zoo' – modern breeding stock supply the vast majority of the mass market.
- Rare-breed pigs have enhanced eating quality.
- Some consumers are prepared to pay a hefty premium for 'rare breed' pigmeat – link such production to these consumers.
- Remember 'the boar is half the herd'.
- Keep a good balance of productive sows of different ages within the herd.

3 Making the Most of Nutrition

Since feed costs represent over 70 per cent of the overall cost of pig production, anyone involved in the modern pig industry who does not have a basic grasp of nutrition and feed cost is living dangerously. Pig feeding should be regarded as a biological engineering process in which energy, protein, mineral, vitamins and water are efficiently converted into lean meat. In any one year around two tonnes of feed are consumed by each sow and the weaners it produces, and over the same timespan, the finishing pigs produced by each sow consume around three and a half tonnes of feed.

The sow must be appropriately fuelled to produce a plentiful supply of viable piglets over her lifetime, and every effort must be made during the young pig's short life-span to maximize efficient conversion of feed. However, most important is feed utilization efficiency in the finish-

ing house, since the tonnage of feed used there is so great. In all, astute buying and allocation of feed has a marked impact on the profitability of pig farming.

THE ALIMENTARY CANAL

In order to make the best use of feed, a basic knowledge of the digestive system of the pig is required. A journey through the alimentary canal starts at the mouth. The pig's instincts to root make it particularly adept at chewing and grinding ingested food which is moistened by alkaline saliva; starch is broken down by an enzyme within the saliva called amylase. Once the food is broken into smaller fragments, muscular movements known as peristalsis force it along the gut, which is basically a tortuous tube; there is much biochemical activity both along the length of the gut and across the gut wall. Moisture from saliva eases the process of swallowing and the passage of food into the stomach. Food fragments arriving in the stomach of the adult pig find themselves in a muscular sac with a capacity of around 8 litres. It is helpful to think of the stomach as a 'holding pen', a checkpoint prior to the small intestine.

The stomach has a very acidic environment, and this acidity helps to suppress harmful bacteria such as *E. coli*; in partic-

Approximate Feed Requirement (tonnes/month)			
Herd size (Sows)	Sow	Weaner	Finisher (to 68kg (150lb) deadweight)
50	5	4	15
100	10	8	29
150	15	12	44
200	20	16	58
400	40	20	117

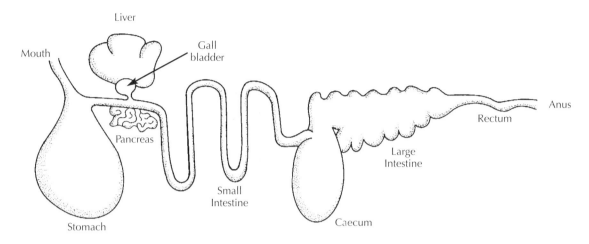

The anatomy of the digestive system of a pig.

ular, it helps the enzyme pepsin to start to work on the breakdown of protein. Once feed leaves the stomach and arrives in the small intestine, several digestive juices flow into the gut from the gall bladder and pancreas; within these juices, pancreatic amylase completes the breakdown of starch into sugars under alkaline conditions, trypsin breaks down protein into amino acids, and lipase turns fat into fatty acids. These are then ready for absorption.

In all pigs, and particularly baby pigs, it is vital that digesta does not shoot through the gut before it can be absorbed. Nature slows down the throughput by increasing the absorptive surface area of the small intestine: it does this by lining it with a series of finger-like projections known as villi, which are themselves coated with further projections called microvilli. These facilitate the transfer of nutrients to the blood system, which then conveys them to the appropriate sites for

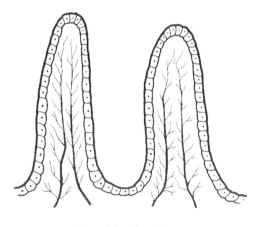

Normal healthy villi
with a good capacity
for absorption

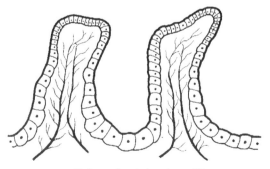

Deformed and shrunken villi
with a reduced capacity
for absorption

Diagram of villi – nature's answer to traffic calming.

Water is a vital nutrient both indoors and outdoors, and in all weathers. (J. Harvey Engineering)

bone growth and muscle development, as well as for the deposition of fat and the build-up of other tissues. Digesta flows from the small intestine into the large intestine, in which there is much recovery of water and minerals via re-absorption.

No enzymes are secreted into the large intestine, although the digestion process still continues there: bacteria which are the normal inhabitants of the hind gut break down food via fermentation. The cellulose cell walls of vegetable matter cannot be broken down by naturally occurring enzymes in the pig – there is in fact a whole range of carbohydrates generally referred to as 'fibre' which resist enzyme breakdown. However, although the process is not as efficient as breakdown by enzymes, bacteria in the large intestine can ferment fibre and break down its tough walls to form organic acids which can be absorbed into the bloodstream. Throughout the gut there is a vast range of both beneficial and harmful organisms which actually outnumber the cells in the body.

Another benefit of fermentation is that the resultant organic acids increase the acid balance and so help prevent the proliferation of harmful micro-organisms such as *E. coli*. Fibre is also able to mop up water within the gut, and this promotes a safe passage for the digesta through the gut, thus diminishing the likelihood of diarrhoea and constipation. Fibre does have its down side, however, in

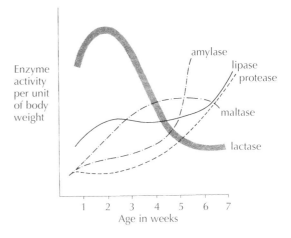

The activity of the digestive system in a baby pig.

53

that it is a low energy feed, so if too much is ingested the overall digestibility of feed will be reduced; excess fibre takes up space in the gut, and growth rate is impaired. This is particularly crucial with young pigs.

Fermentation is most effective in adult stock. Feedstuffs such as grass, quality silage and fodder beet which contain 20 per cent, 28 per cent and 6 per cent, respectively, crude fibre can be fed to sows, and phenomenal intakes of these bulky forages have been recorded in mature sows. The bulk tends to stretch the pig's gut, so if these forages are offered in late pregnancy and stretch the gut, the likelihood is that during lactation the sow will be able to achieve a higher intake of conventional feed, to its benefit. Dietary fibre can also be used in early pregnancy to limit feed intake.

The need to match nutrient supply to changing needs is epitomized in the baby pig. Its immature gut is ill equipped for the digestion of starches, since the enzymes maltase and amylase are initially only present at a low level. On the other hand, it is well equipped with lactase to digest milk sugar, and lipase to break down milk fat. Particularly when indoor pigs are weaned before twenty-four days of age, highly sophisticated, expensive first-stage (starter) rations are needed. The clever bit is knowing when cheaper conventional cereals, proteins and energy sources can be introduced, which means being able to assess exactly when the appropriate enzyme systems have developed, or are capable of being switched on. Formulating and feeding rations to baby pigs is therefore both an art and a science. Since dehydration is a major problem in newly weaned pigs, recent developments have focused on the concept of feeding a porridge to baby pigs in an attempt to boost feed intake; a gradual reduction in its water content gently coaxes the digestive system on to solid food.

The breakdown of food may perhaps be summarized thus:

- Much physical breakdown occurs in the mouth, and the biochemical breakdown also starts there.
- The acidic environment of the stomach helps kill harmful bacteria.
- Villi slow the passage of food through the small intestine and increase the absorptive area.
- No enzymes are secreted in the large intestine: some digesta is fermented there, and it is a site of absorption.

ENERGY

Fats, proteins and carbohydrates are all potential sources of energy. During the process of oxidation they are broken down and energy is released. The following equation outlines the associated biochemistry:

$$C_6 H_{12} O_6 + 6O_2 = 6 CO_2 + 6H_2O + ENERGY$$

In the absence of a mechanism to trap this energy, it would simply be released into

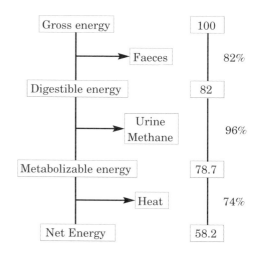

Energy evaluation principles.

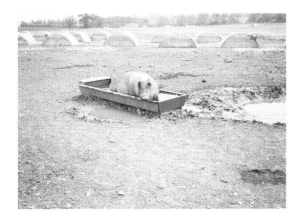

Wallowing in the drinking water –
definitely not recommended!
(PIGSPEC)

the environment as heat. However, at cell level there is a complex provision for storing it: a substance known as adenosine diphosphate (ADP) combines with inorganic phosphate to form adenosine triphosphate (ATP); it follows the biochemical pathway

$$ADP + H_3PO_4 = ATP + H_2O$$

This process traps the energy within the living cell and so minimizes the generation of waste heat, and is known as oxidative phosphorylation. Less heat energy is lost from a fat-based source as compared to other sources of energy.

Energy is subsequently released in the pig and is used for body maintenance, growth or milk production as required. Different feedstuffs have different energy levels, and the term for quantifying this energy is MJ/kg of DE (megajoules per kilogram of digestible energy). So what does this mean to a pig?

If a sample of pig feed were burnt, like a lump of coal, it would give out heat: this is known as its gross energy. Using a steel chamber containing an atmosphere of oxygen, it could be fired in a laboratory to release its gross energy content. A mathematical equation involving a term for the associated temperature lift enables a figure to be calculated for its energy value. Not surprisingly, this 'raw energy' is of little value to the pig – the very reason why coal does not feature in pig-feed ration formulation!

When a pig eats, there is an inevitable energy loss in the form of a waste gas, methane. There is also heat energy loss in the faeces in the form of indigestible components that still have a gross energy content. Digestible energy is the energy remaining that the pig can actually use for maintenance and production.

Fibrous substances such as grass meal have a digestible energy around 5.99 MJ/kg, whereas dried whole milk has around 22.1 MJ/kg, and wheat around 14.3 MJ/kg: therefore feed ingredients should be carefully selected for optimum utilizable energy. Getting the energy/protein balance right is also vital for efficient pig production.

The energy content of ruminant and poultry feeds is usually expressed as metabolizable energy (ME), and takes account of energy losses in urine and other nitrogen losses. So far in the UK this system has not been widely used by the pig industry; however, 'ME (Pig)' could be a term which pig farmers will see more of in the future after more metabolism trials have been completed on various feeds for pigs. The energy that the pig ultimately makes use of in order to fuel growth and other metabolic processes is known as the 'net energy'.

The pig's utilization of energy may perhaps be summarized thus:

- Fats, proteins and carbohydrates are all potential sources of energy.
- Some heat energy is lost from food, but the pig has a mechanism for storing energy.
- Pig rations should have the optimum balance of protein and energy otherwise inefficiencies will arise.

PROTEINS

The protein content of pig feed is eventually broken down to small peptides and amino acids in the gut, and these pass into the bloodstream. In growing pigs and adult breedingstock these amino acids are subsequently removed from the blood and pass into the liver where they are 'built up' and deposited in various tissues, thereby facilitating growth. Imagine them as building blocks loaded onto a pallet before being used to build a well-bonded wall: growth comprises the build-up of amino acids into body proteins, mainly muscle, connective tissue and blood. Amino acids are also used in the manufacture of enzymes and other substances essential to the regulation of life processes.

Like other mammals, the pig has only a limited ability to store protein, and so surplus amino acids have to be broken down. This situation arises because of a process known as deamination which takes place in the liver and kidneys. It involves a biochemical reaction between oxygen and amino acids to form uric acid, which does not contain any ammonia; the acid is then converted into urea, and is ultimately excreted through the kidneys. Deamination is an energy-dependent process, and if excess or unbalanced protein is fed, the cost of disposing of the surplus has to be borne.

Protein utilization is actually a complex process. In growing pigs, protein requirements vary according to their sex and liveweight, and are governed by their different genetically driven potentials for lean meat production. However, 'lean is lean', and so the relative amounts of different amino acids will be the same in all instances. This makes it possible to establish an optimum balance of essential amino acids which, when supplied with sufficient nitrogen for the synthesis of non-essential amino acids, would consti-

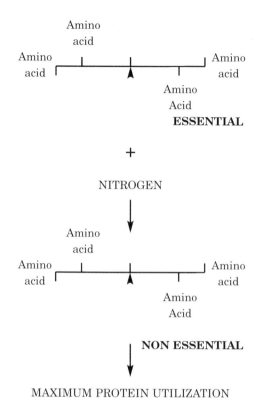

Ideal protein.

tute an 'ideal protein'. Essential amino acids cannot be produced within the animal and must be supplied from within the list of dietary constituents; thus the ideal protein represents the perfect supply of essential amino acids and non-essential nitrogen for the productive process under way – which might be growth, pregnancy or lactation. If individual components of protein are then added or subtracted over and above that already present as the ideal protein package, its quality cannot be impaired, nor can the performance of the pigs to which it is fed. Hence pigs of different classes require different amounts of ideal protein, though the quality of the protein remains the same.

The ratio of the most important amino acids in an ideal protein is expressed in relation to the lysine content, lysine being

Amino Acid Requirements in Ideal Protein for Growing Pigs		
Amino Acid	*Relative to Lysine = 100*	*% Inclusion in Ideal Protein*
Lysine	100	7.0
Methionine	50	3.5
Tryptophan	15	1.0
Threonine	60	4.2
Total non-essential amino acids	–	59.6

Source: Fuller & Chamberlain

understood to be the first limiting amino acid. Not surprisingly, the optimum ratio of amino acids in feed is very similar to that in the lean tissue of the pig. Quality proteins such as fish meal and milk products have this characteristic profile.

Protein breakdown has two distinct phases. First, the pig's own enzymes in the stomach and small intestine get to work on the feed, generating protein subunits that are available for absorption. Once the digesta enters the terminal ileum it is no longer subjected to attack by these enzymes. Beyond the ileum much of the undigested protein is broken down less efficiently into urea and ammonia by fermenting bacteria that produce enzymes of their own. Hence the best estimates of digestibility take account of the ability of proteins to donate their amino acids prior to entering the large intestine. Any value thus determined is known as the ileal digestibility.

The most important points regarding protein may therefore be summarized thus:

- Essential amino acids have to be supplied in the diet.
- The pig cannot store much protein and so any excess has to be eliminated – with an energy cost.
- Ideal protein contains the optimum ratio of amino acids.
- The quantity of ideal protein required depends on genetic and environmental factors.

THE BALANCED DIET

Protein and Energy

Getting the balance right between protein and energy is vital, and there are penalties for getting it wrong. When there is too much energy in relation to ideal protein, what protein is there, will be used efficiently; but growth rates will be depressed because of the shortfall in ideal protein. Conversely, if there is too much ideal protein and not enough energy, again there will be poor growth rate; but this will be accompanied by a loss of protein components through de-amination. If the energy level of the diet is increased, the surplus energy will be stored as fat, with consequent detrimental effects to the acceptability of the carcase at slaughter.

The concept of 'choice feeding' allows the pig itself to select the ideal blend of energy and protein, and the respective

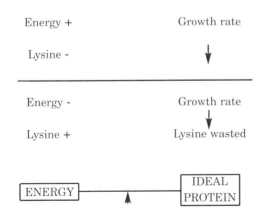

Protein: Energy balance.

fractions are made available in separate hoppers. As the pig grows it is able to adjust its feed selection so that it endeavours to ingest the optimum energy/protein balance within the confines of the composition of the diets on offer. Such an approach is not foolproof since the pig is not the perfect judge of its own needs, and research and farm trials have yielded variable results.

P stands for Pig

P stands for Pig, as I remarked before,
A second cousin to the Huge Wild Boar
But pigs are civilised, while Huge Wild Boars
Live savagely at random out of doors,
And in their coarse contempt of dainty foods,
Subsist on truffles, which they find in woods.
Not so the cultivated Pig who feels
The need of several courses at his meals,
But wrongly thinks it does not matter whether
He takes them one by one or all together.
Hence, Pigs devour, from lack of self-respect,
What Epicures would certainly reject.

MORAL

Learn from the Pig to take whatever Fate Or Elder Persons heap upon your plate.

Hilaire Belloc, *A Bad Child's Book of Beasts* (1940)

Initially the daily lysine requirement increases in the growing pig; however, once the rate of lean deposition starts to decline, the take-up of lysine tails off – that is, the ratio of lysine per unit of energy declines. Hence a ration which is appropriately balanced for the pig at 30kg (66lb) cannot be right at 90kg (198lb). Particularly on a continuous throughput breeder/finisher unit, a frequently changing ration specification is difficult to implement. The practical compromise has therefore been simply to lower the protein content after an arbitrary mid-point in the growth of the pig, for example, when it has reached about 45kg (99lb). Even given

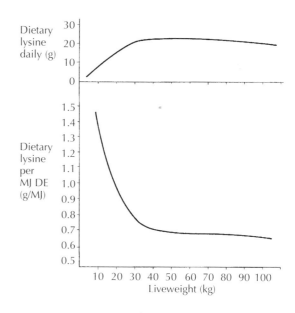

The relationship between dietary lysine and energy in a growing and finishing pig.

this measure, in the early stages lysine tends to be in short supply, whereas in the late finishing stages it is excreted from the body in the form of urea, due to excess.

The setting-up of 'contracted pig schemes' practising all-in/all-out management has provided a cost-effective and practical opportunity for regularly changing ration specifications for finishing pigs. The broiler industry presented a useful role model, since frequent alteration of ration formulation was routine practice in a production system in which all-in/all-out management was the 'norm'.

Phase feeding is a practice becoming more commonplace in the pig industry, and one that takes advantage of the opportunities provided by all-in/all-out systems. In its simplest form it involves changing the specification of feed in the bulk bin for contemporary batches of pigs. A more complicated arrangement involves the use of sophisticated machinery for blending differing proportions of feed

---

Bulk Bin Management

What to avoid:

- Siting the bins in direct sunlight.
- Defective welding of seams leading to deterioration.
- Porous and rusty surfaces.
- Lorries entering the pig unit to fill the bins.
- Feed sticking to the bin sides and lodging on internal surfaces.
- Moisture, heat and condensation causing damp and hot spots leading to mould contamination and mycotoxin production.
- Mites in the feed.
- Unappetizing odours in stored feed.
- Last-minute ordering of feed.
- Compromising on safety when managing bulk bins.

How to avoid problems:

- Regularly inspect the bins – at least once monthly.
- Every spring and autumn thoroughly pressure-wash the inside of the bins; ensure internal surfaces are dry before refilling.
- Check the inlet and outlet to the bin for blockages and wear and tear.
- Try to ensure that bins are emptied, or almost emptied, between feed deliveries.
- Regularly use smoke bombs for fumigation control of insects, particularly mites.
- Dust the inside of a clean, dry bin with mould inhibitor.
- Practise a hygiene protocol for pig feed hoppers.

---

from two or more bulk bins or liquid feed stores. This allows feed of different specification to be fed automatically within the same room. Hence pigs of different genetics, sex, or those intended for specific market outlets, can be fed appropriately. Furthermore, the need to reduce nitrogen and phosphorus levels in effluent has caused this system to be taken up in the Netherlands, thereby assisting with environmental damage limitation.

Vitamins

Vitamins are organic compounds necessary for maintaining normal processes such as growth, health and fertility; generally, however, they cannot be synthesized by the pig, so it is essential that they are provided in a balanced diet. Small amounts of biotin and some B vitamins are synthesized by bacteria in the gut, but ration formulators cannot depend on this unpredictable contribution, hence supplementation of the diet is the norm.

Vitamins are natural, biologically active substances, and each one undertakes a specific task unique to that particular micro-nutrient. They were first discovered in the early twentieth century, and were first classified according to letters of the alphabet. As more vitamins have been discovered in modern times, they are increasingly referred to by their chemical names. Pig feed compounders are well versed in vitamin requirements, and commercial pressures are such that they strive to keep abreast of new developments. Vitamins are first mixed in small quantities with mineral mixtures, and then with other feed ingredients. How long the vitamins remain efficacious depends on these other substances, and on various environmental factors such as exposure to heat, light and moisture. Inevitably there is always a certain time lag between manufacture, the mixing of the vitamins, and their consumption by the pig. Hence home mixers should always heed the 'use by' date on the paper sack, and in particular co-product (by-product) feeders should specify those vitamins and minerals which make up for any shortfall in the overall ration.

Typical Vitamin Specifications in Rations for Modern Pigs

Vitamin (iu / kg)	Weaner First Stage	Weaner Second Stage	Grower	Finisher	Dry Sow	Lactating Sow
A	15,000	15,000	10,000	8500	10,000	10,000
D_3	2,000	2,000	1850	1875	2,000	2,000
E	250	150	100	50	70	70
Selenium (mg/kg sodium selenite)	0.3	0.25	0.25	0.20	0.20	0.3*

* 0.3 mg/kg in single combined sow diet

Source: Various UK Feed/Mineral/Vitamin Companies

Vitamins added to feed usually have a 20 per cent safety margin over and above that required for good health and production. Some producers on high-output systems strategically inject a multi-vitamin booster subcutaneously in productive gilts after weaning their first litter: this is a one-off, high-level 'shot' given immediately after the drain of lactation.

Despite these 'good measure' strategies, under certain circumstances vitamins appear to be deficient. The main culprits are vitamin E (tocopherol), vitamin B12 (cyanocobalamin) and biotin. Symptoms of vitamin E deficiency sometimes arise, particularly in diets with high levels of unsaturated fat where soya bean oil or full fat soya are used at significant rates of inclusion. Because of the trend against using animal protein in pig diets, rations are increasingly based on soya beans and cereals, and these are more likely to lack B12. Especially when sows and boars are housed on concrete, they should be examined for cracks in the keratin on the cleats of their feet: this would indicate a biotin deficiency.

Breeding sows require supplementary vitamins throughout their lifetime so that they are able to sustain high output over several parities. This approach seems to provide variable results on the same farm and between farms, not all of which are directly related to nutrition. Increasingly, particularly on high output units, specific supplementary vitamins and minerals are being fed just for a limited critical period. A target time is the first thirty days of pregnancy in an effort to minimize embryo loss and boost implantation rates. The decision whether or not to administer booster doses of vitamins and minerals must be taken on an individual farm basis, and will reflect the current output of that particular farm.

Minerals

Most minerals are present in solution in an ionic form, and carry out the general function of maintaining a constant osmotic pressure and pH. It is very important that the correct ionic balance is maintained in blood, lymph, tissue fluids and cells. However, minerals such as calcium and phosphorus which form bone, iron in the blood, trace elements in enzymes and phosphoric complexes associated with energy metabolism, actually form organic compounds.

Calcium and phosphorus together make up around 75 per cent of the mineral content of the pig. Other important minerals include potassium, sodium, magnesium, chlorine and sulphur. Ration formulators take great care not only to ensure that the required levels of mineral are supplied, but that the proportion of various minerals is also correct; for example, excessive levels of calcium can lead to urinary problems.

Details of mineral inclusion levels are supplied with purchased diets, and are usually expressed as a percentage of the diet. Trace elements – including iron, copper, cobalt iodine, manganese, zinc, sele-

nium and molybdenum – are measured in parts per million (ppm) or milligrams per kilogram of diet. Nevertheless, deficiency of a trace element can have a hugely deleterious effect on pig health and productivity. Moreover, any savings from home-mixing cereals or incorporating by-products can be rapidly eroded if the mineral status is inappropriate. Mineral levels must be related to the raw materials fed, and specialist help is recommended. Maximum levels of inclusion of trace elements are maintained within the Feedingstuffs Regulations of the Agricultural Act.

Bone comprises around 50 per cent water, 20 per cent protein, 26 per cent ash and – as every smart dog knows! – about 4 per cent fat. The ash fraction contains around 85 per cent calcium phosphate, besides calcium carbonate, magnesium carbonate and some citrate. Providing the right minerals for good bone formation in rapidly growing, genetically improved pigs and high-output breeding stock is vital.

The provision of water specifically for suckling pigs encourages creep feed intake. (Bernard Partridge)

The nutritional balancing act might be summarized as follows:

- Vitamins and minerals are important in any balanced diet; moreover, co-product feeds usually require special attention.
- The efficacy of vitamins declines if they are stored too long before feeding: read the label.
- Inadequate levels of vitamins, minerals and micro-nutrients can impair production and pig health.
- Temporary additional supplementation may be a good idea in some high-output systems.

Water

Trial work in both Britain and Denmark in the distant past suggested a trend in favour of better daily liveweight gain for self-watered pigs. Similarly, farmers running high-output breeding units indicate higher feed intakes and milkier sows when water is not restricted in the farrowing house. Since the original trial work, the amount of carcase lean in genetically improved pigs has increased by over 25 per cent. Lean meat contains over 70 per cent water, and sow's milk over 80 per cent, hence it follows that water has become an increasingly important nutrient. Moreover, water is essential as an agent for 'flushing' toxins or mineral burdens from the gut. It seems logical, therefore, to adopt a professional approach to the provision of water. A good approach is to focus on the seemingly unimportant aspects of water, and to do something about them.

The Pig Welfare Code is more concerned with the general well-being of the pig than with maximizing output of lean meat with respect to watering recommen-

---

Water: Getting the Right Quantity and Quality

- Provide unrestricted access to water.
- Install a header tank or anti-sucking-back device between the mains supply and the pigs.
- Insulate and lid the header tank. Where mineral content is known to be high incorporate a filter and drain tap.
- Check flow rates frequently.
- Check and adjust drinker heights.
- Undertake laboratory analysis to check water quality.
- Consider adding a flavour enhancer when water is not palatable.
- Be prepared for interruptions in supply – winter and summer bring their own special problems.
- Particularly on an all-in/all-out system, consider fitting a water meter, and check whole house consumption every day.

Requirements for Water

Stage	Drinker height (cm)	Minimum flow rate (millilitres/minute)
Weaners	35–45	500
Growers	50–60	700
Finishers	65–75	700
Dry sows/boars	80–90	1000
Lactating sows	80–90	1500

- Height settings are approximate – check with manufacturers.
- Spray/nozzle drinkers for lactating sows are usually sited in, or just above, the feed trough.
- Adjust settings according to piglet behaviour.
- Check for excessive spillage and agression near the drinkers.

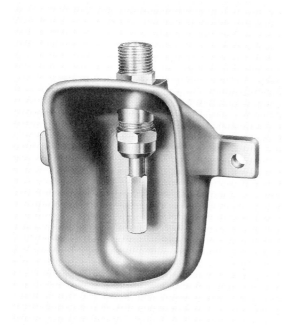

A novel drinker designed to minimize spillage and contamination of water. (Arato Drinkers)

Improved nipple-drinker design ensures minimum spillage, and that clean water is always available. (Bernard Partridge)

dations. According to the code, 'Pigs should have sufficient clean water, or other whole liquid, for their daily needs.' And where water is not freely available, then at least $2^1/_2$ litres ($^1/_2$gal) of water should be available for each kilogram of dry feed. The guideline *minimum* daily recommendations for sows are:

Non-pregnant   5 litres (1gal);
Pregnant   5–8 litres (1–1$^3/_4$gal);
Lactating   15–30 litres ($3^1/_4$–$6^1/_2$gal).

Trials and practical experience indicate that there is tremendous variation between individuals in the amount of water they consume, or at the worst remove from the drinker. At least one drinking point must be available for every ten pigs, and audit schemes usually demand more than one source of water in each pen of pigs. Even where liquid feeding is practised, and especially where co-products are used, additional drinking water must be provided.

In a necessarily precise industry, rules of thumb tend to be taboo. Having said that, a guideline for the water needs of any pig is to estimate its bodyweight in kilograms, and then divide this figure by ten: the answer in litres corresponds to the approximate daily water requirement. Thus:

50kg (110lb) liveweight = 5 litres (1gal) of water/day;
90kg (198lb) liveweight = 9 litres (2gal) of water/day.

This is a useful mathematical aid, particularly when calculating the water storage capacity needed in a header tank supply-

Correctly sited nipple drinker. (Arato Drinkers)

ing a known number of pigs. An absolute minimum of twelve hours' water storage is recommended, and a strategy should be developed for emergency water supply during periods of temporary disruption. On remote sites, or where, for instance, tractor driving responsibilities necessitate long absences, an unobserved disruption to water supply could have very serious consequences.

Given the choice, pigs prefer to drink from a bowl rather than a nipple drinker; they also prefer to drink clean water rather than foul water. If the design and siting of a bowl drinker is such that it rapidly becomes soiled with dung, most pigs will back off and reject it. Many of the original drinking bowls for pigs 'borrowed' their design specification from the dairy industry. However, pigs and cows not only have a different anatomy, they also behave markedly differently: in pig pens, such bowls within minutes of 'de-bunging' become a receptacle for dung and unwholesome food debris. Fortunately a new generation of bowl drinkers designed for cleanliness and spillage-free accessi-

bility has emerged onto the market in recent years. Furthermore, relatively drip-free nipple or bite drinkers have made great advances.

Generally, nipple drinkers should provide a hygiene bonus, but if flow rates are excessive and spillage arises, pigs readily opt for the easier but more hazardous option of drinking from the floor. The provision of filtering devices prior to the header tank reduces the likelihood of the plumbing nearest the pig from becoming blocked by dissolved and suspended solids. Water containing high levels of dissolved solids tends to be unpalatable and expensive to purify, particularly when the suspended solids exceed 1,000 ppm. If possible, such sources of water should be avoided.

If a drinker is not set at the right height and the correct angle, water spillage can be a problem; not only is this expensive, but it also tends to exacerbate pollution problems. Given that a pig increases its bodyweight by about 70-fold between birth and slaughter, and 150-fold by the time it becomes a mature breeding animal, drinker heights need widely differing settings for the various stages of production. Recommendations for particular drinker heights must be checked with manufacturers. The correct height approximates to the distance between ground level and the top of a pig's snout when it is standing normally. Ideally, drinkers should be set at right angles, or at about 15 degrees below the horizontal.

Trials have indicated that baby pigs given water with inadequate flow rates soon tire and lose interest. Finishers are prepared to stand their ground for longer at a drinker, but since this denies access to others, it is not the ideal solution. Generally flow rates should be such that, given the need, pigs could obtain their daily water requirement within twenty minutes. It is logical to suggest that the high water requirement of lactating sows will not be easily met by poor drinker design; any consequent behavioural disturbance will lead to poor milk let-down and the potential for over-laying offspring. In hot weather it is advisable to provide extra water, to help dissipate higher body temperatures.

To summarize, the following watering points should be observed:

- Do not allow water to be an afterthought: regard it as a vital nutrient.
- Recognize that lean meat and sow's milk have high water contents, and make the most of this opportunity.
- Plan for failure: formulate a strategy for dealing with plumbing emergencies in both hot and cold weather and on Bank Holidays!
- Avoid spillages of clean water: when allowed to mix with dirty water, it becomes a pollution hazard.

One finishing building with two feed lines to improve nutritional specificity.
(TXU Europe (formerly Eastern Group))

Finishers fed ad lib in naturally ventilated, insulated portal-frame building. (TXU Europe (formerly Eastern Group))

FEED SYSTEM STRATEGIES

Scientific advances in nutrition, genetics and feeding equipment bring with them new opportunities for feeding pigs, and the inevitable complications associated with these choices. Even before the revolution in pig genetics, the consensus was that floor-feeding of meal was a wasteful process, and economics at that time favoured replacing this system with a pipeline and troughs, and opting for wet feeding. Financial appraisals then indicated that a change from floor-feeding finishing pigs on pellets to a wet-feeding regime could not be justified: it was assumed that after 70kg (154lb) liveweight there was no opportunity for ad lib feeding since excessive backfat was inevitable. Restrict feeding was the order of the day.

> Never eat anything more at one sitting that you cannot lift.　　　(Miss Piggy)

Consumer awareness, and an acceptance of the need for 'due diligence' during the on-farm stages of the food chain, have together caused the practice of floor-feeding to be questioned: it does not square with wholesome meat production, and could lead to the proliferation of disease organisms such as those responsible for

Single-space hoppers have proved popular on ad lib feeding systems.
(TXU Europe (formerly Eastern Group))

swine dysentery and salmonellosis. Furthermore, the allocation of feed in this system is governed more by the need to keep the pen floor clean, than the opportunity to make the most of the genetic potential of the pig.

Feed Conversion Efficiency

The challenge faced by today's pig farmers feeding modern pigs is that of cost effectively maximizing the production of lean meat. In order to do this, the farmer has to ascertain how much feed the genetics will be able to make use of efficiently in a particular environment and with pigs of a certain health status.

On the graph overleaf, the solid line represents 'daily liveweight gain' (DLWG) and the dotted line 'feed conversion efficiency' (FCE). At low feed intakes, little growth rates take place since much feed is used simply for maintenance; hence feed conversion efficiency is poor. At higher feed intakes, more nutrients become available for growth, daily liveweight gain increases and so feed conversion efficiency improves. This situation increases until a crucial stage is reached when the rate of fat deposition takes off; this happens later and later in genetically advanced pigs. Fat deposition demands energy, and inherently has a higher nutrient requirement, being some threefold

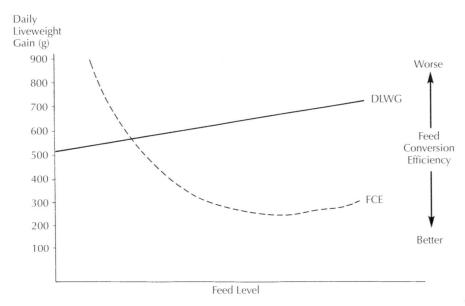

Influence of feed level on feed conversion and growth rate.

higher in dry matter than lean tissue. Eventually a stage is reached when the rate of energy uptake demanded exceeds that associated with the earlier rapid growth rates; feed conversion efficiency then starts to deteriorate.

Prior to the amazing advances in pig genetics, the dotted feed conversion efficiency line used to take the form of a 'V' shape. These days it has become more of an 'L shape', which opens up great possibilities for ad lib feeding to higher weights without substantial deterioration in grading profiles.

A pig-activated circular feed hopper providing good access with minimal spillage. (Pyramid Systems (Malton) Ltd)

Typical Analysis of Pig-Feed Raw Materials

Feed product	Digestible energy (MJ DE /kg)	Dry matter	Crude protein	Available lysine	Ether extract (oil)	Crude fibre
		<------------------------------%------------------------------>				
Barley	14.5	86.0	12.3	0.37	2.5	5.1
Wheat	16.0	86.0	13.0	0.30	1.8	3.0
Wheat feed	11.5	86.0	17.5	0.50	3.5	9.0
Maize	17.1	89.0	9.6	0.50	4.1	2.5
Chilean fish meal	17.0	91.0	73.0	5.30	10.0	0.5
Extracted soya bean meal (high protein)	15.5	90.0	55.0	2.90	2.4	4.0
Field beans	15.8	86.0	29.0	1.65	1.8	9.0
Sugar beet pulp (molassed)	13.1	90.0	11.0	0.35	0.4	15.0

Source: Dr W. N. Ewing, *The Feeds Directory*

Wet versus Dry Feeding

The widespread emergence of ad lib feeding of genetically improved pigs has fogged the issues regarding differences between wet and dry feeding. Unrestricted hopper feeding of meal or pellets with an unlimited water supply is now commonplace, and 'slop feeding, whereby drinkers are located within a dry feed, single space hopper, has become popular. This system arose because of the need to minimize dirty water production on intensive units in the Netherlands, again for reasons of pollution control.

Traditionally the only option for wet feeders was wet feeding a gruel via a pipeline system discharging into a long trough; bacon pigs were each provided with 300mm (1ft) of trough space, though this tended to elongate the lying area. The development of 'zig-zag' trough divisions made big inroads into the problems of bullying at the trough, and the associated variations in feed intakes. However, the basic concept was seriously flawed in that

Maximum Inclusion Rates in Pig Rations

% Recommended upper inclusion rate

Feed product	Creep	Weaner	Grower	Finisher	Sow
Barley	20.0	25.0	30.0	30.0	25.0
Wheat	6.0	55.5	50.0	50.0	50.0
Wheat feed	5.0	10.0	25.0	25.0	20.0
Maize	6.0	50.0	409.0	25.0	35.0
Chilean fish meal	10.0	10.0	7.5	4.0	3.0
Extracted soya bean meal (high protein)	20.0	25.0	30.0	30.0	30.0
Field beans	0.0	0.0	7.5	10.0	10.0
Sugar beet pulp (molassed)	0.0	10.0	10.0	15.0	25.0

Source: Dr W. N. Ewing, *The Feeds Directory*

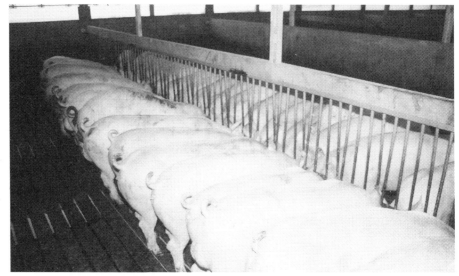

Traditional wet feeding in long troughs with zig-zag divisions. (Pyramid Systems (Malton) Ltd)

Guidelines of the Nutrient Requirements of Gilts and Boars (split-sex feeding)

Nutrient	Gilts 50–75kg (110–165lb)	Boars 50–75kg (110–165lb)	Gilts 75–100kg (165–220lb)	Boars 75–100kg (165–220lb)
Moisture %	12.8	12.8	12.8	12.8
Oil A %	5.1	5.1	4.6	4.6
Oil B %	5.7	5.7	5.3	5.3
Fibre %	4.2	4.2	4.8	4.8
Ash %	5.8	5.8	5.8	5.8
MJ DE/kg	13.8	14	13.5	13.7
Mcal DE/kg	3.29	3.35	3.22	3.27
Starch %	34.2	34.2	34	34
Linoleic %	1.33	1.33	1.21	1.21
Crude protein %	18.5	19.5	17.5	18.5
Total lysine %	1.1	1.25	0.95	1.1
Methionine %	0.41	0.46	0.35	0.41
Meth/cyst %	0.61	0.69	0.52	0.61
Threonine %	0.77	0.87	0.66	0.77
Tryptophan %	0.22	0.25	0.19	0.22
DG-lysine	0.96	1.09	0.83	0.96
DG-methionine	0.36	0.41	0.31	0.36
DG-met/cys	0.54	0.61	0.45	0.54
DG-threonine	0.66	0.75	0.57	0.66
DG-tryptophan	0.19	0.22	0.17	0.19
Lysine (g)/MJ DE	0.8	0.9	0.7	0.8
Lysine (g) Meal DE	3.34	3.73	2.95	3.37

Source: JSR Healthbred Limited

the need to provide generous trough space for simultaneous restrict-feeding governed the layout of the building. The desirability of matching pig numbers and appropriate lying area with the available trough space also played havoc with optimizing stocking densities: the result was a long, thin lying area in a wide building with insufficient dunging area. The necessarily long narrow pens often had fouled lying areas because of the long challenging trek to the designated dunging area.

The resultant wide buildings also proved difficult to ventilate, particularly in hot weather when dirty pigs often became a problem.

The arrival of short-trough, ad lib wet feeding has simplified the problems of pen layout. The system can be installed in slatted, insulated, compact buildings, or for bedded pigs kept in large groups in straw yards. Whilst little is known about the feeding behaviour of pigs on such systems, it has great potential for encourag-

Dietary Specifications for Maiden Gilts and Sows

Nutrient	Gilt Rearer 80–140kg (175–309lb)	Gestation	Lactation
Moisture %	12.8	12.8	12.8
Oil A %[1]	5.3	5.3	5.5
Oil B %[2]	6.1	5.9	6.2
Fibre %	4.7	6.5	4.1
Ash %	6.1	6.5	5.9
MJ DE/kg	13.5	13.2	14.2
Mcal DE/kg	3.23	3.11	3.40
Starch %	33.3	31.7	36.4
Linoleic %	1.38	1.35	1.65
Crude protein %	16.5	13.1	18.5
Total lysine %	0.80	0.55	1.05
Methionine %	0.31	0.19	0.35
Meth/cyst %	0.53	0.30	0.58
Threonine %	0.57	0.41	0.63
Tryptophan %	0.17	0.11	0.19
DG-lysine	0.72	0.45	0.87
DG-methionine	0.28	0.16	0.31
DG-met/cys	0.46	0.36	0.51
DG-threonine	0.54	0.33	0.54
DG-tryptophan	0.14	0.09	0.16
Lysine (g)/MJ DE	0.60	0.42	0.74
Lysine (g)/Meal DE	2.47	1.77	2.94

[1] By ether extraction
[2] By acid hydrolysis

Source: JSR Healthbred Limited

ing very high feed intakes, in particular into young pigs, without impairing grading.

Facts on feeding systems may perhaps be summarized as follows:

- Good grading and ad lib feeding are both attainable with many modern pigs.

- Floor-feeding is an inefficient process, and detracts from wholesomeness.
- New technology is changing the options available in feeding systems.
- The chosen feeding system can have a substantial impact on building layout.

Guidelines for the Nutrient Requirements of Weaners, Growers and Finishing Pigs

	Weaner 12–20kg (27–44lb)	Grower 20–45kg (44–99lb)	Finisher 45–100kg (99–220lb)
Nutrient			
Moisture %	12.8	12.8	12.8
Oil A %	6.1	5.9	4.6
Oil B %	6.89	6.7	5.3
Fibre %	3.2	3.6	4.8
Ash %	5.2	5.8	5.8
MJ DE/kg	14.7	14.4	13.7
Mcal DE/kg	3.51	3.44	3.27
Starch %	35.7	34.8	34
Linoleic %	1.75	1.58	1.21
Crude protein %	21.5	20.7	18.5
Total lysine %	1.45	1.29	1.08
Methionine %	0.53	0.48	0.39
Meth/cyst %	0.87	0.78	0.65
Threonine %	1.01	0.91	0.76
Tryptophan %	0.29	0.26	0.21
DG-lysine	1.32	1.17	0.93
DG-methionine	0.46	0.42	0.34
DG-met/cys	0.78	0.69	0.59
DG-threonine	0.83	0.72	0.61
DG-tryptophan	0.26	0.23	0.18
Lysine (g)/MJ DE	0.98	0.89	0.79
Lysine (g)/Meal DE	4.13	3.78	3.31

Source: JSR Healthbred Limited

FORMULATING PIG RATIONS

Those charged with formulating pig rations for use on everyday commercial farms have a challenging role. Traditionally, rations have been formulated on the basis of the *apparent digestibility* of raw materials. However, their protein and energy content is variable, and digestibility is very much influenced by the conditions prevailing during test conditions. Moreover this says very little about how a particular ingredient might be utilized alongside various other foodstuffs. In particular, amino acid digestibility varies with low digestibility raw materials, and nutritionists cannot accurately predict how such feeds will perform at individual farm level. The use of *true digestibility* or *ileal digestibility* is increasingly helping to improve the efficiency of pig ration formulation.

Since the digestive system of young pigs is not well suited to breaking down starches and fibre, there is a need to impose constraints on the inclusion levels of certain raw materials. Ration formulators aim to maximize profit for the pig farmer by increasing the inclusion level of cheaper raw materials once the gut can cope with them. The table indicates a recommended upper limit of 5 per cent for wheat feed in creep, whereas 25 per cent would be acceptable in finishing rations.

Examples of the nutrient specification of rations suitable for healthy, genetically improved pigs are listed. Modern pig feeding is concerned with matching nutrition with the genetics on a particular farm at a particular time, and as a result is an increasingly precise business. The concept of altering the ration specification in the late finishing stages is shown, as is the opportunity to modify rations to maximize lean meat production on split-sex feeding regimes.

The following points might summarize the procedure of formulating pig rations:

- Enlist expert help when deciding about ration formulation.
- Ensure that samples of raw materials and rations fed are chemically analysed.
- Change ration formulations to suit current circumstances on any particular farm.
- Exploit genetic potential by maximizing lean meat production on finishing units.

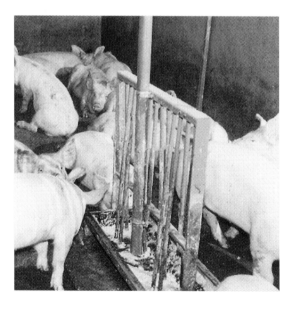

Ad lib wet feeding in short troughs. (Hampshire Feeding Systems Ltd)

Notes for Novices

- To get the best out of pig feed you must understand 'how a pig works'.
- New babies and infants need special feeding arrangements – so do baby pigs and weaners.
- Nutrient requirements vary in relation to the genetics of the pig and the stages of production.
- The protein/energy balance is a key factor.
- The correct blend of amino and fatty acids must be provided.
- Vitamins and minerals are important.
- Feed quality control is vital, particularly for home-mixers and by-product feeders.
- Only licensed swill-feeders may feed meat-based products to pigs.
- Feeding pigs to lay down fat is an expensive process – most consumers demand lean meat.

4 Management: Pigs and People

It takes a very special sort of person to look after pigs and do the job consistently well: unless their activities are pig-centred, failure, disillusionment and financial loss will be the inevitable outcome. Particularly on larger units, the job is concerned with establishing an appropriate routine and keeping to it with meticulous attention to detail. Smaller pig producers have the benefit of intangible extra rewards arising from their close involvement with their stock, which helps to offset the burdens of inefficiency inevitably associated with small scale production.

Pig keeping is concerned with problem prevention: anticipating problems, recognizing them as they arise, and responding to them positively whilst steadfastly maintaining high standards, however depressed the market may be. Primarily it is a job for those who enjoy their pigs and want to get the best out of them. The industry has no place for clock-watchers, brutes or the squeamish, and a pig farming venture should always be regarded as a joint venture with the pig; like all partnerships, it is about relationships and developing mutual trust. Pig farming takes place in an increasingly aggressive market place, and the rest of the world must be regarded as the competition.

STOCKMANSHIP

Stockmanship is a key factor, because, no matter how otherwise acceptable a system may be in principle, without competent, diligent stockmanship, the welfare of the animals cannot be accurately catered for.

(Pig Welfare Code)

Hemsworth and Coleman (1998) regard stockpeople as professional managers of livestock who have generally not received worthy recognition for their unique skills. This observation is supported by their recommendation of key features in a duty list for a modern stockperson:

- A good general knowledge of the nutritional, climatic, social and health requirements of the farm animal.
- Practical experience in the care and maintenance of the animal.
- Ability to quickly identify any departures from normal in the behaviour, health or performance of the animal, and to promptly provide or seek appropriate support to address these departures.
- Ability to work effectively, independently and/or in teams, under general supervision, with daily responsibility for the care and maintenance of large numbers of animals.

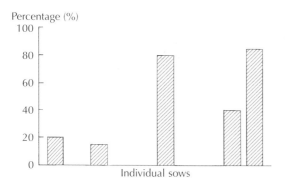

Behavioural studies with sows. Approach rate – aversive handling.

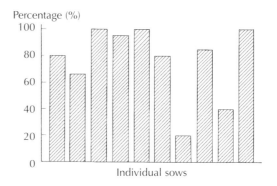

Behavioural studies with sows. Approach rate – pleasant handling.

Stockpeople must be sure they have a basic understanding of the pig's needs regarding nutrition, environment, health and housing – and regularly update it – and a knowledge of its social and sexual requirements: indeed the list is formidable, and remarkable observation skills are required. The owner of the pig unit is additionally charged with the twin challenges of financial and personnel management. People endowed with these qualities must be well motivated and have a good attitude to the pigs in their care.

> Give to a pig when it grunts and a child when it cries, and you'll have a fine pig and bad child.
>
> (Danish Proverb)

Inadequately motivated staff are characterized by:

- poor observation of pigs;
- low technical competence;
- a diminished ability to recall information;
- a reluctance to use their skills; and
- an aversive handling of pigs.

If people burdened with the above characteristics are entrusted to look after pigs,

the pigs in their care will perform less well and will be more difficult to handle. Dr Martin Seabrook of the University of Nottingham has shown that the quality of human–pig interaction varies markedly, and can be linked to pig performance: at the worst, some pigs are fearful of humans, whereas sows handled consistently gently remain more docile. Seabrook and Mount (1993) undertook behaviour studies with indoor pigs in a standardized, unsophisticated environment, and their work indicated that pigs which were roughly handled exhibited higher levels of the hormone corticosteroid. This can cause chronic stress,

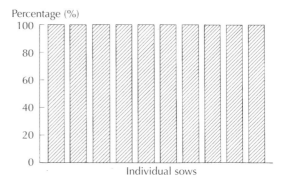

Behavioural studies with sows. Approach rate – with food.

Many people just like pigs. (Eastbrook Farms)

since the elevated levels of corticosteroids sap energy from the pig and impair the synthesis of amino acids into tissue. Thus bad stockmanship upsets pigs, and this eats into profits.

Seabrook and Mount's research with sows indicated that they had a strong ability to identify different people; in particular they were able to differentiate those they associated with pleasant handling from those they associated with aversive handling. Generally, quietly handled sows were much more willing to approach an experimenter – though not all sows were uninhibited, and some were backward at coming forward even though they had never known rough handling. Again there was great variation between individual responses when sows were subjected to the same test after they had previously experienced aversive handling. Most were reluctant to approach the experimenter – however, it seems that the sows had not subjected themselves to excessive fear. Once food was made available it appeared that previous bad experiences were temporarily forgotten.

Even punks like pigs. (PIGSPEC)

Types of People on Pig Units		
P	Piggie Person	'I just love my pigs'
I	Idle b*****r	'It's not my job, the manager will do it'
G	Groupie	'I like teams, I can avoid responsbility'
P	Procrastinator	'I'll leave it, the problem will go away'
E	Experimenter	'My ways are best, it'll be easier if I do it my way'
O	Orally oriented	'It won't work, we cannot be expected to do that'
P	Plodder	'I'll just get on with what I have always done'
L	Loner	'I like being alone with my pigs'
E	Equipment person	'That is a good machine, it'll make my life easier'

The key features inherent in good stockmanship may perhaps be summarized thus:

- Stockmanship is the key to successful production.
- Modern stockpersons must be knowledgeable and able to apply their skills.
- Stressing pigs causes hormone imbalance, upsets pigs and reduces profits.
- Most roughly handled sows are reluctant to approach people.
- Minor aversions are not a barrier in the quest for food.

IDENTIFYING APPROPRIATE ATTITUDES

Understanding the qualities required in a person for them to keep pigs well, or not so well, should help promote the right attitude towards pigs. Self-management, or the management and motivation of others on the pig farm, depends on how well the unit owner understands the personalities of the people involved – indeed, the pig industry must present psychologists with a host of investigational opportunities! The strengths and weakness of individuals must be identified, and appropriate attitudes developed for different people.

Thus a pig-unit owner or employee who lacks confidence needs support and encouragement, a situation that could be remedied by some formal training or part-time study aimed at increasing the knowledge base. On the other hand, the self-assured individual who is obviously competent and confident will almost certainly rise to the occasion if given more responsibility, or asked to become involved at the cutting edge of a new development. Conversely, this would be a daunting prospect for a person suffering a confidence crisis.

The good qualities and personal burdens of stockpersons have been identified by Seabrook (1990) who undertook detailed research on this fascinating aspect of pig production. Checklists were developed to characterize individuals, and a summary of Seabrook's findings are given.

Interaction and Personality Characteristics	
Good Interaction	Poor Interaction
Confident	Under-confident
Consistent	Inconsistent
Emotionally stable	Less emotionally stable
Independent	Dependent
Not affected by the system	Affected by system
Low aggression	High aggression

Source: Seabrook, 1990

78

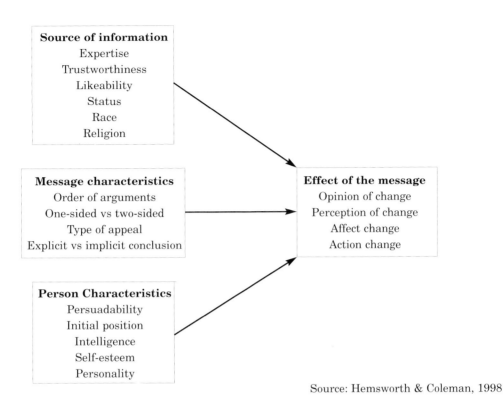

Source: Hemsworth & Coleman, 1998

Factors that affect attitude changes.

The table identifies a diverse range of people types with various strengths and weaknesses, and each individual will require different motivational strategies in order to make them good pig keepers, and to enable them to continue in that mould.

Question
How can attitudes to working with pigs be changed?
Answer
Only with a great deal of effort aimed specifically at the individual.

In order to implement behavioural change it is necessary to look at the personalities involved and their specific circumstances; a model for implementing change has been developed in Australia (Hemsworth and Coleman, 1998). In fact, persuading pig people to change established behav-iour patterns is more than just telling them what they should really be doing: it involves helping them to cope with the reaction of others who recognize such changes, and who might be eager to tell colleagues – as in 'Fred has been rolled over by the boss again', for instance. Due allowance must therefore be made of personal circumstances, external factors such as rates of pay, profitability within the industry, and the adequacy or inadequacy of the facilities available to the labour force.

Hemsworth and Coleman recognize increasing pressures regarding the employment of people on pig farms: these people must be adaptable and conscientious, and must want to treat pigs well at all times. They point out the lack of structured selection procedures for identifying staff most likely to be good pig keepers – sophisticated techniques that are com-

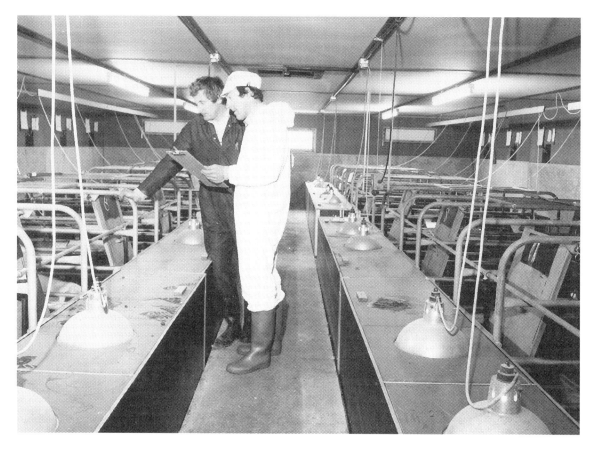

Today's managers need both good communication skills and technical knowhow. (TXU Europe (formerly Eastern Group))

monplace in other industries. In view of this, they advocate the establishment of user-friendly, formalized selection protocols and staff training programmes.

> He knows not a pig from a dog.
> (English proverb)

A large survey undertaken in Australia by Hemsworth and Coleman indicated that although pig stockpeople expressed a dislike for some aspects of their work, an impressive 86 per cent enjoyed working with pigs. A great opportunity therefore awaits the pig industry, the challenge being to identify the right sort of people who will find pig keeping an enjoyable and rewarding career. Once identified,

every effort must be made to deliver their training needs, and to ensure that bad practices are not allowed to develop on account of the relative isolation and repetition associated with pig work.

How to attract the best pig people, and then keep them motivated, may perhaps be summarized thus:

- Recognize that pig people have varying motivational needs.
- Check procedures regularly to ensure good working practices.
- Put much effort into facilitating change; it's not easy.
- Consider using formalized selection procedures and individual training schemes.

PEOPLE WELFARE

If a quality labour force is to be recruited and retained they must be protected by their employers. Whilst this is a moral obligation and also good for business, recent legislation demands safeguarding the well-being of people within any working environment. The pig industry has, like other industries, become enmeshed in a web of employment legislation. Whilst such laws are well meant, if wrongly interpreted they can be a recipe for inactivity and prohibitively high costs. If ignored, they can be a personal disaster for those damaged by bad working practices. Accidents sometimes ruin lives and ruin businesses. Criminal proceedings can be brought against alleged offenders by the Health & Safety Executive who act as enforcement agents. Offenders can also face civil law suits for damages from victims of bad practices. Those ignoring these safeguards live dangerously.

The Control of Substances Hazardous to Health (1989) Regulations demand that

Very toxic	Toxic	Harmful	Irritant	Corrosive

Symbols for hazardous substances.

any working practices that might involve a health hazard should be assessed and reviewed. Any products marked with illustrated warning labels should be treated with great respect and avoided if safer alternatives are available. The employer and labour force must work together to promote a culture that eliminates the likelihood of mishaps and accidents.

An accident can be identified as an unplanned and uncontrolled event which has led to, or could have caused, injury to persons, damage to plant or other loss.

Research shows that for every accident involving a major injury, there are twenty-nine resulting in minor injuries, and 300 resulting in no injuries. In other words, for some, good fortune eventually runs out. The Health & Safety Executive have, therefore, good reason for taking an interest in all accidents on the pig farm.

Any farmer who employs five or more people is required to undertake 'risk assessment' and record it. Furthermore, a document must be provided regarding the farm's health and safety policy, and a copy must be made available to all employees. Part-time employees – that is, anyone on the payroll – are included in the staff total.

Some diseases of the pig, such as certain strains of pig influenza, are transmissible to humans; these are known as zoonoses. The risk to human health from pig zoonoses must be assessed, and measures must be taken to prevent or adequately control exposure. There is every likelihood that more stringent EU regula-

---

COSHH Regulations in Practice

What you need to do	*How to do it*
• Gather information	• Undertake risk assessment
• Evaluate it	• Identify potential hazards
• Decide what to do about it	• Decide who might be vulnerable
• Record your decisions	• Query whether existing precautions are adequate
• Repeat the exercise regularly	• Review and revise as necessary

Control of Substances Hazardous to Health (COSHH) Risk Assessment Checklist for Pig Producers

POTENTIALLY HAZARDOUS SUBSTANCES		RISK TO PEOPLE
Noxious gases:	ammonia	Inhalation
	carbon monoxide	
	hydrogen sulphide	
	carbon dioxide	
Dust from straw, feed and pigs		Inhalation
Glass wool insulation, asbestos etc		Inhalation
Animal medicines		Contact and/or ingestion
Disinfectants/fumigants		Contact and/or ingestion
Vermin, birds and other pests		Disease transference
		Leptospirosis (Weil's disease)
Sick/dead pigs		Disease transference *e.g.* meningitis
Micro-organisms/moulds		Disease transference *e.g.* botulism, abortion carcinogenicity

MAIN RISK AREA

Noxious gases: Poorly ventilated buildings; agitation of slurry.

Dust: Straw stored over kennels; compact fan-ventilated buildings; densely stocked buildings; continuous throughput buildings; lax cleaning procedure.

Glass wool insulation, asbestos etc.: Installing insulation or asbestos products; working in defective buildings containing such materials.

Animal medicines, disinfectants, fumigants etc.: Ignoring manufacturer's instructions; self-injection; inappropriate disposal of needles.

Vermin, birds and other pests: Spillage of feed; lack of systematic rodent/pest control policy.

Sick pigs: Delayed euthanasia; lack of personal hygiene; failure to clean and rest hospital units; poor ventilation, inadequate drainage.

Micro-organisms/moulds: Poor bulk bin management; lack of feed hopper management; using mouldy bedding.

MONITORING NEEDS – Written reports/record sheets to be retained in all instances.

Noxious gases: Summer and winter assessment on annual basis; detailed assessment of new buildings when first used.

Straw, feed and body dust: Inspection of straw at harvest; regular checks to ensure that straw stored above kennels is not allowed to remain there indefinitely.

Glass, wool insulation, asbestos etc.: All staff to have access to 'repairs book' in which any defects can be recorded with date noted. Regular monthly inspection of building fabric.

Animal medicines/disinfectants/fumigants: Continuous records maintained in specially provided book; management spot checks.

Vermin birds and other pests: Written report from specialist contractor after, e.g. one visit every six weeks according to the severity of the problem. Emergency attention to damaged bird-proofing noted in monthly building fabric report.

Sick/dead pigs: Regular pig herd health surveillance via routine visit by specialist pig vet, e.g. four times per year. Prompt disposal of deadstock. Annual medical examination for pig unit staff.

Micro-organisms/moulds: Regular microbiological analysis of feed/bedding, routine check on empty bulk feed bin before refilling, detailed check e.g. four times per annum with defects noted. Weekly visual check for contaminants in empty ad lib hoppers.

Fixtures and fittings as well as dung contain fat residues. (Antec International Ltd)

tions on zoonoses will be enforced in the future. Indeed, a new proposed EU Zoonosis Directive is in its draft stage, and initially contained two specific targets for pig herds. The incidence of salmonella serotypes must be reduced to 5 per cent of herds by January 2007, and 1 per cent by January 2012.

Promoting a legal, healthy and safe life on the pig farm may perhaps be summarized thus:

- The law of the land requires that pig farmers should safeguard the health and safety of personnel.
- Some written evidence about health and safety measures is a legal requirement.
- Good employers see this as an opportunity to demonstrate how much they value their staff.
- Anticipate tougher regulations on health and safety in the future.

Strategies for Managing Zoonoses

- Minimize infection by keeping pigs healthy.

- Ensure a high standard of personal hygiene.

- Issue and wear personal protective clothing.

- Immunize people at risk, e.g. tetanus injection.

- Promptly inform the doctor of any mystery illnesses.

- Especially inform children and visitors to pig farms about avoiding zoonoses.

MANAGING TO SUCCEED

The lifestyle people choose determines the degree of stress they are likely to encounter. Similarly, the way a pig unit is originally set up has a massive impact on productivity potential, disease incidence, quality of work and staff morale. People, pigs and pig places cannot achieve the impossible, and it is unrealistic to depend on 'fire-brigade' input from the unit veterinary surgeon if the basic set-up is flawed – there is no future in using antibiotics and other medicaments simply to 'buy pig performance' when the environment is inadequate and unsuitable.

Within Europe the scene is set for a much reduced dependence on antibiotics. Increasingly, factors such as hygiene, all-in/all-out management, ration formulation, stocking rates, house temperature and draught exclusion will assume greater importance. Positive herd-health management is the popular expression, and a change towards all-in/all-out management looks like being a cornerstone of this strategy.

Continuous Throughput vs. All-in/All-out

Whereas the highly efficient broiler industry has for years regarded all-in/all-out production as a vital component of the management regime, this has not been the case with the pig industry. Relatively small numbers of pigs produced each week, and the need for economy of labour, particularly on breeder-feeder units, have conspired to discourage all-in/all-out production. The compromise has been systematic depopulation of the farrowing and weaner housing but continuous throughput in the finishing house. Thorough cleaning and resting of finishing accommodation has in the past been a rarity, though it has sometimes arisen by default when an acute disease crisis has forced the issue. The need to reduce antibiotic use, and the trend towards bigger pig units, both indoors and outdoors, has led to greater uptake of all-in/all-out management.

Research at the University of Adelaide has highlighted the potential of all-in/all-

Pig Growing/Finishing Management System			
	All-in/all-out cleaned	All-in/all-out not cleaned	Continuous flow
Growth rate (g/day)	658	619	610
Dust (mg/cu m)	1.80	2.31	2.51
Respirable particles (mg/cu.m)	0.210	0.265	0.290
Viable bacteria (colony forming units $\times 10^3$/cu.m)	132	177	201
Gram-positive bacteria (colony forming units $\times 10^3$/cu.m)	82	109	122

Source: Cargill and Banhazi 1998

All-in/all-out production has been widely practised in broiler production for years. (Antec International Ltd)

out systems of pig production, particularly when linked to an appropriate hygiene routine. Pigs housed in clean accommodation on an all-in/all-out system had a 6.3 per cent improvement in growth rate. But if the housing was not cleaned between batches, the growth performance benefit was reduced to 1.5 per cent. Pigs on a continuous throughput regime had to tolerate a dustier atmosphere, and growth rates were significantly depressed. Differences were not detected in the incidence of pneumonia but lung lesion scores were lowest in the all-in/all-out system. The need for all-in/all-out management increases markedly as the age of the pigs decreases; warm farrowing houses and rearing accommodation are particularly prone to bacterial build-up.

Hygiene programmes for pig buildings have tended to be regarded as power-washing and disinfection – a worthwhile undertaking for someone else! In future, however, the procedure must be regarded as part of a comprehensive biosecurity programme. Specialist advice should be taken from product manufacturers regarding the efficacy and compatibility of the array of products currently available. Products designed specifically for farm use must be chosen since the farm environment presents a wide range of surfaces with different characteristics: some are non-porous, such as wood and metal; others are semi-porous, for instance, surface-damaged concrete and wood. The pig farm environment is much more variable than that in most industrial situations. The enormity of the task in hand must not be overlooked, the objective being to reduce micro-organism levels to 0.0001 per cent of their original level. Most micro-organisms are easily removed, but some are much more persistent. Yet washing only with water can reduce the bacterial load by up to 60 per cent.

Washing only with water can reduce the bacterial load by up to 60 per cent. (Antec International Ltd)

Since modern diets are often fat-sprayed, special measures must be undertaken to reduce fat residues in dung and to get them off fixtures and fittings. An effective, heavy duty detergent is required to increase the likelihood of subsequent disinfectant being effective against stubborn bacteria. If a detergent is encouraged to foam, contact time is increased and dirty water production is reduced. Detergents contain sanitizers that are not strong enough to be effective disinfectants in their own right, but are adept at cost effectively reducing the bacterial load prior to full disinfection. Allowing cleaned buildings to dry out thoroughly, and giving them a rest from pigs should be enshrined in the management protocol.

STOCKING DENSITY

In checking the suitability of an existing pig unit, a clip board, tape measure and calculator are useful tools. Ultimately the pig business involves the efficient production of pigmeat from a given area. A good starting point, therefore, is to assess the annual output of pigmeat required, and break this down into weekly targets. The associated numbers must then be related to the stocking density at various stages of production. If calculations indicate that The Pig Welfare Code minimum space allowances are violated, either pig numbers have to be reduced or the space provided has to be increased. In particular, overstocking in the rearer, grower or finisher stage is bad practice: it compromises the welfare of the pig, and leads to mediocre performance and disease. EC

Area/pig
(m²)

Line A

Average weight (kg) of pigs in group

Minimum total floor area in relation to pig liveweight.

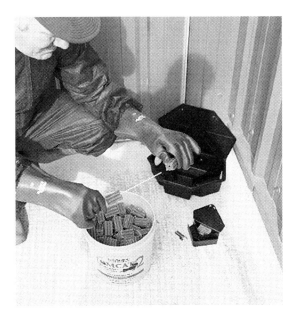

A systematic approach to vermin control is required. (Antec International Ltd)

Directive 91/630 spells out the requirements for *total* floor area in weaner, rearer and finishing pig housing, and the minimum space allowances are based on a series of bands defined by the average weight of the pigs in the group.

If the total floor area provision is below that shown in line A (*see page 86*) at any time, it could result in enforcement action and prosecution. If there are welfare infringements, where the space allowance

---

Pig Welfare Code – Minimum Lying Area

Liveweight	Area	
(kg/lb)	(m²)	(ft²)
20 (44)	0.15	1.6
40 (88)	0.25	2.7
60 (132)	0.35	3.8
80 (176)	0.45	4.8
100 (220)	0.50	5.5

Pig Hygiene Programme Cleaning a Room

Preparation
1. Turn off all electrical circuits other than the room lights.
2. Remove all portable equipment from the room for cleaning.

Cleaning
1. It is vital to remove as much dust and organic matter as possible using a shovel, scraper and brush.
2. Turn off the water supply to the header tank and drain the water system. Scrub the header tank with a detergent solution. Refill the system and flush through. Refill the system and add the required amount of disinfectant.
3. Soak the room using the required amount of detergent through a pressure-washer. Start at the roof at the furthest point from the door, working backwards down the wall to the floor. Pay particular attention to corners, cracks, and the underside of crates and gates.
4. Leave to soak for 30 minutes.
5. Drain the water system, making sure disinfectant is flushed through every drinker. Refill with fresh water and flush through the water system making sure fresh water is flushed through every drinker.
6. Pressure wash the room, starting at the roof, working down the wall to the floor working towards the door.

Disinfect
1. Fill a knapsack sprayer with the required amount of disinfectant and water.
2. Disinfect all surfaces of the room, starting at the roof at the furthest point from the door, working backwards down the walls to the floor. Ensure extra coverage on corners and cracks and the underside of equipment.
3. Allow the room to dry overnight.
4. Restock.

Source: Newsham Hybrid Pigs Ltd.

After power-washing and disinfecting, pens should be allowed to dry out and rest.
(PIGSPEC)

is above line A, in the UK, veterinary officers of the State Veterinary Service are empowered to demand that the pig farmer must implement an action plan. Schedule 3 of the EC Directive 91/630 specifies that pigs must have access at all times to a lying area which is clean, well drained or provided with dry bedding.

So how does the commercial pig farmer find a way through this catch-all red tape? The need for clear-cut recommendations for total lying areas on pig units operating a wholly slatted system was long overdue. However, the impact of this requirement on units where there is a separate designated solid lying area is somewhat academic. Usually where slats or a push-through dung passage is provided *in addition to* the designated lying area, the total space allowance will be met, provided each pig has sufficient lying area. The key issue in such instances is ensuring that

A meticulously clean batch-finishing pig unit.
(PIGSPEC)

Particularly on small units, old converted buildings can provide an appropriate environment. (Allen & Page)

the pig is provided with the minimum lying area as specified in EC Directive 91/630.

Since the minimum lying area requirement between 40kg (88lb) and 100kg (220lb) liveweight literally doubles, if floor areas are to be used cost effectively, the implication is that during this period either pig numbers will have to be reduced or pen size increased. And the need to address this practical challenge will not go away. Indeed, since slaughter-weights are predicted to increase in the future, if changes are not made, the problem will be exaggerated. The opportunity to match pig ration specification more closely with the changing needs of growing pigs, plus the desirability of operating an all-in/all-out system, provide an extra incentive for addressing the issue of optimizing pig space provision.

Positive herd-health management may perhaps be summarized thus:

- Make sure the pig unit facilities allow the management plan to be implemented.
- Check pig numbers and the space available at all stages of production.
- Try to implement an all-in/all-out system of production.

- Adopt a more professional approach to cleaning and disinfection.
- Providing minimum space allowances at all times is crucial.

UNWELCOME VISITORS

Despite the fact that rats spend most of their time eating, sleeping and breeding, they still manage to spread nasty diseases such as leptospirosis, salmonella, hanta virus, plague and murine typhus. Although baiting is a key stage in the control programme, other equally important stages must precede it. These comprise:

- inspection;
- identification;
- sanitation/cleaning;
- rodent proofing;
- baiting.

Inspection

Inspection should not be confined to the buildings, but must extend beyond them, and outdoors is probably the best place to start. First, areas of vegetation, feed storage, water, refuse, wood piles and so on should be identified and searched, since

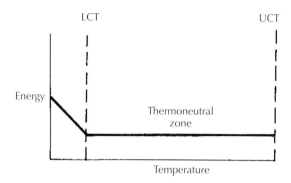

The thermal environment of pigs.

Identification

Identification is the next stage in the control programme. The presence of pointed droppings about 6mm long indicates the house mouse is a pest, whereas pointed droppings 12mm long confirm the presence of the roof rat.

Cleaning up and Rodent Proofing

If palatable pig creep feed and other food sources are readily available to pests, why should they be attracted to rodent bait? The removal of unused pig feed is important, as is the lidding of feed barrows and hoppers. Within the UK, some ad lib feeding systems now store the pig feed within a sealed system, and only small amounts of feed are made available to the pigs on demand.

Making rubbish heaps outside the pig unit should be avoided, and vegetation within 1m of the buildings should be removed so that units are surrounded by a 'clean' perimeter. If any tree branches overhang the building, these should be removed. Rats are attracted to water, stagnant pools, farm ponds and ditches, and these should be checked. Breeder/feeder pig units with continuous throughput are the most difficult to keep vermin-free. On these units pig feed is always available, and there is no break in

each of these could prove attractive to rodents. Locating where rats enter the pig building or feed store is an important first stage in the control programme.

the cycle. Just as keeping disease out of a herd comprises part of the pig-unit health strategy, stopping rodents entering pig buildings should be part of the management philosophy.

Baiting

Once rodents enter a pig building, unless they are prepared to consume a bait, effective control will be impossible. The USA government require a minimum of 33 per cent acceptance rate of vermin baits, but some UK baits claim to have an acceptance rate of 70 to 80 per cent, and achieve a 100 per cent kill.

Resistance can develop when anti-coagulant baits are repeatedly used on the same pig unit. Some rodents are not killed by the bait: they continue to reproduce, and their offspring are also resistant to the poison. Resistance is best avoided if the anti-coagulant bait is periodically withdrawn and briefly replaced with an acute poison. A systematic approach to rodent control is required, otherwise control measures will not be effective. Sometimes resistance is wrongly blamed for control failure when eradication measures have been too casual.

After rodents eat an acute bait, the intention is that the victims will die quickly since they would become ill shortly after eating the bait. Sometimes a lethal dose is not consumed, however, and although the rodents feel ill, they stay alive; they associate their illness with the bait and so take care never to eat it again. Even with the most palatable acute baits, some rodents will choose not to eat a lethal dose, and so beat the system; this is known as 'bait shyness'. This is yet another indication that effective vermin control is most likely to be achieved after a systematic and meticulous approach to infestation problems.

Spilled feed, pig feed in hoppers, and storage areas are also attractive to wild birds, and this can lead to disease risk. For instance, the link between starlings and transmissible gastroenteritis is acknowledged, and during autumn and winter the British starling population is boosted by some forty million migrant birds from Europe. Exclusion is the key to bird control. Proofing measures involving mesh with hole sizes not exceeding 19 by 19mm are effective with sparrows, and 22 by 22mm if starlings are to be excluded. Plastic strip curtains and plastic eaves fillers known in the building trade as a 'comb' are also helpful in keeping birds away from pig units.

These are the key points about pest exclusion:

- Problems with pests lead to problems with neighbours.
- A systematic approach to rodent control is required.
- Inspect, identify, clean, rodent proof and then bait.
- Baiting programme should take account of outdoor rodent refuges, besides the more obvious ones indoors.
- Birds spread disease, steal food and contaminate pig units.
- Shooting invading birds might provide a sense of revenge, but preventing access to pig feed is the best control measure.

AN ENVIRONMENT FIT FOR A PIG

Many people ask at what temperature they should run their pig buildings, but this is dependent on so many variables it is almost impossible to answer; in fact pigs operate productively over a wide range of temperatures. The producer should aim to find the temperature band that suits the pig: this band is known as the thermoneutral zone (*see page 90*), or comfort zone, and is the one within which

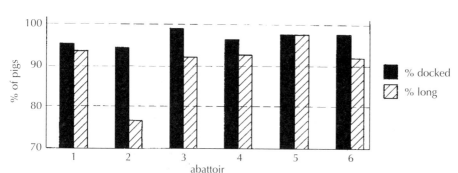

Percentage of pigs with no tail damage.

■ % docked

▨ % long

Source: Cambac Research

the pig does not have to produce extra heat to keep warm, or dissipate waste heat to keep cool.

Research has shown that in the UK it is most economical to keep pigs just above their lower critical temperature (LCT): this encourages adequate feed intake, efficient feed conversion and good growth rates. On ad lib feeding systems, room temperature can be used as a mechanism for controlling feed intake. Keeping pigs below their LCT results in either the unproductive use of feed or the breakdown of tissue to generate heat. (LCTs

have been derived from pioneering work undertaken at the former Scottish Farm Buildings Investigation Unit (Centre for Rural Buildings), Aberdeen and Babraham Research Institute, Cambridge.

When pigs carry sticks,
the clouds will play tricks;
when they lie in the mud,
no fear of a flood.

(English weatherlore)

The upper critical temperature (UCT) is

Factors Influencing Pig Lower Critical Temperature and Upper Critical Temperature

Lower Critical Temperature

Group size	An isolated pig in a farrowing crate is more sensitive to low temperatures than pigs in a group.
Feed intake	Newly farrowed sows and just-weaned pigs eat less and so are more prone to stress from low temperatures.
Air speed	Cold draughts make pigs feel more sensitive to low temperature – that's why they huddle.
Flooring	Pigs on slatted floors need higher room temperatures than those on straw. Wet floors make pigs feel cooler.

Upper Critical Temperature

Stocking density	A reduction delays the onset of heat stress.
Feed intake	A reduction in feed energy intake makes pigs less sensitive to excessive heat.
Air speed	Increasing air speed at pig level makes pigs feel cooler under hot conditions.
Bedding removal	This allows pigs to dissipate heat through the floor.
Water	Wetting the pig or wetting the floor makes the pig feel cooler.
Shade provision	Natural or artificial shelter is particularly helpful in keeping outdoor pigs cool.

Additional ventilation of ark units can be helpful in hot, still weather. (PIGSPEC)

at the top end of the range, and once it is exceeded, pigs feel uncomfortable and take desperate measures to increase heat loss. In outdoor situations they tend to wallow, but this is an 'emergency' need and they probably wouldn't do it if shade were provided. 'A pig that has been washed goes back to roll into the mud.' (2 Peter 2: 22): St Peter, who did not have the benefit of agricultural research, presumably penned this verse after making observations on a hot summer's day, in a treeless environment.

When heat-stressed, indoor pigs attempt to flood the waterbowls and create a wet lying area. Pigs are 'natural biochemists', and modify the extent of their lying area and other behaviour patterns according to the prevailing temperature. For instance they have very tidy dunging habits, particularly in hot weather, choosing to find a comfortable lying area and going somewhere else to dung.

Temperature recommendations must therefore be related to the overall environmental circumstances. In fact the behaviour of the pig is a useful guide to the suitability of its environmental temperature, and good stockmanship involves noting any behaviour changes and reacting appropriately.

When growing pigs are ad lib fed and have a dry, draught-free straw bed to sleep on, their temperature requirements differ markedly to those of pigs in more testing environments.

Pigs see the wind.

(Wiltshire saying)

Furthermore, ad lib fed, straw-bedded dry sows thrive in draught-free conditions just above 10°C. Under similar circumstances but given restricted feed, the

Typical Lower Critical Temperature Ranges for 50kg (110lb) Liveweight Pigs				
Feed level (kg/lb day)	Floor type	Air speed	Building insulation	LCT (°C)
1.4 (3.0)	slats	draughty	poor	22
	slats	draughty	good	20
	slats	low	poor	19
	slats	low	good	17
2.08 (4.6)	slats	draughty	good	15
	slats	low	poor	13
	straw	draughty	good	11
	straw	low	poor	8

Naturally ventilated pig finishing house. (PIGSPEC)

house or kennel temperature would need to be 15°C. And before and just after farrowing, sows need a room temperature of 20°C if lying on dry, insulated concrete, and 21°C on perforated metal. Within a week of farrowing, 15°C and 17°C is acceptable for well fed sows and thriving offspring on a draught-free concrete floor or slatted floor, respectively. Once the temperature exceeds around 24°C in the farrowing house, sow feed intake is impaired.

Whilst pigs are naturally boisterous animals, providing them with a comfortable, if not enriched environment, has a tremendous bearing on their behaviour

A raised dung passage roof with natural cross-flow ventilation. (PIGSPEC)

Automatically controlled, naturally ventilated weaner house with curtain sides. (PIGSPEC)

towards other pigs and the people caring for them, as well as their immediate environment. Building materials, equipment, fixtures and fittings which are widely used in industry often fail 'the pig test', and if factors such as stocking density, room temperature, air speed at pig level and equipment suitability do not meet

with the approval of the pig, it is only too ready to inform its keeper of any shortcomings.

Strew no roses before swine.

(Dutch proverb)

Air quality has a major impact on the

Spray-foam roof insulation in a portal-frame pig building. (PIGSPEC)

Pig Environment and Pig Health Interactions

PIG BEHAVIOUR
Are they huddling and stacking because they're too cold?
Are they stretched out because they're too warm?
Are they aggressive?

Check: water quality
flow rate
availability
lighting regime
vice incidence
bedding
draughts
air quality
rodent infestation

PIG APPEARANCE
Are they starey-coated and hairy?

Check: room temperature
draughts
body temperature
bedding
feed – quantity
quality
mineral/
vitamin content
accessibility

PIG DUNG
Location – if it's in the wrong place:

Check: wetness
dryness
blood staining
mucous presence
water
diet

behaviour and health of pigs, and pig people. When ammonia levels reach the 10–15ppm range, the respiratory health of the pig can be seriously harmed: ammonia can cause rhinitis, which impairs the pig's sense of smell and, as a result, interest in feed diminishes and nutrient intake reduces.

Within free air, carbon dioxide concentration is 0.03 per cent, and the design specification of modern pig buildings aims for a carbon dioxide level not exceeding 0.3 per cent at the minimum ventilation rate. This target is a 'trade-off' between air quality, thermal comfort and draught incidence. If the gas goes much above 0.3 per cent, a heavy, stuffy atmosphere results, and the pig's feed intake suffers. Always be suspicious of buildings where the stockman subconsciously spends the minimum amount of time inside, or can be seen in the doorway taking a regular 'top-up' of fresh air.

As faeces break down, hydrogen sulphide is produced. Regular emptying of slurry channels helps prevent any build-

Floor-fed finishers. (ABN Ltd)

up of this foul gas, which most people can smell once it reaches the 3–5ppm range. Levels as high as 20ppm impair feed intake. When 'stale' slurry has been agitated within a pig building, elevated levels of hydrogen sulphide have been known to kill people and pigs unlucky enough to be in there.

These days, gas heating in farrowing and weaner housing is not so commonplace. However, if it is used, and gas burners become defective, elevated levels of carbon monoxide can be produced. Once levels reach the 150 to 200ppm range, there is a high risk that unborn piglets could die *in utero*.

Outbreaks of tail biting arise because of a number of environmental factors, including poor air quality. This vice was first identified over 100 years ago. Recent surveys indicate that up to 81 per cent of pigs are tail-docked in an effort to minimize tail biting. An abattoir study undertaken by Dr Jane Guise of Cambac Research involved the examination of 62,971 tails, and it concluded that the odds of a docked pig not being bitten were 2.73 times better than the odds of a long-tailed pig being bitten! Tail docking is an unpopular job, but on the basis of this massive research project it is undertaken for good reason. Thus the pig industry is still challenged with finding the reasons why tail biting continues to happen; no doubt more detailed survey work based on diverse environments and genetically diverse pigs will eventually help find the answer to this mystery.

Like a pig's tail, going all day, and nothing done at night.

(Lancashire proverb)

Kennelled finishing accommodation under a portal-frame structure. (ABN Ltd)

Dust is the scourge of pig farming, and pig buildings suffer the highest dust concentration of all livestock buildings: feed debris, skin fragments, bedding materials and dried faeces conspire to produce this smelly irritant. Dust carries bacteria, which increase the risk of disease and irritate the respiratory tract. There is also much concern about the impact of dust on human health, and this has led to a requirement under the COSHH Regulations to monitor dust levels. Minimizing the production of dust and lessening its effects remain major challenges for the pig industry.

To summarize, the following environmental checks should be made on a regular basis:

- Relate house temperature to the stage of production, nutrition, bed quality, draught incidence and pig behaviour.
- On outdoor units provide shade and wallows to prevent heat stress.
- If people find air quality unpleasant, so will the pigs.
- Monitor the environment regularly.
- Bad environments encourage bad behaviour, poor health and low productivity.

Package deal, totally slatted finishing system. (Pyramid Systems (Malton) Ltd)

Automatic control of natural ventilation on a finishing house.
(Pyramid Systems (Malton) Ltd)

Control equipment is best located in a different environment to the pigs. (TXU Europe (formerly Eastern Group))

Notes for Novices

- Liking pigs is the starting point.
- An eye for detail is crucial, plus a sense of dedication.
- 'Happy pigs' produce the best pigmeat.
- If you provide the wrong environment pigs rarely hesitate to let you know.
- Growing pigs increasingly need more space allowances.
- Whilst pen temperature is crucial for pigs it must always be related to draughts, bedding, group size and feed level.
- Before embarking on an outdoor venture, look at the proposed site after days of incessant rain.
- Remember, pig people can make a pig business sink or swim.

5 The Breeding Sow —

When sows freely roamed woodland territories, environmental challenges were such that piglet mortality rates were high. Nature coped with this by endowing the sow with great prolificacy, and enabling her to mate at a time which would ensure that piglets would be born when there was an abundance of food. Raising pigs within an organized farming system overcame many of the obstacles of nature, but led to new challenges in view of the changed environment.

The modern industry demands a lot from the genetically improved breeding sow. In any one year, each sow is expected to rear in excess of twenty-two weaners; it is routine for her piglets to double their birthweight within the first week of their life, and her progeny is expected to yield in excess of one and a half tonnes of saleable pigmeat each year. Consumers nowadays demand lean meat, and this has had to be reflected in the genetics of the sow, thus modern sows are bred to produce a slaughter generation which has a low body fat content and a high lean tissue growth rate. This manifests itself as a 'protein drive', since lean meat necessarily has to be deposited as the sow strives to achieve an increased mass of body protein.

Gilts and young sows continue to lay down protein long after they reproduce for the first time; and if the protein is not available in the diet, the sow responds by breaking down body protein – for instance, to sustain milk production. As might be expected, this catabolism of body

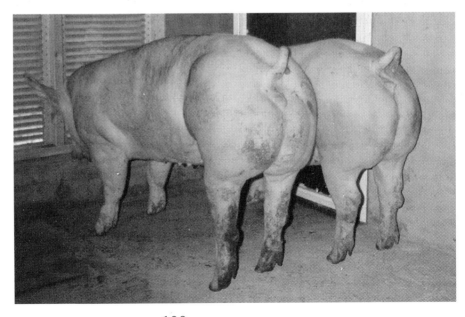

Bulbous hams help maximize lean meat yield. (SEGHERS genetics)

100

protein impairs reproductive efficiency, and this manifests itself as silent heats (anoestrus), failure to conceive, lighter and smaller litters and impaired milk production. Managing the modern sow to maximize her lifetime productivity, and so that she raises pigs with super-lean carcases, is a demanding and complex business.

Given the high level of lean meat production demanded by pig producers, and the need to safeguard the welfare of the pig, sow feeding cannot be a 'hit and miss' affair: the management regime must provide the sow with quality nutrients in the right amounts and at the right time.

PREPARING GILTS FOR BREEDING

Lifetime reproductive efficiency is concerned with the establishment and conservation of fat reserves, and the avoidance of lean depletion. Although the main impact arises during her time in the breeding herd, preparing the pre-pubertal gilt for lifetime productivity is nonetheless important: if she is not set up for life correctly, the battle is lost before it has begun. The days of leaving gilts in the fin-

ishing house to prove their potential alongside contemporary slaughter pigs have gone. Whereas money is hopefully made when slaughter pigs efficiently convert feed into lean meat, this phenomenon actually delays the onset of puberty in gilts.

Modern gilts are late-maturing. Maximum protein deposition rate is thought to occur between 100kg (220lb) and 140kg (309lb) liveweight in genetically improved gilts, and unless a gilt has a protein mass of at least 35kg (77lb) she will be unlikely to achieve her reproductive potential.

Fast growth rates in pre-pubescent gilts must be avoided. Studies undertaken in France indicate that:

- only 28 per cent of gilts weighing 100kg (220lb) in 140 days or less reached their fourth litter;
- 45 per cent of gilts that were grown more slowly to reach 100kg in 170 days made it to their fourth litter;
- staying power was significantly increased when gilts had 18mm or more backfat at 100kg liveweight.

Research has shown that modern sows have a higher bodyweight and a reduction

The Changing Characteristics of Sows in UK Nutrition Experiments				
	1967	*1983*	*1988*	*1993*
Weaning parity 1 weight (kg/lb)	150 (330)	153 (337)	160 (353)	185 (408)
Backfat (mm/in)	–	25 (0.9)	19 (0.7)	15 (0.5)
Weaning parity 3 weight (kg/lb)	180 (397)	190 (419)	195 (430)	242 (534)
Backfat (mm/in)	–	22 (0.8)	19 (0.7)	17 (0.6)

Source: Edwards, 1995

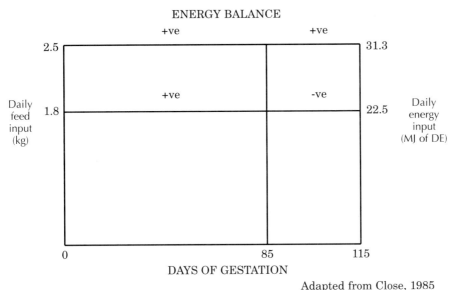

ENERGY BALANCE

Adapted from Close, 1985

Energy studies in pregnant gilts – individually housed at 20°C.

in backfat, and such changes call into question the validity of the conclusions drawn from older trial work with sows. Research undertaken by Dr William Close suggests that, even when housed in a warm environment and fed individually, modern gilts are often in negative energy balance at the end of their gilt pregnancy. Hence there is a need to increase feed levels in late pregnancy.

If maiden gilts are to mature into productive sows they require a specialized management and feeding regime. During the gilt rearing phase, the ration specification must be tailored to the lifetime needs of a breeding regime that differs markedly from that of a pig producing lean meat for slaughter. After around 75kg (165lb) liveweight, specialized gilt rations should be fed on a restricted basis: this tends to reduce weight at puberty. Earlier restriction can reduce weight at puberty and also increase age. The mineral and vitamin content of gilt rations must also reflect the need for lifetime productivity, and so their specification must mirror that of a breeding sow rather than a finishing pig. Gestation and lactation have widely different physiological needs,

and in order to optimize production, ration specification must match these specific needs.

INTRODUCING BREEDING STOCK

When purchased gilts are introduced to a breeding unit, a strict three-phase management protocol is required, consisting of:

• an isolation period;
• an in-contact period;
• an integration period.

Isolation premises must be run on an all-in/all-out basis, and should be sited at least 50m (160ft) from other resident pigs. Isolation provides a 'one-off' opportunity to keep disease out of the main pig herd. If purchased pigs show signs of disease, as a last resort they could be slaughtered to safeguard the health of the main herd. Newly arrived pigs, both gilts and boars, must be kept separate from established resident pigs for at least two weeks, and a detailed scheme for introducing purchased breeding stock drawn up in connection with the unit's veterinary surgeon. Any injections must be administered using separate needles for each batch of pigs.

During the isolation phase, good stockmanship is vital in order to acclimatize the potential breedingstock both psychologically and pathologically within their new 'foreign' environment. Once reassured that the pigs are not the bearers of disease, the 'in-contact' procedures can be implemented. If the introduced stock are from a herd of very high health status they should first mingle with mature sows for two weeks. Thereafter they should mix with weaners, which tend to be particularly apt at furnishing a potent cocktail of the 'bug profile' of the herd.

Once challenged with the resident bugs, newly introduced stock should be given time to recover from any disease challenge after the 'in-contact' pigs have been removed; ordinarily this period should last from four to eight weeks. During this phase, oestrus should be

stimulated by allowing around fifteen minutes per day of within-pen contact with a mature boar. Service should be delayed until at least the third heat, which should take place after introduction to the main herd.

Modern, late-maturing gilts should not be served until aged between 210 and 230 days, although age alone is a poor indicator of maturity. Trials on eight farms with Camborough gilts suggest that mating after seven months of age gave better gilt and sow productivity. At that stage, gilts should weigh at least 130kg (290lb) liveweight and have 16–18mm backfat at the P2 position. This liveweight and body condition would be consistent with a steady growth rate of 500–600g per day from around 85kg (187lb).

Gilts seem to respond positively to daylight: for example, oestrus appears to be longer and more predictable if gilts are subject to an eighteen-hour day as compared to a six-hour day, though light seems to have less impact on the cycling behaviour of sows as compared to gilts. Keeping gilts in the dark can delay puberty by up to a month. The best practical option is to ensure that some natural light is provided in both gilt housing and service areas. During winter some artificial lighting should be left on overnight.

Oestrus is stimulated by 'flushing', that is, feeding the gilt enhanced energy levels prior to mating. This helps maximize the ovulation rate. The ad lib provision of a gilt or lactator diet for twenty-one days prior to the first service is recommended. Pig keepers must always be vigilant for the tell-tale signs that oestrus is imminent; not all pigs read text books, so never be surprised to find a sow or gilt on heat earlier or later than you might have expected it.

There are two hormones that together are responsible for stimulating the release of ova: the follicle stimulating hormone (FSH) and the luteinizing hor-

The Relationship Between Age at First Mating and Litter Performance

Age at mating (days)	Number of gilts	Pigs born alive (first litter)	Pigs born alive (litters 1–3)
<200	93	10.6	11.2
201–210	126	10.8	11.1
211–220	313	11.7	12.2
221–230	152	10.7	11.1
>231	93	11.0	11.6

Source: PIC International

Hormone activity in the sow.

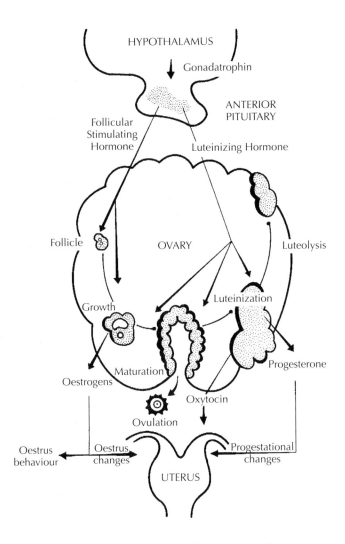

mone (LH), controlled by the anterior pituitary at the base of the brain. Sub-fertile females have lower levels of these hormones; this is particularly true of gilts just weaning their first litter. However, the shortfall in hormone levels can be rectified by injecting naturally occurring hormones, ideally the day after weaning.

Management of gilts may perhaps be summarized thus:

- Gilts should be built to last, and need a special feeding regime programmed for steady growth.
- When gilts first arrive on a breeding unit, care should be taken to keep out any new disease and to attune gilt health to that of the herd.
- Modern gilts are late-maturing, and continue to deposit lean tissue.
- Service should be delayed until the third or fourth oestrus.
- Oestrus is usually predictable, but is sometimes spontaneous.

THE CHALLENGE OF BOAR MANAGEMENT

Although most boars *think* they are ready for work from five to eight months of age, in actual fact their semen quality is usu-

	The Signs of Oestrus		

Pro-oestrus		**When training Tick Off**	3
	In gilts, the vulva swells but this is not consistent in the sow.		
	The vulva becomes congested or red.		
	The udder develops in gilts.		
	The female becomes nervous and easily disturbed.		
	She is ridden by other sows but does not stand.		
	Vaginal walls become reddened (congested).		
	Clitoris becomes more prominent.		
	Vaginal fluids thicken; produce strands between fingers.		
Oestrus			
	The vulva reddening starts to subside.		
	There is a slight mucus vulva discharge.		
	The female becomes more active.		
	The female starts to mount other sows and if mounted starts to stand.		
	Emits a characteristic high-pitched grunt.		
	She actively seeks boars.		
	Has a decreased appetite.		
	Stands to back pressure, particularly in the presence of a boar.		
	In a Large White (Yorkshire) she pricks her ears.		
	Rub marks evident on skin.		
	Has a clean vulva in outdoor units (post-service).		
	Rubs and is attracted to stockpeople.		
	Allows coitus.		

Source: Garth Pig Stockmanship Standards

ally suspect until they reach at least ten and a half months. Thereafter it continues to improve until they reach around eighteen months of age. Systematic use of boars should therefore be regarded as a key aspect of quality control in the modern breeding herd.

Ordinarily, purchased breeding boars arrive on the commercial farm at five and a half to six months of age; however, the temptation to work them early must be resisted. An analysis of 5,000 mating records processed the data collected into an Index of Performance: this took into account factors such as returns to service, farrowing rate, and numbers of piglets born alive. The results indicated a consistent improvement in productivity when older boars were used to sire litters.

When purchased boars arrive at a farm, the first priority should be to isolate them, followed by in-contact and integration phases. However, because boars are very often housed on their own, their social integration is also a priority since prolonged isolation could lead to the boar becoming afraid of other pigs and people, thereby having a negative impact on his libido.

Boars destined for breeding should be fed on a lactator sow diet from five to six months of age, to ensure that adequate levels of calcium and phosphorus are provided. Most boars have a voracious appetite and their feed intake has to be carefully regulated and generally limited to around 30 MJ of digestible energy per day. In practice, indoor boars are fed 2.5 to 3.5kg (5.5 to 7.7lb) per day depending on body condition and housing environment.

Farrowing Rate Numbers Born Alive and Performance Index by Age of Boar

Age of boar (months)	Farrowing rate (%)	No. born alive per litter	Index of performance	Age of boar (months)	Farrowing rate (%)	No. born alive per litter	Index of performance
6	56	10.03	5.62	14	82	11.45	9.40
7	71	10.75	7.63	15	83	11.58	9.61
8	72	10.90	7.85	16	84	11.64	9.78
9	70	10.93	7.65	17	84	11.64	9.78
10	80	10.90	8.72	18	86	11.85	10.19
11	81	11.00	8.91	19	89	11.86	10.56
12	82	11.06	9.07	20	90	11.90	10.71
13	84	11.31	9.50	21	94	12.11	11.38

Source: Cotswold Pig Development Company Ltd, 1987

In winter, feed rates would be higher for outdoor boars, and should be pitched towards the top end of the range if boars are working particularly hard. There is some evidence that supplementary levels of methionine and cystine can boost boar fertility; a well tested practice is to 'top dress' the starter rations of a hard-worked boar with about 250g of fish meal per day. Some producers advocate 'treat feeding' boars with supplementary greenstuffs to boost vitality.

The housing needs for boars present a conundrum in pig welfare – though the recommendations in Section 51 of the Pig Welfare Code appear clear cut:

As a guide, individual accommodation for an adult boar should have a floor area of not less than 7.5m² (81ft²) if used for living purposes only. If used for both living and service purposes, the floor area should be not less than 10m² (108ft²) with the shortest side not less than 2.5m (8ft 2in). In either case the pen divisions should not be less than 1.5m (4ft 11in) high. Boar pens should not be sited or constructed in such a way as to isolate the boar from sight or sound of other stock or of farm activity.

These are very demanding requirements that are expensive to incorporate. The practical problem is that of housing an individually penned pig in a dual-purpose space – i.e. a living and serving area. A generous floor area is required for pre-mating and mating activities, but the thermal requirements of the boar have to be met at other times. The reality is that a boar, given average feed levels and when housed on a dry, draught-free concrete floor, would start to feel cold at around 14°C and below, and to catabolize its body reserves.

The pragmatic approach is to ensure that the Welfare Code pen dimensions are not breached, that the boar is not housed in a draught, and that it is provided with a dry floor on which to lie and work. If a boar is thermally challenged, a short-term remedy is to increase feed levels. Sometimes a raised bedded area is provided within a boar pen, with some additional gating to confine the boar to facilitate safe introduction and removal of sows and reduce the injury risk to the labour force. Boar pens should be checked regularly for unnecessary protuberances, rough concrete and blockwork, as well as sharp metal projections.

Conception Rate and Litter Size in Relation to Quality Score at First Service			
Quality score	*Number of first services*	*Conception rate %*	*Mean born alive and dead*
1	7	86	7.67
2	28	75	10.11
3	49	92	11.46
4	16	75	11.50
Total	100		

Source: University of Aberdeen, 1994

Like the labour force, boars often suffer a 'post-induction crisis'. Each boar should have its own induction programme, and should be worked gently and gradually into the herd. In its lifetime a boar has the potential to sire between 500 and 1,000 offspring, and so must be carefully nurtured. When a boar is first put to work at seven and a half months, it is recommended to provide him with a mature sow showing a strong heat. Until ten months of age, two ejaculations per week must be regarded as the maximum; this work rate can eventually be doubled in the following year. Around five matings per week seems to be the upper limit for a mature stock boar. After a period of heavy workload, a two- to three-day rest is needed. Boars given longer rests have a tendency to 'fire blanks' – meaning that dead sperm has first to be expelled before their work is effective.

Experienced pig keepers observe that sows given a 'quality' service, and provided with a calming environment after the event, tend to produce most piglets.

Pigs love that lie together. (English proverb)

Surprisingly little research has been undertaken on service management techniques. An observation study at Aberdeen University graded 'quality of service' from one (poor) to four (excellent), depending on the apparent effectiveness of coitus. Sows were mated and a follow-up service given on the second day, and a 76 per cent conception rate was achieved. Those that did conceive were subjected to a one-minute courting ritual and a one-and-a-half minute courting ritual prior to penetration at the first and second service, respectively. At the first service there was a significant relationship between how long the boar stayed inside the sow and subsequent litter size: this increased by

Boar saliva is a source of pheromones. (SEGHERS genetics)

107

Service pens on mainland Europe. (SEGHERS genetics)

0.48 piglets for every minute increase in duration of intromission. Those pig keepers generally considered successful try to keep the sow and boar locked together for as long as possible, and the Aberdeen research confirms that this is a wise policy.

Boar management may perhaps be summarized thus:

- The quantity and quality of boar feed should be carefully regulated.
- Boar fertility improves between puberty and eighteen months of age.
- Young boars should be worked less than experienced boars.
- Welfare Code Recommendations for boars are very specific.
- Litter size can be increased with good service management.

Loose-housed sows on electronic sow feeding (ESF) system. (E. Collinson & Co. Ltd)

ARTIFICIAL INSEMINATION

Globally there has been a massive increase in artificial insemination of sows and gilts in recent years, particularly on large, vertically integrated units. Compared to other European countries and the USA, AI usage in Britain had tended to be confined to breeding companies, enthusiasts and small producers needing to boost their boar power; AI use in the UK is now thought to account for 15 to 20 per cent of all inseminations. By comparison, the 1998 annual report of the National Committee for Pig Breeding Health and Production indicated 46 per cent of inseminations from AI in Denmark; the figure is around 80 per cent for Belgium.

Several factors have influenced the growth in AI uptake. These include encouraging research findings, improved diluents for semen, reduced disease risk, increased use on large outdoor units, and more on-farm (DIY) collection of semen. Whilst in the past the term 'artificial insemination' was quite appropriate and acceptable, it is presently regarded by some as apt to misinform and confuse discerning consumers. There has been much 'greening' of the terminology associated with AI, and various breeding companies now market 'gene transfer' and 'enhanced mating systems' that involve the indirect introduction of top quality semen.

Another factor which has reduced the keeping and use of stock boars on commercial farms has been the high cost of appropriate boar accommodation. The demanding welfare requirements described earlier dictate that a boar housing and service pen swallows up the floor area of up to six sows. Low stocking density in a service house inhibits room temperature lift, and this has an impact on

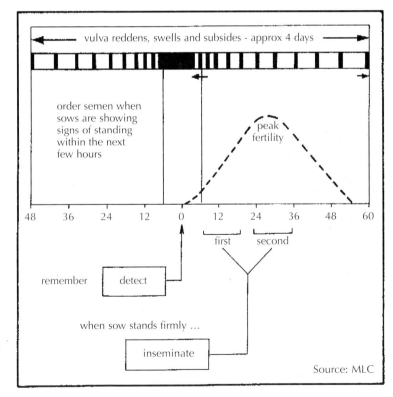

Detecting heat, ordering the semen and timing the insemination.

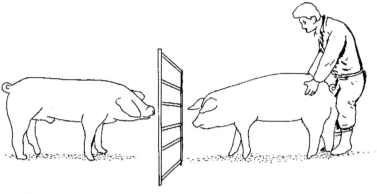

Boar presence not only stimulates oestrus, it also assists the AI process

Source: MLC

Standing to back pressure within sight, sound and smell of a boar.

feed usage. However, some continued boar presence in the service house remains a key feature of service via AI: not only is a mature boar helpful in stimulating oestrus, it also provides a vital role in stimulating oxytocin release in the sow at the time of mating by AI or otherwise. This hormone helps stimulate uterine contractions, which help transfer semen from the cervix to the site of ovulation.

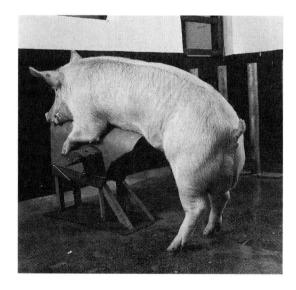

An AI boar mounting a 'dummy' sow. (Newsham Hybrid Pigs Limited)

Progress with AI

The general aspects of AI have not changed much over the years, and in particular demand much observation of the sow over a four-day period. What *has* changed has been the development of specialist equipment to increase the efficiency of AI, and a better understanding of the key elements of the procedures involved. Plastic 'flatpacks' have been developed for storing and infusing boar semen. Compared to using a plastic bottle to coax semen into a sow, as was common practice in the past, a flatpack encourages a more natural physiological uptake, and this has resulted in improved conception rates and numbers born. (It is important to follow closely the guidance of the manufacturers of specialist equipment and the breeding companies supplying the semen.) Research has shown that if semen is pre-warmed, less back-flow is encountered, and this boosts both conception rates and numbers born.

Equipment manufacturers have not been slow to apply this research, and now supply insulated containers which feature both refrigeration and heating apparatus. By maintaining the semen at 17°C and protecting it from sudden temperature changes, sperm viability is increased. The facility to keep semen warm is particular-

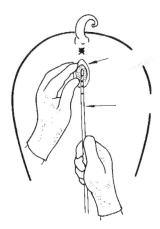

Wearing gloves , the vulva must be cleaned with a dry paper towel before the lubricated catheter is inserted

Source: MLC

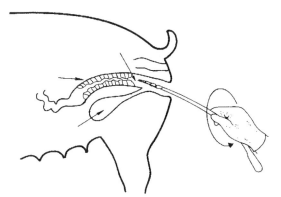

After entry the catheter should be gently pushed into the vagina as far as the cervix

Source: MLC

Preparation for AI.

Inserting the catheter.

ly helpful for outdoor production.

Semen diluents extend the life of the ejaculate and preserve the viability of spermatozoa. Five-day diluents have long been regarded as the 'norm', but if longer-life diluents could be developed, this would boost AI programmes both in terms of boar availability and despatch of the semen. Research in Denmark has investigated the impact of the diluent 'Androhep', as compared to standard EDTA diluent. Trials involved Friday-collected mixed semen from Duroc boars, compared to Monday-collected EDTA semen: in all instances the semen was transported at a fixed time on Mondays for use on the same day or on the next day.

Early indications relating to 250 litters per group showed no significant differences in sow productivity between the two diluents or collection times. This work was undertaken by Denmark's National Committee for Pig Breeding, Health & Production, and is typical of worldwide research programmes with a common commercial objective.

Research programmes also aim to

reduce the risk of artificial insemination spreading disease. If in-feed use of antibiotics on pig farms is to be reduced, treating collected semen with antibiotics such as neomycin sulphate to reduce the

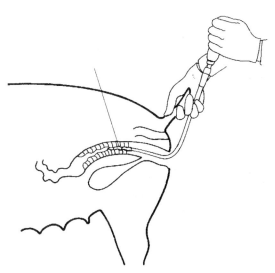

The semen pack should be raised above the sow's tail

Source: MLC

The insemination process.

111

The Impact of Pre-Warming Semen for AI (200 sows per treatment)		
	Control 17°C	Pre-warmed 35.2°C
Signs of irritation at insemination (%)	18	2
Backflow during insemination	7	2
Subsequent farrowing rate (%)	87.2	89.4
Litter size (parities 2–7)	11.2	11.9

Source: Behan, University of Aberdeen, 1991

spread of pathogens could be an alternative. In particular, antibiotic treatment of collected semen might become an effective weapon against the spread of the troublesome salmonella DT104.

Research and commercial experience has established that pooled semen rather than single-boar semen tends to give improved results. A significant factor associated with the increased use of AI has been an improvement in efficiency when AI is used in combination with natural service. The table overleaf summarizes data relating to services with AI only, natural service, and AI combined with natural service. After adjusting the data for parity differences, conception using AI only was shown to be less than with natural service or an AI top-up. It seems very likely that AI use in the UK will increase further, particularly in combination with natural service.

On-farm collection of AI has seen an upsurge in popularity in recent years. This is not a job for amateurs, but those that undertake it seriously, as a means of reducing labour and housing costs, minimizing disease risk and making the most of superior genes, have achieved commendable results. Several specialist companies now provide apparatus and expert advice for on-farm collection of AI. The equipment needed includes plastic disposable gloves, a 'dummy' sow and a thermos

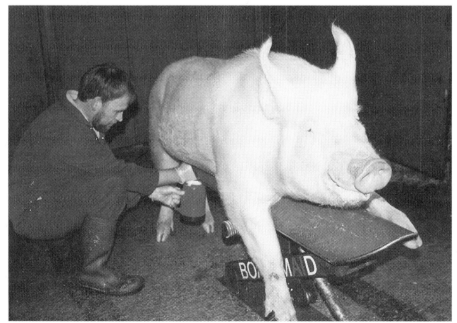

Semen collection from AI boar. (Rattlerow Farms Ltd)

Litter Size Analysis by Service Type

	Average parity	No. of litters	Average born per litter	Average born alive per litter	Average weaned per litter
AI only	3.74	20,623	11.49	10.85	9.61
Natural service	3.62	93,637	11.76	11.07	9.76
AI + natural	4.07	63,540	11.87	11.10	9.97

Source: PIC Management Yearbook 1998

flask or polystyrene box for collecting the semen. Once collected, a clean 'laboratory' area housing a microscope with a phase-control facility is required to check the motility of sperm. The practice demands a disciplined approach, great attention to detail, and strict hygiene measures. Some operators now use hygiene monitoring kits which give an indication of the incidence of protein residues contaminating various surfaces.

How to get the best out of AI may perhaps be summarized thus:

- Regard AI as a specialist technique requiring specialist training and apparatus.
- Use boars to stimulate oestrus, to get the best out of the sow during the AI process, and for natural mating to boost the effectiveness of AI.
- Keep a look-out for research developments involving long-life diluents and effective antibiotics for semen.

The AI laboratory of a major breeding company. (Rattlerow Farms Ltd)

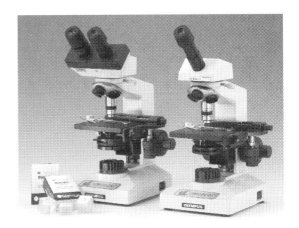

A good quality microscope allows sperm motility to be assessed. (Unitron (UK) Ltd)

- On-farm collection of semen offers great opportunities, but only for the dedicated.

PREGNANCY DIAGNOSIS

In the last quarter of the twentieth century, MLC Pigplan records indicated an improvement in litters per sow per year from 1.90 to 2.25. This impressive advance represents a saving of thirty unproductive days, and this can be attributed to shorter lactations and fewer 'empty' days in the average annual output of breeding herds. Early identification of non-pregnant sows has been a major reason for this improvement in efficiency. The discovery of empty sows at the time of moving to farrowing pens used to be a relatively common occurrence: modern technology has enabled such mishaps to have become a rarity.

Pregnancy detection devices initially

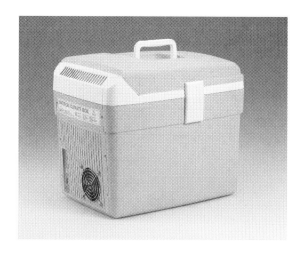

Fixed temperature storage box for on-farm collection of semen. (Unitron (UK) Ltd)

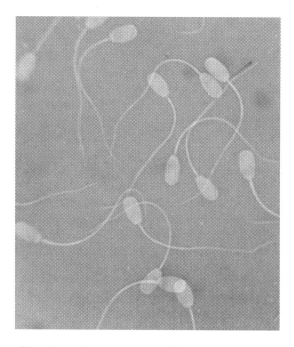

Checking for sperm motility. (SEGHERS genetics)

had a widespread impact on the pig industry in the early 1970s. The first generation of these comprised 'pulse echo' devices which depended on the detection of the presence of fluids in the uterus to confirm pregnancy, since a relatively large echo resonates from a fluid-filled space; between day thirty and sixty, the uterus of pregnant sows is filled with fluid. Unfortunately the bladder and the intestines of the sow also contain fluids, and so there is a risk of recording false positives. The simplest devices were hand-held, and 'confirmed' pregnancy by means of a bleep or glowing light. More sophisticated types could be linked to oscilloscopes. This basic apparatus, when used correctly, could confirm pregnancy thirty days or more after service; however, the technique did not actually identify the presence of foetuses.

Whilst allowing a sow and boar some 'head to head' contact, as well as limited 'in-pen' contact, still remains an effective method of detecting predicted or unscheduled oestrus, the arrival of electronic devices brought a new discipline to pregnancy management. Systematic checking

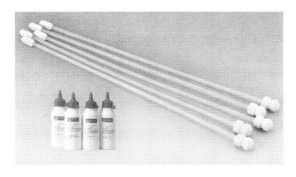

Disposable foam-tipped catheters are now commonplace in AI management. (Unitron (UK) Ltd)

and a 'hands-on' approach to individual sows became part of the progressive herd manager's routine.

'Doppler Ultrasound Pregnancy Detectors' were next on the scene, and they have remained popular with many operators. These more sophisticated devices involve the use of a hand-set and probe which is positioned externally on the abdomen and directed at the uterus. As blood moves through the uterine artery in a wave-like motion, there is a change in frequency as ultrasound waves bounce back from it. This manifests itself as a characteristic 'whooshing' noise with which the operator will already be familiar from a training audio-tape supplied with the kit.

Doppler devices can be used to good effect generally from twenty-five days after service until the end of pregnancy, or during the actual farrowing process. After forty days of gestation the device can also detect the characteristically fast heartbeats of individual foetuses. Sometimes false positive readings are obtained, since a sow on heat can be confused with a pregnant sow. The best practical safeguard is to pregnancy-test at both twenty-eight days and thirty-five days; if two positives are observed, then it is reasonable to assume that the sow would be pregnant.

More recently the pig industry has greatly benefited from medical advances in the pre-natal care of infants. Parents-in-waiting and their medical attendants now have real-time scanning at their disposal, whereby foetuses can be seen on screen, sexed and even photographed from an early stage in pregnancy. Although not quite so sophisticated, scanners are now in use on go-ahead commercial pig units. Obviously they are more expensive than alternative devices, but they offer a much more unequivocal approach to pregnancy diagnosis. This is not only helpful in the technical sense, but it also has psychological implications in that pregnancy diagnosis is often perceived as a check on the labour force: those employed to get sows in pig experience psychological pressures for them to confirm they have done just that. A system of pregnancy diagnosis which is much more clear cut, helps combat this reality of human nature.

'Farm-proof' portable scanners have been developed that can be operated by one person: these comprise compact devices weighing less than 4kg (9lb) including batteries. Their great advantage is that they can confirm pregnancy in

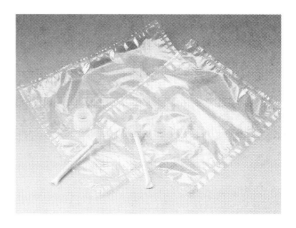

'Flat packs' have become popular on AI systems. (Unitron (UK) Ltd)

Scanner for pregnancy detection.
(Unitron (UK) Ltd)

sows as early as the nineteenth or twentieth day after service. A hand-held probe is placed in contact with the sow's abdomen, and an image of the uterus and its contents appears on the screen: foetuses can be identified within five seconds, in addition to any uterine infection. The device can also be used during the farrowing process to check whether parturition is complete.

Where there is an obvious fertility problem in a herd, a pregnancy diagnosis technique borrowed from the dairy industry can be employed. In conjunction with the unit's veterinary surgeon, a testing kit can be used to detect empty sows, and identify those needing treatment or culling. This involves a reaction between one drop of sow's blood and a chemical reagent which produces a colour change dependent on progesterone levels. In particular, it is helpful to identify whether or not valuable stock should be culled, or retained in the herd. This particular technique can be applied after just seventeen days following service. Since the actual total cost of an empty day has been estimated at between £4 and £5 per sow, there is good reason for the early identification of non-pregnant stock.

Ways to minimize emptiness may be summarized thus:

- Sow/boar contact must always play a major role in oestrus detection.
- A regular, systematic 'hands-on' approach with individual sows will in itself help to detect emptiness.
- Dependable, sophisticated devices and techniques are now available which enable early detection of pregnancy by trained operators.

FARROWING TIME

Three months, three weeks and three days after service – that is, after about 115 days – comes the next challenge: farrowing. Whereas accurate service dates help in the planning process, ultimately sow behaviour is the key; for instance, well exercised group-housed sows tend to have shorter pregnancies than individually housed sows.

Body Condition

Sows and gilts must be managed so that they are in a suitable body condition at farrowing: 'sow condition-scoring' charts can act as an aide-memoire for checking body fat cover. Excessive feeding in early pregnancy can have a negative impact on implantation rates, particularly in gilts; furthermore, over-fat sows tend to suffer a troublesome confinement and to experience extreme back-fat loss during lactation. It has already been highlighted that gilts tend to be in negative energy balance during the last month of pregnancy. However, getting them fat during pregnancy only to suffer uncontrollable weight loss in lactation is not the answer, since it is energetically very inefficient.

The pragmatic approach to reduce the risk of sows entering the farrowing house with inappropriate body condition is to use mid-pregnancy as a buffer zone. At that stage, feed levels can be adjusted on an individual basis as required, so optimum body condition should be achieved as the end of pregnancy approaches. The last days of pregnancy are characterized by a marked increase in the development and weight of intra-uterine fluids and membranes as well as mammary tissue. Generous feeding in late pregnancy can help boost birthweights and prepare the sow for lactation – during the last two weeks of pregnancy the foetus actually deposits about 40 per cent of its eventual birthweight.

A study involving 400 pigs was undertaken by BOCM Pauls Ltd. It indicated 40 per cent mortality in piglets with birthweights under 1kg (2.2lb), whereas only 1.8 per cent mortality was recorded in pigs born at a weight of between 1.3 and 1.5kg (2.9 and 3.3lb). There was also a marked increase in days to slaughter in the pigs with lower birthweights.

At MLC's Stotfold Pig Development Unit, the strategy is to feed 30.5MJ of DE/kg containing 0.55 per cent lysine throughout most of the pregnancy; this helps to ensure that for most genotypes, lean tissue growth rates remain below potential. However, in order to boost birthweights and prepare the sow for lactation, feed intake is increased from 2.25kg (5lb) per day, to 2.75kg (6lb) per day of the specified ration for the last three weeks of pregnancy.

As farrowing approaches, sows tend to be listless and to exhibit inappetance: hence it is sound practice to reduce feed levels around forty-eight hours prior to farrowing, and to feed a sloppy mix of bran that reduces the likelihood of constipation and milk fever.

The Farrowing Environment

The farrowing environment is the ultimate compromise. It is designed to provide individual housing for the sow and litter, and to cater for their separate welfare needs. It reduces the likelihood of piglets being crushed or savaged by the sow, it provides a relatively hygienic environment, and it facilitates good stockmanship. It is an expensive environment, however, with a capital cost per sow-place up to five times that of a place in the dry-sow house. And therein lies the dilemma, because the commercial need to minimize capital expenditure on the most expensive building resource on the farm is as much a priority as to reap the maximum benefit from that unique resource. There is also a welfare requirement to settle the sow into its new quarters prior to farrowing, to help stimulate an immune response to the new 'bugs' in that alien environment. Ultimately this benefits the piglets, as 'passive immunity'.

The practical approach is to manage farrowing rooms on an all-in/all-out basis. This is generally associated with weekly batches, with service and farrowing dates inevitably ranging over a few days. If possible, clean pregnant sows should be housed in their farrowing environment for five days prior to parturition; two days must be regarded as exceptional, and the absolute minimum. If pregnant sows are introduced to damp farrowing rooms, the results could be disastrous, since a warm, humid environment rich in organic matter provides a fertile breeding ground for disease. Every effort should be made to drain surface water from the farrowing room and to expel unseen moisture by providing some bracing ventilation before pigs are reintroduced.

Efficient pig farmers regard empty farrowing places as an insult to their management and a drain on finances. Unintentional vacant farrowing pens must be regarded as:

- A failure of service management.
- A visual reminder of earlier, unproductive use of dry sow accommodation.
- The most expensive pig-place resource on the farm remaining unused for around four weeks.
- A penalty to other sows in the farrowing room, since they miss out on a temperature lift contribution of about half a kilowatt for each empty sow place.

The likely knock-on effect for each empty sow place would be:

- Ten empty spaces in the nursery and weaner housing.
- Ten empty spaces in the finishing house.
- Ultimately ten fewer pigs to sell.

Assistance at Farrowing

Assuming a full farrowing house and farrowing well underway, what degree of assistance do sows require? The temperament of outdoor sows, and of outdoor pig keepers too, promotes a 'leave them alone and let them get on with it' philosophy. Conversely, indoor producers tend to adopt a more interventionist approach, encouraged by the fact that every piglet has cost up to about £15 by the time it is born, dead or alive.

The MLC *Pig Year Book* for 1998 adds further food for thought: in MLC-recorded herds, 10.8 per cent of piglets born alive outdoors died prior to weaning, compared to 11.6 per cent of indoor-born piglets. These results from commercial farms further question the need for high technology and the engagement of human interference during the actual farrowing process. The metabolic changes taking place in the sow are well documented and readily recognized by trained stockmen: bed- or nest-making activities, increased restlessness

Maternal Behaviour of Sows		
Phase	*Duration*	*Characteristics*
Nest site seeking	24–16hr before farrowing	Voluntary isolation and selection of nest site
Nest building	16–3hr before farrowing	Vigorous nest construction activity
Parturition	3hr before farrowing until end of farrowing	Total pre-occupation
Nest occupation	Parturition to 10 days after	Sow and piglets keep together in close proximity to the nest
Social integration	10 days to 8 weeks post-partum	Introduction of the litter to the herd
Weaning	5–17 weeks	Gradual and subtle

and the onset of abdominal contractions signal the imminence of parturition. The presence of milk in the udder, and a body temperature rise of 0.5°C are also useful pointers.

Dr Per Jensen of the Swedish University of Agricultural Science spent years studying the material behaviour of sows in semi-natural enclosures. He identified six distinct behavioural phases, each with its own characteristics, some of which provoke certain questions regarding the management of farrowing in commercial situations.

The strategy for engaging human intervention at farrowing depends on an array of factors, including sow and stockman temperament, overall hygiene status and pen design. Biochemical assistance to synchronize and speed up the farrowing process is an option certainly available to all indoor producers with accurate service dates. However, the best approach is to undertake a 'farrowing audit' on each individual unit, and to set up an appropriate protocol.

The agreed procedures must match the ability of the management and labour force, and should reflect training programmes. A fundamental requirement is that there should be universal understanding about what is supposed to be done. The agreed procedures should involve the unit veterinary surgeon, and any fundamental revision or fine-tuning should only be implemented after discussion with all concerned. A written procedure would further ensure consistency.

THE CHALLENGE OF LACTATION

Lactating sows need nutrients to sustain milk production and avoid body fat loss. Genetic advances and the trend towards hyperprolific strains aim to increase the number of piglets weaned. Furthermore,

Estimates of Dietary Energy Requirements of a Young Sow (MJ DE/day) to Prevent Maternal Bodyweight Loss and Satisfy Various Levels of Litter Performance

Piglet weaning weight (kg)	Litter size			
	9	10	11	12
6	80.5	87.2	93.8	100.5
7	93.2	101.3	109.4	117.5
8	106.0	115.5	125.0	134.4

Source: MLC

high piglet weights at weaning have a positive influence on days to slaughter. Hence much is demanded of the modern sow in lactation, in terms of maximizing numbers weaned and weaning weights, without impairing lifetime productivity.

It figures that lactation feed levels must reflect litter size and weaning weight as well as sow body condition, and obviously these will vary from sow to sow. Immediately after farrowing the sow is not enthusiastic about feed intake, and the demands for milk production are low. But this gradually changes, and any lactation feed programme must reflect this, meaning that each sow must be treated as an individual.

Daily energy requirements throughout the lactation of sows with defined litter sizes have been calculated by MLC. The data relate to a model sow weighing 160kg (350lb) liveweight and producing piglets weighing 1.3kg (2.8lb) at birth on a twenty-four-day weaning system. These calculations were used to develop the 'Stotfold Feeding Strategy', used at MLC's Stotfold Pig Development Unit.

In the first ten days after farrowing, all

The Stotfold Feeding Scale for Lactating Sows

| LACTATION FEED SCALE | | | | | | | | | | | | |

First 10 days (All Sows/Gilts)						Sow Identification:						
Day	Kg	Fed				Total Fed:						
1	2.5					Date Farrowed (Day 1)						
2	3.0		NOTES:									
3	3.5											
4	4.0											
5	4.5											
6	5.0											
7	5.5											
8	6.0											
9	6.5											
10	7.0											

Gilt < 10 piglets Sow < piglets			Gilt 10 piglets Sow 9 piglets			Gilt 11 piglets Sow 10 piglets			Gilt 12 piglets Sow 11 piglets			Gilt 13 piglets Sow 12 piglets		
Day	Kg	Fed	Day	Kg	Fed	Day	Kg	Fed	Day	Kg	Fed	Day	Kg	Fed
11	7.0		11	7.5		11	7.5		11	7.5		11	7.5	
12	7.0		12	7.5		12	8.0		12	8.0		12	8.0	
13	7.5		13	8.0		13	8.5		13	8.5		13	8.5	
14	7.5		14	8.0		14	8.5		14	9.0		14	9.0	
15	8.0		15	8.5		15	9.0		15	9.5		15	9.5	
16	8.0		16	8.5		16	9.0		16	9.5		16	10.5	
17	8.5		17	9.0		17	9.5		17	10.0		17	10.0	
18	8.5		18	9.0		18	9.5		18	10.0		18	10.5	
19	9.0		19	9.5		19	10.0		19	10.5		19	11.0	
20	9.0		20	9.5		20	10.0		20	10.5		20	11.0	
21	9.5		21	10.0		21	10.5		21	11.0		21	11.5	
22	9.5		22	10.0		22	10.5		22	11.0		22	11.5	
23	9.5		23	10.0		23	10.5		23	11.0		23	11.5	
24	9.5		24	10.0		24	10.5		24	11.0		24	11.5	
25	9.5		25	10.0		25	10.5		25	11.0		25	11.5	
26	9.5		26	10.0		26	10.5		26	11.0		26	11.5	
27	9.5		27	10.0		27	10.5		27	11.0		27	11.5	

Source: MLC

sows are fed to a standard scale: on day one, 2.5kg (5.5lb) are fed, and this is increased by 0.5kg (1lb) daily, so that by day ten 7kg (15lb) is provided. After that stage, the demands of the litter exert a greater influence on the sow's metabolism. Hence, from ten days each sow is treated as an individual such that feed levels reflect litter size and target weaning weight.

Such high feed intakes in lactation are only achieved with a great deal of effort and attention to detail, particularly with respect to farrowing-room temperature regulation and the provision of water. Once-daily feeding of lactating sows is no

Comparison of Litter Performance with MCL recorded herds			
	Stotfold	*Top Third*	*Average*
Pigs reared per litter	10.3	9.95	9.53
Average weaning age (days)	24	23	25
Total litter weight weaned (kg/lb)	81.4 (180.0)	61.7 (136.0)	61.9 (136.5)
Piglet weaning weight (kg/lb)	7.0 (17.0)	6.2 (13.7)	6.5 (14.3)

Source: *Stotfold Feeding Strategy* MLC

longer an option for committed producers, and those achieving high feed intake levels in lactation choose to feed two or three times per day, and promptly remove any rejected food before it has a chance to go stale.

The result of maximizing lactation feed intake on the Stotfold scale is an increase in litter growth rates and weaning weights. It is a superb example of applied science making the most of research and stockmanship. Litters weaned from the Stotfold system were 32 per cent higher than values calculated from MLC records for average and top third herds. Also, individual piglet weights were 24 per cent higher as compared to MLC-recorded herds. The Stotfold feeding system also tends to produce more uniform weaning weight, moreover it minimizes weight loss in the sow, and so keeps her in good condition ready for early re-breeding.

The following are salient points regarding farrowing and lactation:

- If sows are too fat before farrowing they will suffer excessive weight loss in lactation.
- Increased feed levels in late pregnancy help elevate piglet birthweights.
- The farrowing house is an expensive resource and requires judicious use.

- During lactation, room temperature regulation has a marked impact on sow feed intake.
- In lactation, sows should be fed in accordance with their individual needs with respect to body fat, age of litter, piglet numbers and weaning weights.

Notes for Novices

- Unless gilts are 'built' properly they will fail to thrive as sows.
- Don't be surprised if gilts come on heat at any time.
- Boars thrive on regular work – if your herd is too small to keep a boar active, consider AI.
- A breeding boar needs four to five times the overall space allowance of a sow.
- Unless sows are in pig they won't produce piglets – but they will still need feeding!
- Efficient service management and pregnancy diagnosis are important aspects of production.
- Although service, pregnancy, farrowing and lactation are separate stages, try to think how they impact on each other, and on the next cycle.

6 Raising Piglets

In the wild state, the natural maternal behaviour of sows helped to ensure survival of the species, rather than maximize production. The commercial practice of confining the sow and litter in a farrowing crate for a three- to four-week period has two benefits: it encourages a sustained milk flow, which pampers the litter, and it reduces the likelihood of piglets being crushed. Even so, deaths due to crushing still comprise a major proportion of piglet loss. Obviously, new-born piglets are particularly susceptible, so if maximum numbers are to be kept alive, human intervention is best directed at the period from the onset of farrowing until piglets are forty-eight hours old. Considering that a mature, newly farrowed sow could weigh up to two hundred times more than each piglet she produces, she must be regarded as a source of danger as well as a lifeline to new-born piglets.

When sows have unrestricted freedom of movement, piglets tend to get crushed. (Allen & Page)

THE STILLBIRTH PROBLEM

A unit suffering a 10 per cent mortality of live pigs, on average, also loses 0.75 piglets per litter due to stillbirths. In other words, total deaths per litter represent around two piglets – within the United Kingdom this amounts to over three million dead pigs per annum.

> Theer's more ways o'killin pigs than chokin' 'em 'ooth [with] butter. (Shropshire proverb)

As sows age, their muscle tone declines and so farrowing takes longer. Typically once farrowing is underway in a gilt, piglets emerge about every twelve to fifteen minutes. Older sows take around another nine minutes. As sows age, the incidence of stillbirths increases, particu-

Risk Factors that Influence the Birth of Stillborn Pigs	
Factor	*% Risk*
Parities 1 & 2	15
Parities 3 & 4	25
Parities 5 & 6	35
Parity 7 and over	45
Stillborn in previous litter	+30
Previous litter size >12	+15
Blackwell University of Minnesota (1986)	

The start of the search for colostrum. (ABN Ltd)

larly after about seven litters; sows generally should only be retained beyond this stage if they do not have a history of high levels of stillbirths.

Research from the University of Minnesota advocates a mathematical probability approach to reducing stillbirths, since analysis of American farm records indicated that risk factors were accumulative. Whereas stillbirths were not a problem in the majority of litters, some sows appeared to be particularly susceptible. The commercial producer

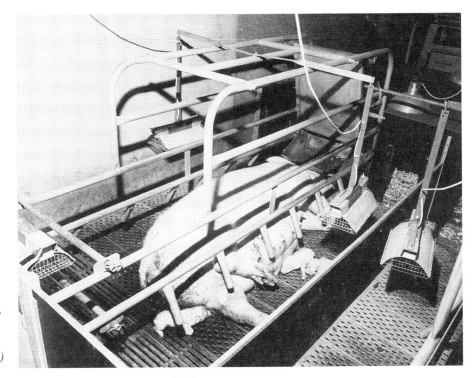

Supplementary heat in the neonatal period helps reduce piglet mortality. (TXU Europe (formerly Eastern Group))

Farrowing Monitor		
Birth Number	Time Checks	Comment
1		
2		
3		
4		
5		
6		
7		
8		
9		
10		
11		
12		
13		
14		
15		
16		

NOTE: The last-born piglets are the most vulnerable. If there is a 30-minute delay between deliveries near the end of farrowing, then assist. Discuss the farrowing pattern with your vet.

must therefore identify 'high risk' sows, and organize an appropriate culling programme. On the basis of the Minnesota data, if a parity seven sow which had previously produced stillbirths were retained for breeding, subsequent stillbirth problems would be highly likely.

Professor Peter English of Aberdeen University has undertaken much applied research into piglet mortality. One outcome has been the development of a simple form to monitor progress during farrowing. Any early indication of a protracted farrowing should prompt the attendant to monitor progress – if difficult farrowings are observed, noted and monitored, it is more likely that a sow will be provided with the help she so obviously needs. Very often piglets that are stillborn were actually perfectly healthy, but expired as a result of oxygen starvation during the farrowing process; so adoption of this technique could well lead to a marked reduction in such stillbirths. For instance, it

Piglets, straw and heat input are a recipe for good welfare in the absence of farm fires. (ABN Ltd)

124

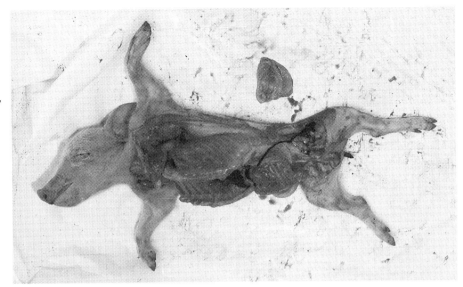

A dead piglet with an empty stomach has never, ever suckled. (TXU Europe (formerly Eastern Group))

has been shown that where piglets are being born at fairly regular intervals, the interval prior to a stillborn piglet emerging is often twice as long as that before a live one. Stillbirth incidence also tends to increase during the last third of parturition. Bear in mind, too, that oxytocin injections should be used sparingly, because although this hormone does

enhance uterine contractions, its administration could result in the severance of the umbilical cord, and so lead to stillbirths.

Irritable sows tend to have a higher incidence of stillbirths. Thus sows troubled with skin parasites, or agitated because they are not provided with suitable nest-building material, are more likely to have prolonged farrowings.

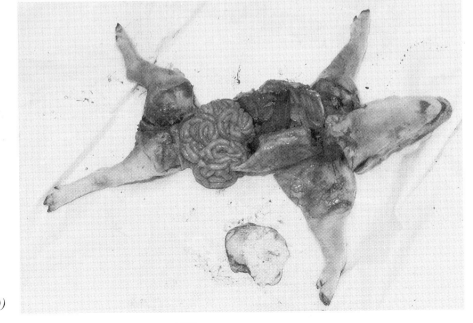

Clotted milk in the removed stomach of a dead pig indicates suckling had taken place. (TXU Europe (formerly Eastern Group))

Excessively high temperatures in the far-rowing room also tend to make sows restless: this can upset the hormonal balance and lead to extended farrowing. Finally there may be situations where management is excellent, yet stillbirths and mummified piglets continue to be a problem; in which case the possibility of injecting for parvovirus must be considered.

COPING WITH POOR COMPETITORS

There is a tendency to record any pigs found dead at the back of a sow as 'born deads'. However, this may be exaggerating the incidence of stillbirths and could well be 'wrong-footing' the management. Piglets that died well before farrowing are usually mummified and their status is clear cut, whereas pigs born alive but which fail to 'get going' are not so easily distinguished. If the sac enclosing the piglet has been ruptured in the vicinity of the piglet's front claws, the chances are that it briefly lived.

A simple post-mortem examination can also help provide an answer. If the lung tissue floats when immersed in a bucket of water, this is indicative of lung infla-

Energy Stores in the Newborn Pig and Infant		
	Pig	*Infant*
Glycogen (g/kg)		
Liver	4.5	4.2
Muscle	26.5	10.0
Total	31.0	14.2
Available energy (KJ/kg)	377	167
Fat (g/kg)	15	150
Available energy (KJ/kg)	<80	5440
Total available energy (KJ/kg)	460	5607
Source: Mellor and Cockburn, 1986		

tion, meaning that the piglet has breathed independently. Opening the abdominal cavity and examining the stomach can also be informative: for instance, milk in the stomach clots rapidly and is easily observed, which would confirm that a piglet was born alive, and that it suckled, too. On the other hand, many dead piglets are found to have totally empty stomachs. Often they appear to be quite normal, but failed to thrive because evidently they did not suckle and so died from starvation and hypothermia.

At birth, pigs are physiologically immature, and only limited body energy reserves are present as glycogen and fat. This deficiency makes them poor competitors – compared to human infants they miss out on that vital 'kick-start' that energy provides. Within twelve hours of birth, three-quarters of the meagre liver glycogen energy reserves will have been utilized, and nearly half the muscle glycogen depleted. Piglets born to sows that

A novel farrowing crate design from Germany. (PIGSPEC)

were underfed in late pregnancy have particularly low glycogen reserves. New-born pigs also have low fat reserves, since their bodies contain only 1.5 per cent fat as compared to 15 per cent in babies; moreover, most of the fat in neonatal pigs is present as structural fat, and as such is not readily available for mobilization. By way of comparison, total energy reserves in new-born pigs are only around 8 per cent of those in human infants. Hence introduction to life is a great challenge to neonatal pigs, and should always be regarded as a traumatic experience. A good birthweight markedly increases survival rates.

In the uterus, pigs have been nurtured at 39°C. A newly dropped piglet might find itself on its own: it might not have the benefit of huddling with littermates, it will not have an immediate supply of nutrients, and it will certainly never enjoy the benefit of any blood-warming, affectionate licking from its mother. Under such bleak circumstances, even in still air at 34°C, the piglet would start to break down body reserves in order to maintain body temperature, and given its disadvantaged starting point, inevitably this can only be a short-term emergency expedience.

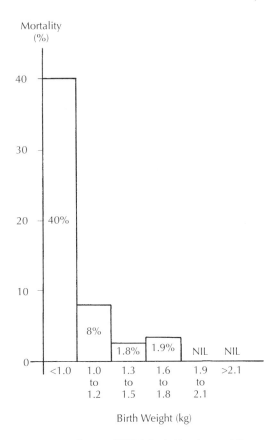

Source: BOCM-Pauls Development Farm

The influence of birthweight on piglet mortality.

The priorities of a newborn piglet are therefore:

- getting dry and clean;
- keeping warm and out of draughts;
- taking in more energy (suckling);
- avoiding getting crushed.

This is potentially achievable by huddling with its mother and littermates, and suckling as soon as possible. Unfortunately the baby pig is born into a wet, dirty and hostile environment. First of all, before it has a chance of instinctively boosting its energy reserves, it has to negotiate the hazardous journey to the sow's udder. Invariably, Darwinian com-

A forward/side-creep farrowing pen with a shared access passage. (Pyramid Systems (Malton) Ltd)

127

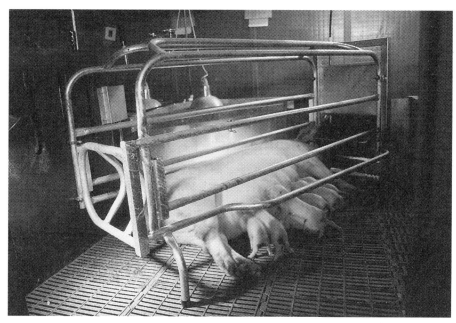

Farrowing crate offering newborn piglets a normal degree of protection from crushing. (G. E. Baker (UK) Ltd (Quality Equipment))

petition rules come into play: sharp metal slats, rough concrete and inappropriate bedding materials can all injure the soft, delicate skin of the new-born piglet as it courageously paddles its way to the teat. Open wounds quickly become a contact point for infection, and so a disease cycle

gets under way. Not surprisingly, many piglets find the challenge too great and never reach the teat, and so perish from starvation or get crushed because of their lack of alertness.

However, Nature has a mechanism for boosting this nutritional shortfall and

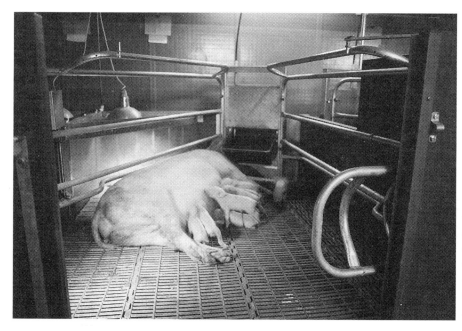

The same crate with its hinged sides opened to give the sow more freedom. (G. E. Baker (UK) Ltd (Quality Equipment))

Labour-saving European farrowing pen. (SEGHERS genetics)

also has provision for reducing the piglet's susceptibility to disease (since it is born with little immunity): the first milk, or colostrum, has enriched levels of proteins and total solids as compared to the sow's 'ordinary' milk that will 'come in' later. Within the colostrum, large protein molecules called 'immunoglobulins' are present, particularly during the first few days of life when the piglet has a temporary facility to absorb these directly through its gut wall. During its first twenty-four hours, the piglet consumes around 250 millilitres of colostrum, which equates with around 20 per cent of its bodyweight, and the immunoglobulins therein provide it with passive immunity to combat the pathogens of its mother. At between twenty-one and twenty-eight days of life these immunoglobulin levels subside, but thereafter gradually rise again as the piglet develops active immunity in its own right.

Many apparently normal piglets that die soon after birth do so because they are poor competitors and fail to receive that vital first intake of colostrum. When farrowing is induced and help is at hand, these non-viable pigs can be identified and revitalized with a 20 millilitre feed of colostrum via a stomach tube. Provided such piglets are separated at an early stage, and after assisted feeding are put under a heat lamp, they have a high recovery rate. Note that stomach-tube feeding is not a job for amateurs and must only be undertaken by trained operators. There are also various products available on the market aimed at boosting survival rates in lethargic piglets; these are in the form of a bottled liquid suspension, and are easy to administer under the piglet's tongue via a user-friendly plunger, nozzle and extension tube. These energy-boosting potions often comprise highly digestible fats known as short-chain or medium-chain triglycerides (MCTs) that are enriched with a blend of vitamins.

Attention to detail in the farrowing pen can be the difference between average and top-third performance. The majority of piglets readily thrive, despite the perils that their new, challenging environment imposes upon them; others require additional, tender loving care. Provision of a temporary supplementary heat supply

The rest of the litter are not quite so photogenic. (SEGHERS genetics)

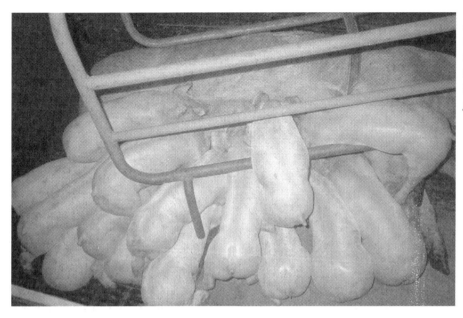

Prolificacy and low piglet mortality are key objectives. (SEGHERS genetics)

behind the sow at farrowing works wonders for drying the skin and raising the critical temperature of particularly vulnerable piglets. When piglets are born onto slats, a temporary hygienic cover such as a plastic sheet or board is helpful in reducing the effects of chilling draughts.

During the piglets' early hours of life, the very first priority is to attract them to the 'milk bar', though because of the sow's bulk and clumsiness, unfortunately this must also be regarded as a danger zone. Professor English's work has shown the benefit of providing extra heating at the side of the sow for the first forty-eight hours after parturition, as this encourages piglets to lie within 'commuting distance' of her udder but hopefully clear of the danger zone. A word of warning here: pig farmers are renowned for their versatility in creating quite remarkable supplementary heating devices, but when luck runs out, piglet and sow mortality can be total. Straw bedding, temporary heat lamps and the pigs themselves are an acknowledged source of farm fires. Hence much effort has to be made in making all creep lamps safe as well as effective.

Underfloor heating offers great advantages in terms of its safety features, effectiveness, running costs and resistance to moisture attack. However, many farmers baulk at the prospect of installation complications, and the hassle of electrical repairs that often entail breaking up concrete.

FACILITIES FOR FARROWING

In 1997 the EU's Scientific Veterinary Committee produced a report entitled 'The Welfare of Intensively Kept Pigs'. In particular, committee members had been invited to appraise current practices for farrowing and lactating sows, and to assess pig behaviour. Inevitably they focused on the low levels of piglet mortality regularly achieved on both unsophisticated outdoor systems as well as more intensive indoor systems. Well managed, crated farrowing systems have consistently produced litters with low mortality rates.

The committee accepted that piglet mortality was likely to be higher in sows

Weaners raised on slatted floors have a more hygienic environment. (ABN Ltd)

that were not restrained at farrowing, but they expressed some instinctive reservations about crated systems. They recommended the further development of farrowing systems which would liberate the sow and enable her to undertake normal nest-building behaviour. However, the quest to free the sow from the farrowing crate has been hampered by several 'breakthroughs' in loose-housing equipment that although eye-catching, ultimately failed to benefit the piglets. Hence any future changes must be made with great caution.

The Dutch are perhaps making progress: workers at the Research Institute for Animal Production investigated a novel layout for a farrowing room,

Weaners raised on straw fare better as long as they are well managed, but the labour input can be high. (ABN Ltd)

A portal-frame building housing weaners in kennels. (PIGSPEC)

Piglet bungalows with 'automatic control of natural ventilation' (ACNV). (Pyramid Systems (Malton) Ltd)

where farrowing nests were arranged radially round a central piglet feeding area. When the youngest piglets in the batch were one week old, partitions between litters were removed, as was the back-board behind the sows. Key points which emerged from the trial were:

- Sows accepted a farrowing nest if the design and layout and the nest-building material were attractive.
- Sows in farrowing nests must have their back end projecting, yet have the capability to move freely through the house.
- Piglet savaging did not seem to be a problem.
- Some sows sought privacy when farrowing, others did not.
- Newly farrowed sows were reluctant to leave their litters in order to seek food. The feeding area needed to be close to the nest.
- Given further refinement, group-housed farrowing systems could be an alternative to individual crates.

The possibility of group housing in lacta-

tion persuaded scientists at the Scottish Agricultural College to take another look at multiple suckling. They studied the impact of mixing sows and litters two weeks after farrowing, and came to the following conclusions:

- There was considerable disruption in established suckling patterns.
- Competition at the udder was increased, since there was unrestricted opportunity for more piglets to suckle.
- Whilst the mixing of piglets from individual litters was in itself disruptive, the impact of increased competition because of extra numbers was far worse.
- Sows were most troubled by extra piglets suckling in the first twenty-four hours after mixing; thereafter problems declined, although disruption persisted for the next two to three days.
- There was a marked dip in piglet growth rates for one week after mixing.

Given the demise of multiple suckling the first time round, the results of these Scottish trials provide little incentive for

132

re-inventing the practice and developing group-housing systems for lactating sows.

More recent experience from commercial farms in the UK is indicating that non-confined but individual farrowing facilities could be a practical option for the future. This could have big implications for consumer perceptions, and must be seen as a research priority. There seems to be a new sense of direction towards sow-friendly farrowing crates designed to allow the sow to turn round without hindrance. Before and after farrowing, these systems restrain the sow for as long as is necessary to protect the litter. Thereafter a pivot device allows the crate side to be opened to facilitate free access. Inevitably, such systems favour smaller pig breeding enterprises; on larger set-ups, questions remain regarding the labour input required to keep such pens clean, as well as the Health and Safety issues for those personnel who enter the pens.

FOSTERING STRATEGIES

Fostering is a useful management aid, but its impact depends very much on sympathetic timing. It is a technique more generally adopted in large indoor units, particularly when synchronized farrowing is practised; in smaller herds a lack of suitable nurse sows at the right time makes cross-fostering difficult. Nevertheless, a strategy for coping with small pigs in large litters needs to be drawn up in every pig unit.

Shift-suckling is one practical option, its main drawback being the demands it takes on the operator's time. During the first twenty-four hours of life, heavier pigs – and particularly those in big litters –

All-in/all-out management is standard practice in nursery units. (TXU Europe (formerly Eastern Group))

133

**Runts Left on Their Natural Mothers
Compared to Runts Reared on a Nurse Sow**

Age	Piglet weights (kg/lb)	
	Left on sow	*Fostered on to nurse sow*
At start – 7 days old	1.84/4.05 (37)	1.78/3.9 (16)
Two days later	2.15/4.7 (37)	2.32/5.1 (15)
Eight days later	3.37/7.4 (36)	4.16/9.2 (12)

Pig numbers shown in brackets

Source: International Pig Veterinary Congress, 1998

are temporarily moved to a heated creep area, and left there for one to two hours; the disadvantaged piglets can then obtain their share of colostrum under much less competitive circumstances. This practice helps reduce within-litter variation, and lightweight piglets are less likely to die.

At the 1998 International Pig Veterinary Congress a trial from the University of Guelph in Canada was reported. At seven days of age, runt piglets were either left on their mothers or transferred to make a whole litter of runts on a nurse sow. Within just two days of moving to a nurse sow, piglets were 0.16kg (0.3lb) heavier than comparable runts left on their mothers. After eight days this weight difference had increased to 0.79kg (1.7lb) for piglets on nurse sows. Piglet mortality on the nurse litters was only 3 per cent, whereas lightweights left to take their chance on their natural mothers found competition with bigger pigs a problem, and mortality was 25 per cent. Those who still need convincing that competition is the problem rather than low birth weight per se should observe the suckling vigour shown by litters of small pigs of comparable liveweight.

Fostering is best undertaken six to eight hours after birth onto a sow at the same stage as the natural mother, because colostrum is then still available from the foster mother. When fostering is delayed beyond day two, as in the Canadian trial, although weights within the litter are less variable, generally total litter weights are reduced. In commercial situations when piglets are fostered, best results are usually obtained if the lightest pigs are left on their natural mother and the heaviest surplus pigs moved to the nurse sow. Back-fostering older, light-weight, 'problem piglets' onto a more recently farrowed sow can encourage disease to spread within the farrowing room.

Some producers on high-output units put much time and effort into cross-fostering, and find it a cost-effective and satisfying experience. However, on most outdoor units, practical problems conspire to make cross-fostering a virtual non-starter. Despite this, both the outdoor sow and the outdoor producer increasingly send out messages that intensive, state-of-the-art pig units do not have a monopoly on high output. Could it be that low mortality on outdoor units is an expression of the contentment of the sow, rather than the degree of sophistication of the equipment in use?

BLUEPRINT FOR BABY PIGS

- Acknowledge that farrowing can be a hazardous process, and that the first two days of life can be traumatic, particularly for lightweight pigs.
- Differentiate between genuine 'born deads', and weakly pigs that die soon after birth.
- Identify, and do not hesitate in culling, old sows that are prone to stillbirths.
- Appreciate the vital role of colostrum, and make sure it is shared amongst the litter.
- Develop a strategy for dealing with lightweight poor competitors.
- Do not forsake conventional farrowing crates unless alternative proven systems emerge.

Temporary 'comfort boards' help reduce floor draughts just after weaning. (ABN Ltd)

THE IMPORTANCE OF IRON

The very best genetically improved slaughter pigs now have around 60 per cent lean meat content. Since lean is rich in iron, it could be that modern pigs have an increased demand for iron. In trials, when sows have been injected with iron three weeks prior to farrowing, there has been no indication of increased haemoglobin levels. However, some indoor producers observe that if piglets fail to get an iron injection shortly after birth, within ten days they start to lick exposed metal surfaces. If a belated iron injection is provided at this stage, the licking behaviour invariably subsides.

It could be that the iron status of piglets is markedly influenced by their natural behaviour patterns. Practical difficulties and 'green' contract requirements sometimes demand that outdoor-born pigs are never given iron injections. Furthermore, they get no iron from creep feed, since it is generally not provided outdoors. Despite this, impressive weaning weights of 7.5kg (16.5lb) are consistently

Push-through mucking out is best avoided for weaners. (ABN Ltd)

135

Small-scale producers tend to run more labour-intensive weaner housing systems. (Allen & Page)

achieved at twenty-four days on many outdoor units. Could this be a reflection of the different behaviour pattern of outdoor pigs?

In the natural state, weaning is a protracted procedure. Following the first week after farrowing, the sow spends progressively more time away from her litter, and in her absence the natural curiosity of the piglets encourages them to root in the soil. Consequently, they ingest iron and various soil-borne micro-nutrients which stimulate their enzyme system. The behaviour pattern of the outdoor-born pig is more closely aligned with this natural situation, and could reflect why they thrive without supplementary iron and have a digestive system which enables them to 'motor on' when given solid food after weaning.

Particularly on indoor units, commercial products are emerging onto the market to work alongside traditionally injected iron; these generally comprise a paste containing an organic-based iron derivative alongside digestive enhancers, and are often shrouded with a trace of 'muck and magic' that gives them some commercial spirit. There is also interest in boosting iron levels to accelerate post-weaning growth rates; this involves the provision of iron fumarate presented within a cylindrical solid that is activated at drinking time.

CREEP FEEDING

The indoor producer's answer to the pig's lack of opportunity to practise rooting is to offer creep feed. These days the digestible energy content of creep feed can be as high as 17MJper kilogram with up to 10 per cent oil and 24 per cent crude protein. Such highly specified products do not store well, however; they absorb moisture and rapidly putrefy in warm conditions, creating an ideal breeding ground for bacteria. In fact 'slap-dash' creep-feeding practice will often do more harm than good; it:

- wastes time and squanders a costly input;
- provides a breeding ground for bacteria and disease;
- encourages invasions from flies, birds and vermin;
- spreads disease amongst piglets;
- stresses the sow and could lead to piglet crushing.

Creep feeding is where art meets science, and is a process that demands a meticulous approach from all those involved in it. Training piglets to eat solid food can be a very rewarding process, and can yield benefits in terms of increased weaning weights and also by making weaning a less troublesome event. In trials where creep feed was given to piglets from ten days of age until weaning at twenty-four days, weaning weights were increased by 1kg (2.2lb). A trial involving 5,000 pigs indicated that piglets with the highest weaning weights made the greatest weight gains in the first three-and-a-half weeks after weaning. Further analysis showed that over 25 per cent of the variation in days to slaughter could be account-ed for by the variation in weaning weights.

The scale of operation on large pig units is such that the most successful creep feeders, although still offering creep on the 'little and often' basis, actually empty a whole bag of feed in one creep-feeding session; that way piglets are more likely to be attracted to it because of its freshness, whilst added flavouring enhancers can be fully effective. Smaller producers do not have this practical advantage and so have to develop an alternative strategy to maintain the feed's freshness. Once a bag is opened and partially emptied, both creep feed and early weaner feed should be stored in an appropriate environment: the paper sack should be folded down and closed within a small, lidded plastic bin, and kept in a feed store adjoining, but separate from, the heated pig environment. Expensive creep feeds should never be stored within warm pig buildings.

Sows love creep feed, and given half a chance will endeavour to steal it from their litter, thus finding the best place for creep-feed either on the floor or in the trough is not easy. It should be placed away from the heat lamp, be inaccessible to the sow, and well away from the dirty area of the pen. Farrowing room staff find that creep feed allocation is an activity

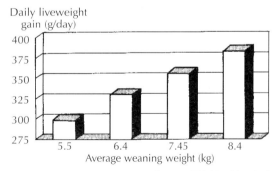

Source: SCA Nutrition Ltd.

The benefit of creep feeding on weaning weight.

Source: SCA Nutrition Ltd.

The effect of weaning weight on post-weaning performance.

Environment enhancement for early weaned pigs. PIGSPEC)

best undertaken some time after sows have been fed; the atmosphere is then generally more relaxed because the sows are more settled and not particularly looking for food. Note that maximum advantage is likely to be gained from flavouring agents if creep is handled with freshly washed hands.

On twenty-one- to twenty-four-day weaning regimes not much creep is consumed, and intakes tend to vary. Nevertheless, creep feeding is still useful in that it helps 'kick-start' the adaptive process of digestive maturation, as well as positively influencing weaning weights. Pigs fed creep have greater stomach capacities than those that just suckle milk, and this helps set them up for solid food digestion after weaning. Creep-eating piglets also have a measurable increase in the output of acid from their stomach, and greatly increased levels of protein-splitting enzymes. At the time of weaning, acid production in the piglet's stomach generally declines. Creep feeding helps to arrest this decline in acidity, and this enables the protein-splitting enzymes to work better.

Creep feeding is somewhere between an art and a science. (Tuck Box Ltd)

Feed a pig and you'll have a hog.

(English proverb)

A recent development which makes the most of the baby pig's instinct to root involves a product known as 'Piglet Peat'. It is marketed in 50 litre sacks, and comprises a semi-moist acidic black peat with protected trace elements including zinc, iron, copper and manganese. Pigs readily consume peat from two days of age, and this appears to provide a nutritional stimulus to the digestive system. The peat must be certified pathogen-free. After about ten days it can be mixed with a conventional creep feed, with the objective of stimulating intake of the creep and so achieving higher weaning weights.

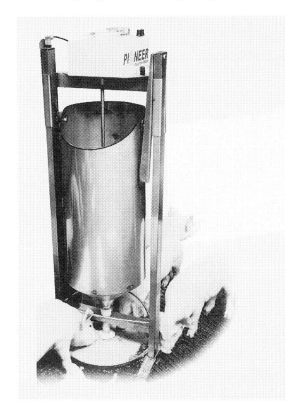

A novel rearing system for early-weaned pigs blends solid feed and water. (G. E. Baker (UK) Ltd (Quality Equipment))

Sophisticated creep and first-stage rations do not come cheap. One of the reasons for their high cost is the need to formulate them with non-antigenic substances. In particular, protein in the form of peptides is sometimes wrongly recognized by the baby pig's immature gut, which identifies them as invading pathogens. The surface of the intestinal villi respond to this false alarm by launching an immune response, and becoming truncated. This slows down the digestion of the wrongly identified digesta, the impact being just the same as when disease is present. Undigested food consequently accumulates in the gut, and nasty bacteria very quickly multiply within it. Other cells from within the digestive system then pour out water in order to flush the debris through the gut – in other words, the piglet starts to scour.

Nutritionists strive, in particular, to avoid incorporating certain cereals into creep feed; similarly, unprocessed soya and cooked fish meal which are known to contain antigenic proteins must also be avoided. Prior to weaning, and for the first seven days thereafter, all cereals in creep feed should be cooked, or receive some form of heat treatment to enhance digestibility. Provision of water is vital in the post-weaning period. Some producers report improved results when piglets are provided with a choice of both first- and second-stage feed about one week after weaning.

The benefits, or otherwise, of creep feeding may perhaps be summarized thus:

- Creep feeding provides a unique opportunity to maximize feed intake when feed conversion efficiency is at its best.
- There are only two choices in pig creep feeding: do it right, or not at all!
- Good creep feeding increases weaning weights and post-weaning growth rates.

- Good creep feeding helps reduce the overall cost per kilogram liveweight gain.

THE POST-WEANING CRISIS

Weaning time for a producer often represents just another busy day in the weekly schedule of never-ending jobs. From the piglet's point of view, however, it is not just an event or a date on the calendar: it is the start of a complex physiological process. A good understanding of this process enables pig keepers to develop empathy with the young traumatized animals entrusted to them at weaning.

Prior to weaning, life for most piglets is as good as it gets: they have the benefit of mother's milk, free access to water, highly nutritious creep feed and a comforting social and climatic environment. But at weaning all this changes, and the producer must prepare the piglets for the challenges they will have to face. Prior to weaning, temperature management in

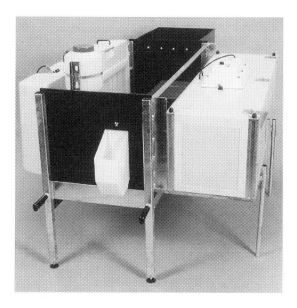

Nurtinger nursery unit for rearing orphan or surplus piglets. (G. E. Baker (UK) Ltd (Quality Equipment))

both the farrowing room and the creep box needs special attention. Lowering the temperature of the creep area before weaning helps stimulate feed intake, and prepares the piglet for the impact of milk withdrawal; by the time of weaning the temperature in the creep box can be lowered to around 24°C, though piglet behaviour is the best guide to both the lower and upper temperature limits. In particular, lightweight piglets need extra tender loving care at weaning.

Research undertaken at Scotland's Centre for Rural Building helps quantify the problems of all pigs at weaning, and in particular the trauma of poor competitors with low weaning weights. The broken line on the graph (left) suggests that a 5kg (11lb) pig on low feed intake – just 126g per day – reduces its body heat production to less than 22 watts. It is highly sensitive to low temperatures at this low feed intake, and consequently has a critical temperature of around 29°C. If the same weight of pig were capable of achieving

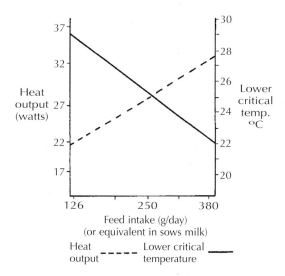

Effect of feed intake on heat output and lower critical temperature (LCT) of a 5kg pig.

140

380g per day of feed intake without suffering digestive upset, its environmental temperature requirements would be markedly different. The left vertical axis of the graph indicates that heat output would be increased to 33 watts per pig, whereas the right axis (solid line) indicates that the LCT would be down to 22°C. In other words, increased feed intake can compensate for the shortcomings of climatic environment. Unfortunately, lightweight pigs deprived of food at weaning do not have this mechanism at their disposal; furthermore, they also have to cope with the challenge of dehydration because they no longer have access to their 24-hour milk-bar. Given the prolificacy of the modern sow and the fact that further increases in litter size are predicted, developing strategies for 'slow stream' pigs becomes a priority.

There have been many attempts to develop specialized rearing facilities – that is, intensive care units for lightweight and disadvantaged weaners. Most of these have been based on the provision of warm or cold milk in liquid form, and have met with only mediocre success. There has also been a tendency to develop systems based on the need to sell high-margin milk-based feed products, rather than on the husbandry needs of the pig.

The use of sophisticated electronics and pumping systems have made intensive care units complicated and expensive. Consequently the commercial reaction has been to share the kit amongst more pigs, and caring for slow-stream pigs in large group sizes is not a smart strategy.

A recent promising innovation has been the development of the 'transition feeder' which aims to address the problem of post-weaning dehydration using robust, unsophisticated apparatus. The device is used for the first two weeks after weaning, and comprises a portable stand-alone feeder which freshly mixes creep and water; it simply connects to conventional electricity and water supplies. A signalling system beckons piglets at the start of the feeding cycle, building on the behaviour pattern developed with the lactating sow. Farm trials have indicated encouraging results when high-quality creeps have been used for particularly lightweight young pigs.

The 'pros and cons' of intensive care units may perhaps be summarized thus:

- Pig-focused strategies must be developed for identifying lightweight/slow-stream pigs at weaning.
- Lightweight weaners rarely thrive in large groups and when in competition with heavier pigs.
- A strict hygiene regime must be practised with 'poor do-er' pigs.
- High temperatures help to make up for low feed intakes.
- Dehydration can be a big problem in disadvantaged and newly weaned pigs.

Notes for Novices

- Many healthy pigs suffocate during the farrowing process – know when to assist.
- Most baby pigs that die are healthy but compete poorly – try to identify these pigs early.
- Ensure that all pigs get their 'kick-start' of colostrum.
- As yet the traditional farrowing crate is the best means of protecting indoor-born piglets – make sure you have sufficient and adequate resting time.
- Creep and first-stage weaner feed is expensive – store it well, feed it judiciously, and regard it as an investment for the future.
- Aim for good weaning weight to ensure fewer days to slaughter.
- Do not regard weaning as just another date on the calendar, consider it as the start of a complex physical and psychological process.

7 Market Considerations

Consumers visit retailers in their millions and purchase pigmeat, and for this reason alone, those involved in pig farming must recognize the close link between the raw material and the packaged goods. Essentially they are food producers, though developing volume sales from the pigs nurtured on farm depends on how well they can co-operate with processors and retailers. These are the people who transform pigmeat into value-added food products.

Pigs and pigmeat need a more specialist approach to marketing than cattle and sheep. Within the European Union the pigmeat sector 'enjoys' a lightweight regime, and does not benefit from the traditional protectionism associated with the Common Agricultural Policy. Pig production is perceived differently from beef and sheep farming, too: consumers tend to link pigs with poultry, and are more inclined to associate pigs with 'factory farming'. The physical output from sows is greater than that from ruminants, and the short interval from birth to slaughter is the envy of the beef industry, although compared to the red meat producers, pig farmers have to live with more stringent welfare regulations. The pig industry has a unique structure, and this is reflected in supply and demand patterns; pigs have always tended to be 'gold or copper'.

As a result of technical innovation, pig-meat in its various forms has become very cost competitive against beef and lamb, and when presented in boneless joints its price compares favourably with poultry. Pigmeat means different things to different people, particularly as it covers a wide range of products that are suitable for further processing. Pig products confer great advantages in terms of convenience and versatility, but then so does poultry meat. Since the poultry industry is better structured and more vertically integrated, there have been more initiatives leading to new product development; for instance, in 1997 across all UK meat sectors, the poultry industry was responsible for 47 per cent of new retail meat products, launching over eight new meal solutions every week. This must be compared to a mediocre 29 per cent share from new pigmeat products. Thus it can be seen that the key to challenging the successful poultry sector is to bring more value-added pig products before consumers.

What can you expect from a pig but a grunt?
(English proverb)

VOLUME SALES

At the time of writing, the big supermarket retailers sell around three-quarters of all pigmeat marketed in the UK; indeed, multiple retailers and butchers are now

Supermarkets attach great importance to visual presentation. (PIGSPEC)

the main vendors of pigmeat. Caterers are major buyers, and it is estimated that around one third of their meat dishes comprise pigmeat. Furthermore, UK food consumption patterns are likely to follow American trends, where 'eating out' is widespread: 'Family Diners' are popular haunts during the week, and in USA city environments, the building of single person apartments without any kitchen facilities is now commonplace. Thus pigmeat sales throughout the catering sector are forecasted to grow, though this will be at the expense of the supermarkets. However, multiple retailers never like to miss a trick, and in recent years there has been a marked increase in the number of restaurants linked to supermarkets. Smaller producers, on the other hand, have great opportunities to supply wholesome, traceable local fare to quality restaurants within their vicinity.

Globally active cost-cutters are also likely to have a negative impact on multiple retailers: they will adopt more vertical integration, and utilize this to increase efficiency. One way or the other, big business will continue to exert a massive influence on pigmeat sales, and UK producers will therefore continue to be confronted with increased pressure to become more efficient.

Household Purchases by Source (Aug 1998 – July 1999)		
	%	
	Pork	*Bacon*
Butchers	18.8	9.3
Multiple Retailers	73.4	76.6
Freezer Centres	3.3	4.1
Independent Grocers	0.3	1.8
Co-ops	1.0	2.8
Others	3.2	5.4
Total	100.00	100.00

Making the Most of the Catering Opportunity

- Ensure continuity of supply.

- Provide a consistent product.

- Become more creative, with imaginative product innovation.

- Get rid of pigmeat's unjustified fatty image.

- Provide larger portions of meat.

- Strive to link producers, processors and caterers more closely.

Retail purchasing patterns in all sectors have changed markedly; for instance, a petrol company now commands the greatest market share of pre-packed sandwiches, whilst a supermarket chain has almost overnight become the biggest vendor of petrol. Who would have predicted such a sea change? Enlightened pig producers must be equally quick to spot any new developments in purchasing trends.

ASSURING THE CUSTOMER

Thinking people in affluent nations philosophize with the benefit of a full stomach, and this tends to influence their viewpoint. Faced with an abundance of low-cost meat presented in a diversity of forms, the consumer has become increasingly bewildered: how, for example, to distinguish between an ethnic serving of highly flavoured pigmeat in a neatly boxed convenience pack, and a wholesome quality cut? The reality is that consumers can now afford to pick and choose what they eat, either when at home or when dining in a restaurant; thus what is acceptable in a busy working household on a weekday evening, and what is demanded by the very same consumers when they become weekend gourmets, can be poles apart. Furthermore enlightened consumers, and particularly those in the UK, seek reassurance regarding:

- good pig welfare: the rearing method must be acceptable;

A silent protest outside a well-known London 'house'. (PIGSPEC)

- the safety of the meat: it must be free from bacterial contamination and drug residues;
- health aspects: pigmeat must be associated with less fat and reduced cholesterol.

In particular, such feelings intensified after the BSE scare in the United Kingdom. Consumers felt they had been duped by the Food Act and let down by an ill-informed government, whilst biological scientists practised intellectual gymnastics and, all in all, they began to feel they were the victims of multiple retailers who were preoccupied in safeguarding their enviable position at the top of the premier league.

The scene was set for change, and there was a great need for some form of credible, independent assurance regarding pigmeat, which would benefit reputable farmers, processors, retailers and consumers. In 1999, the Assured British Pigs (ABP) Scheme came into being. It is part of the Assured British Meat Scheme which conforms to the demanding inter-

UK pig farmers have campaigned for honest labelling. Was this bacon produced in the UK, packed and processed in the UK, or just marketed as English? (PIGSPEC)

national standard EN 45011.

The Food Safety Act (1990) enshrined the need for 'traceability' and 'due dili-

UK pig protestors make their point about pigmeat quality in London's Parliament Square. (PIGSPEC)

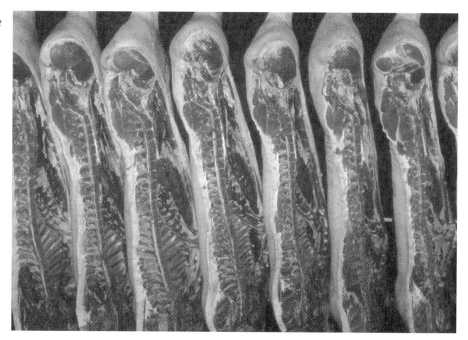

Retailers require leanness and consistency. (SEGHERS genetics)

gence', and the ABP Scheme proved a worthy delivery vehicle, giving pig producers a mechanism for assuring their customers that their production methods conform to appropriate standards. Any UK producer can apply to join the scheme, but to be accepted and retained they have to pass stringent inspections from a private veterinary surgeon and an independent inspector.

ABP is a single, across-the-board scheme: it is not just aimed at the 'big

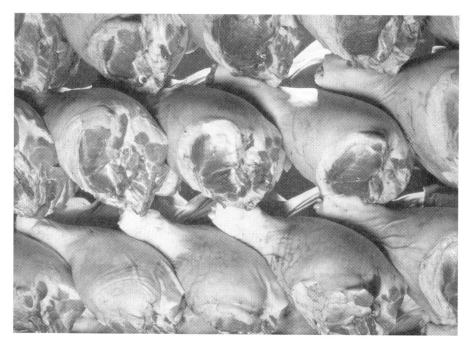

Hams in abundance. (SEGHERS genetics)

EU consumers enjoy a wide range of pig products. (SEGHERS genetics)

boys' and the elite, but is designed to encourage the raising of standards throughout the whole industry. The intention is that ultimately it will attract at least 80 per cent of all pig producers who conform to current legislation and codes of practice. It provides integrated assurance that incorporates compound feed manufacturers, farmers, supermarkets and caterers. Quality pigmeat produced in the UK can now be differentiated by the 'Mark of Distinction': this is an indication to consumers that the production chain conforms to high standards regarding:

- farm assurance;
- transportation;
- slaughtering and processing.

'Farm assurance' includes monitoring of tissue residues, and also transport arrangements. Slaughterers and processors of pork face stringent inspections regarding:

- pig welfare and hygiene;
- slaughtering procedures;
- independent traceability audits;
- carcase dressing;
- organoleptic testing (taste panels).

Participating abattoirs are independently inspected by an official veterinary surgeon (OVS) who monitors their compliance with strict standards.

Bacon and ham is also eligible to display the Mark of Distinction. It is

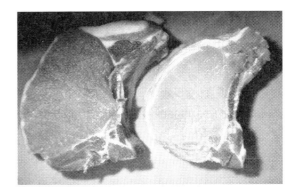

Retailers attach great importance to the colour of pigmeat. (SEGHERS genetics)

147

Assured British Pigs Scheme
General Housekeeping Scores

Category 1

Good, well-maintained modern buildings/structures. Hard-standing perimeter and service roads to most, if not all areas. Evidence of capital investment in modern systems.

Feed vehicles discharge and services accessible from perimeter.

Fenced perimeter. Unit well signed.

Weed growth controlled and managed in all areas.

Good drainage: no 'ponding'. Clear access to all areas.

Storage areas tidy. No excessive accumulations of muck.

No accumulation of scrap equipment, or materials.

Good evidence of regular housekeeping action in all areas of the site. Few, if any, fabric repairs required.

Excellent facilities for staff toilets and canteen area.

Category 2

Sound buildings or structures – some maintenance may be required to fabric in some areas. Some hard-standing areas but may be unlaid roadways and access to certain parts.

Perimeter defined but not necessarily fenced entirely.

Management of perimeter, but some weed growth evident, but not uncontrolled around buildings used for feed or pigs.

Evidence of management of waste, but in certain instances (as indicated in the audit report) there is need for action in the forthcoming three months.

Evidence of pest control scheme/system which is effective.

Basic staff facilities, i.e. toilets and meal arrangements.

Category 3

Older premises where there is a need for essential fabric repairs evident in several areas and certain buildings (in use) needing structure repairs, e.g. broken doors, windows, roof repairs required.

Little definition to perimeter, with poorly maintained service roads.

Some evidence of pest activity, but control measures agreed, investigated or in place but in need of improvement.

Accumulation of scrap, redundant equipment which compromises the ability to control pests. Weed control is required to prevent growth up to and around buildings where pigs are housed or feedstuffs are stored.

Very basic staff facilities.

Category 4

Buildings in poor state of repair. Several items requiring major renovation/repair work to structure. Generally old premises with no obvious investment/maintenance over many years.

Perimeter control poor. Accumulation of muck or general equipment in the pig environment or around the pig buildings and feed stores.

Evidence of obvious pest activity, e.g. mice, flies, rats or birds.

Poor housekeeping in feed stores, evidence of undealt-with feed spillage. Poor pest proofing to areas where pigs are kept.

Waste control poor – significant accumulation of waste, dung, muck.

Feedstuffs exposed to serious opportunities for contamination.

Inadequate facilities for staff.

processed under the British Meat Manufacturers' (BMMA) Charter Quality Scheme, which covers:

- raw materials;
- curing specification;
- maturation time;
- product specification;
- fat and added water content;
- labelling and presentation.

Some supermarket outlets have not enthused about the Mark of Distinction and have been reluctant to use it on their pigmeat. It detracts from their own brand image, and makes it harder for them to confuse consumers by selling undifferentiated imported produce. An 'honest labelling campaign' has brought some government pressure to bear to rectify this.

Quality Assurance embraces due diligence for the whole of the pig's lifetime, and has inevitably forced changes in working practices on some pig units. Supermarkets depend on abattoirs and processors to supply products with consistent quality, and clinically diseased pigs and those with defective carcases are not manifestations of quality production. Hence producers have come under increasing pressure to meet the qualitative aspects of contract specifications. This increased professionalism has worked its way back through the pigmeat production chain. Both weaner producers and finishers now face punitive monetary deductions if such problems are unreasonably passed along the production chain.

'Quality assurance' and 'quality production' might be summarized thus:

- Multiple retailers alone sell around 75 per cent of all UK pigmeat.
- Pig producers must increasingly regard themselves as food producers.
- Catering outlets and product innovation provide opportunities for increased pigmeat sales.
- Independent auditing of quality facilitates product differentiation at retail outlets.

Physical Defects Likely to Trigger Deductions in Quality Pig Production

Pot belly
Belly rupture
Scrotal rupture
Lameness
Abscessed carcase
Open wound
Defective skin
Underweight/overweight
Emaciated and hairy
Deformity/hump back
Blind anus
Clinical disease

ASPECTS OF QUALITY

Pigmeat quality has many components. Ultimately it reflects the superiority of the product as defined by the end user, though over the years it has been adjusted to reflect changing consumer demands, price incentives having been the driving forces behind these changes. The main components of meat quality have been identified by the Meat and Livestock Commission (MLC).

Both genetic selection and the practice of leaving male pigs entire have had a major impact on backfat reduction. Fat depth at the P2 position relates to the sum of fat and rind depth 65mm ($2^1/_2$in) from the mid-line of the carcase, over the head of the last rib. In 1971 the MLC initiated a pilot project involving the measurement of fat depth at P2 using the intrascope. Since then backfat levels have plummeted, though by the mid-nineties had started to level out at around 11mm (0.4in).

The processor's idea of quality. like that of the retailer and the consumer, is a mov-

Components of Meat Quality		
•	Carcase	Composition Dimensions
•	Meat	Sensory Technological Nutritional
•	Hygiene	Pathogens Shelf-life Residues
•	Ethics	Animal welfare Environmental impact Genetic modification

Source: MLC

ing target. The current EU grading scheme based on lean content has led to the introduction of automatic probes such as the 'Fat-O-Meter' and the 'Henessey Grading Probe' which better reflect carcase quality. Carcase monitoring indicates that within the United Kingdom the average lean content is around 58 per cent,

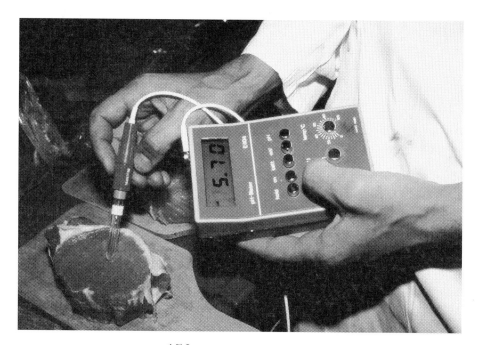

Meat Quality Assessment in the laboratory. (SEGHERS genetics)

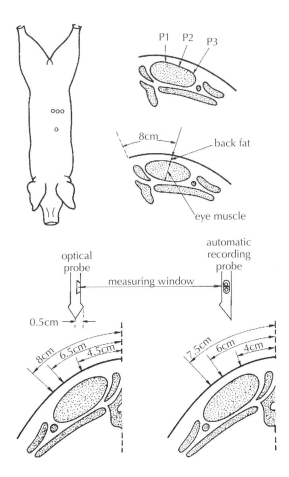

Components of Carcase Quality

- Uniformity

- Freedom from chemical and microbiological contamination

- Maximum yield of high value primals

- High boning yields

- High % lean

---

response in sows on heat; older stock boars tend to secrete high levels of this biochemical since it is associated with sexual maturity. As young boars near slaughterweight in the finishing house, there is a risk that androstenone levels could be problematic in their pigmeat when consumed by certain individuals. European Union legislation demands that male carcases over 85kg (187lb) should be tested for boar taint if destined for the fresh meat market. In particular, in Germany castration of male pigs is still routine practice, and their slaughterweights tend to be higher. This situation

and pigs with up to 69 per cent lean are not unknown. Despite this, there has been no great shift towards paying pig farmers for the lean content of carcases produced.

Sometimes an unpleasant odour and flavour is detectable from pigmeat, particularly from boars. This is known as 'boar taint' and is caused by two substances, androstenone and skatole, acting either separately or in combination. Androstenone is a male pheremone responsible for inducing the standing

---

Lean Meat Percentage and EU Grades

EU grade	Lean Meat Percentage
S	60% or more
E	55–59%
U	50–54%
R	45–49%
O	40–44%
P	Less than 40%

151

has held back the development of the UK's export trade with Germany.

Skatole is a breakdown product of the amino-acid tryptophan produced by fermenting protein in the hind gut. In dirty environmental conditions it can enter the food chain by being absorbed through the skin via urine and dung. An EU boar taint study involving seven countries and supported by the Meat and Livestock Commission indicated that compared to Europeans, British people were less sensitive to boar taint, and that skatole was the principal offender.

Variations in tenderness contribute to a lack of consistency in pigmeat sold to con-

---

Seven-Point Plan for Skatole Reduction

1. *Avoid use of brewer's yeast*
   Brewer's yeast has been shown to increase skatole levels. If the use of yeast cannot be avoided, consider a withdrawal period of seven days prior to slaughter.

2. *Avoid overfeeding protein*
   High protein diets can increase skatole levels. By avoiding feeding excessive protein in the diet the risk of skatole is reduced. This can be achieved by the use of phase feeding.

3. *Provide clean lying areas*
   Pigs lying in dung/urine can absorb skatole through the skin. Clean lying areas help prevent this.

4. *Maintain adequate ventilation rates*
   Especially in the summer months, inadequate ventilation will result in pigs choosing to lie in the moister areas of the pen, i.e. the dunging area. This results in absorption of skatole for those pigs lying in the dunging area and also, due to lack of space, soiling of the resting area.

5. *Design housing to maximize use of dunging area*
   Correct design can reduce dunging in the resting area. This includes:
   - Ventilation that makes the dunging area cooler than the resting area
   - Natural light from windows in the walls encourages dunging in the dunging areas at the outer walls.

6. *Provide correctly positioned drinking facilities*
   Drinkers are better placed in the dunging area to encourage defecation in the correct area.

7. *Use specific feed ingredients to reduce skatole where economic*
   Where cost effective, skatole can be reduced by the use of the following feeds:
   - coconut cake (at 10 per cent of diet);
   - sugar beet pulp (at 20 per cent of the diet or more);
   - wheat bran (at 20 per cent of the diet or more);
   - raw potato starch (at 10 per cent of diet);
   - lupins (at 10 per cent of diet);
   - protein sources that are readily digestible in the small intestine (such as casein).

Source: MLC

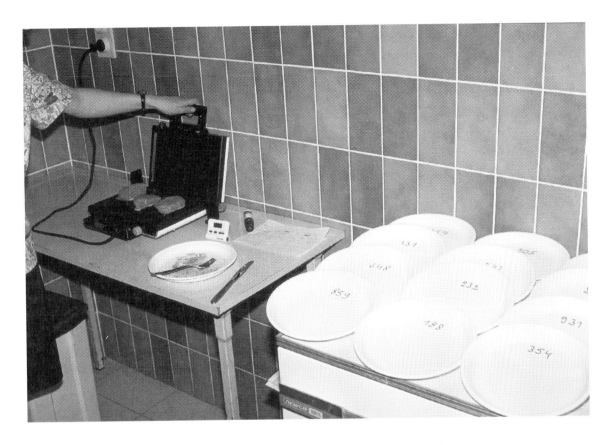

Meat Quality Assessment in the laboratory. (SEGHERS genetics)

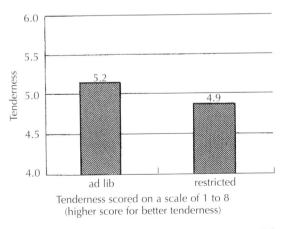

Tenderness scored on a scale of 1 to 8
(higher score for better tenderness)

Source: MLC

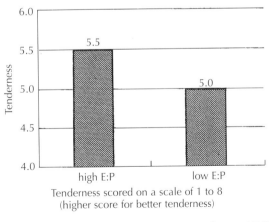

Tenderness scored on a scale of 1 to 8
(higher score for better tenderness)

Source: MLC

*The influence of ad-lib feeding on
tenderness in meat.*

*Impact of protein:energy ratios on
tenderness.*

Pork stirfry. (MLC)

Pork leg steaks. (MLC)

sumers, and evidence is emerging that tenderness – or the lack of it – is regularly associated with particular pig farms. Furthermore, ad lib-fed pigs consistently produce more tender pork than restrict-fed pigs. This might be due to the impact of nutrient intake on growth rate, or because of physiological changes that arise in stressed pigs. Once research has pinpointed the reasons, production systems could then be further refined so that, for example, slow-growing pigs and fast-growing pigs could have specific management regimes. Trials have also shown that increasing the energy/protein ratio in

A variety of lean pork cuts. (MLC)

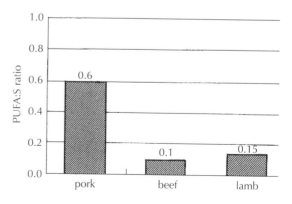

Fatty acid levels in red meat.

154

the feed of finishing pigs improves tenderness.

Compared to other red meats, pork has a healthier balance between polyunsaturated fatty acids (PUFAs) and Saturated Fatty Acids (S). The medical profession recommends a PUFA:S ratio of at least 0.4 in human foods. A typical level in pork is a healthy 0.6. Consumers are being urged to increase their intake of omega-3 PUFAs in order to safeguard their health. Trials have indicated that bacon, chops and sausages from pigs fed a linseed supplement had higher PUFA levels and a higher omega-3 content. This could decrease the shelf-life of pigmeat, though feeding a higher level of the anti-oxidant vitamin E helps overcome this problem. The MLC have outlined a 'Blueprint for Quality British Pork' that takes account of all known aspects of quality.

Loading at the farm has a big influence on pigmeat quality. (ABN Ltd)

TRANSPORT AND LAIRAGE

Pig slaughtering and processing has become a highly specialized activity. There has been massive rationalization throughout the abattoir sector, such that now just eight plants process 70 per cent of all UK pigmeat. Small local mixed-species abattoirs have tended to close, with the result that often there are now much longer hauls to the point of slaughter. This has not helped smaller pig producers, because what happens between the finishing pen and the abattoir has massive implications for pigmeat quality.

There is also a welfare aspect to the transport of pigs, and legislators have not been slow to heed this. EU regulations forbid journey times of more than eight hours for pigs; after this interval they must be unloaded, rested, fed and watered for a 24-hour period. Route plans are required for such journeys which are to a third country or other EU member

Specialist Pig Plants 1991–1998		
Year ending March	*No. of plants*	*Market share%*
1991	46	54
1992	48	57
1993	39	59
1994	34	61
1995	35	67
1996	35	69
1997	29	69
1998	28	70
		Source: MLC

state. If, however, the haulier's vehicle meets certain additional standards, pigs may travel for a maximum of twenty-four hours provided they have constant access to water during the journey. The EU specifies a maximum stocking density of 235kg (518lb)/m^2 for pigs facing a long haul to the abattoir. Inappropriate transport and lairage arrangements can lead to porcine stress syndrome (PSS) which manifests itself as sudden death in transport, and pale, soft, exudative muscle (PSE), particularly in lean pigmeat. PSE results in costly drip losses and off-putting leakages from meat at the point of sale and during cooking. Another less frequent quality problem is that of dry, firm and dark muscle (DFD): this arises when pre-slaughter handling is unacceptably stressful.

Globally, slaughterers and processors have implemented research findings aimed at enhancing pigmeat quality. Slaughtering – or 'harvesting', as the Americans call it – is becoming much more precise. Sophisticated systems which involve gassing a whole pen of pigs, or stunning via electric shock through the floor, now operate successfully in commercial plants. Furthermore, to reduce the risk of pigs being upset by human influence, automatic devices are now often used to coax slaughter pigs into and along races.

Components of quality may perhaps be summarized thus:

- Carcase and meat quality reflect changing customer demands.
- Farmers, processors and pigmeat retailers all see quality issues differently.
- Systems of pig farming, transport and lairage arrangements which provide top quality pigmeat have been defined.
- All those involved in pig production must work together more closely to enhance product quality.

PIG MARKETING

As compared to other red meats, selling pigmeat on a deadweight basis has been a widespread practice for many years in Britain. The Diseases of Animals (Waste Food) Order 1973, and the associated Movement and Sale of Pigs Order 1975 accelerated this trend. Abattoirs and processors saw the opportunity to add value to pigmeat, and consequently looked for a more professional approach to marketing that it was hoped would ensure a continuity of supply.

Co-operatives emerged, initially out of the need to link small weaner-producing units with specialist finishers. These eventually developed into independent marketing groups charged with selling pigs in a fragmented industry, though it was an industry whose structure was rapidly changing. In Denmark and Holland, and to a lesser extent in France, co-operatives continue to dominate the marketing of pigmeat. The production of large numbers of pigs in small countries such as Denmark and The Netherlands necessitated a co-operative strategy and ethos; this was their key to establishing and retaining export markets throughout the world.

In the UK, the pig industry splutters around 72 per cent in pigmeat self-sufficiency, and as a result it has been difficult to develop discipline and the resultant quality associated with exporters and their branded products. UK producers have allowed themselves the luxury of independence in terms of choice of breeding stock, housing systems, feed buying and pig marketing, but where this uncompromising independence, and the resilience of the individuals within it, was once a major strength of the UK pig industry, over time it has become its major weakness.

UK pig marketing groups have always vigorously competed with each other, and

*Stress at the abattoir
must be minimized.
(SEGHERS genetics)*

this has not always been in the long-term interests of the pig farmers serviced by them. Furthermore, pig farmers and marketing groups have tended to engage themselves in commercial warfare with abattoirs and supermarkets, and this whole culture of 'customer bashing' has done little for the long-term viability of the UK pig industry. On the other hand, the establishment of strategic alliances that forge greater collaboration between the various sectors of the industry looks a more likely route to sustainable profitability for everyone in the business.

There is nothing more difficult to carry out, nor more doubtful for success nor more dangerous to handle, than to initiate a new order of things. For the reformers have enemies in all those who profit by the old order and only luke-warm defenders in all those who would profit by the new order. This luke warmness arising partly by fear of their adversaries who have the law in their favour, and partly by the incredulity of mankind who do not truly believe in anything new until they have had experience of it.

Machievelli

In 1999, a potential lifeboat was launched

157

in the form of United Pig Marketing, whose first priority was to eliminate competition between the various marketing groups: once this basic problem was recognized and acknowledged, an opportunity for solving it could emerge. An obvious benefit was that of increased 'clout' brought about by the creation of a greater critical mass within a more professional and disciplined network. It is hoped that eventually this unified group will account for over 30 per cent of pigs marketed in the UK.

This enlightened approach should help maintain markets and establish new ones, and it should provide the industry with a more focused sense of market direction, albeit on a horizontal basis. Despite these structural changes aimed at making UK pigmeat more competitive both at home and abroad, the priority for each individual marketing organization is to safeguard their existing business within a challenging environment. Three approaches to pig marketing typify the modern industry:

- through farmer-controlled organizations;
- through feed industry organizations;
- independently by large pig producers.

Alongside this horizontal restructuring, alternative strategies involving vertical integration are also firmly in evidence. British Quality Pigs (BQP) is but one link in an integrated set-up involving pig production, slaughtering, some processing and marketing. This venture acts as a major supplier of pigmeat to leading supermarket outlets. Pigs are supplied with feed from within the group, which comprises some 25,000 sows spread over 250 farms. The group is also setting up an integrated organic pigmeat initiative.

Another futuristic, vertically integrated venture involves a 'pig to plate' project sourced from a specific genetic source. All

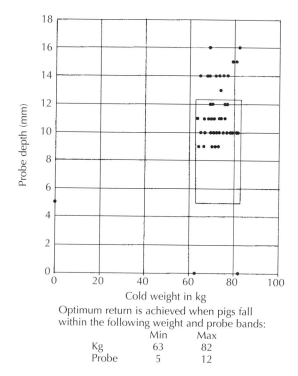

Optimum return is achieved when pigs fall within the following weight and probe bands:

	Min	Max
Kg	63	82
Probe	5	12

Source: Porcofram Marketing

Single probe scatter graph.

pigs within the project are slaughtered at the same abattoir, and the processed pigmeat is marketed through a dedicated retail outlet.

Porcofram Marketing is the largest pig marketing group in the UK, with a 16 per cent market share. This company is pioneering the development of pig marketing software. Their Data Porc Abattoir Profiling Module uses the latest computer technology and helps to make pig marketing less of a 'hit and miss' affair, and more transparent. Software enables up to 30,000 pigs to be compared on the basis of nett price across 100 different contracts. The programme has several features including the facility to help maximize returns within well-defined weight and probe bands within any specific contract. It is a tool for fine-tuning the marketing process.

RISK MANAGEMENT

In recent years UK pig prices have fluctuated between 40p and 150p/kg deadweight; this represents a tidal wave of risk and has resulted in a myriad of business failures and personal tragedies. There is an increasing European and global dimension to pig keeping and trading, and this has increased the degree of volatility of market prices; it has made pig business forecasting more difficult, and encompasses the whole production chain. Chastened bank managers will increasingly look to risk management to safeguard their backs and those of their customers. Farmers in the pig business for long-term profits must therefore develop new strategies for managing risk so that painful and often lethal price fluctuations will be lessened. Signing up to long-term fixed price contracts should help in this respect. Futures trading is another possibility: a futures contract is simply a contract to buy or sell a specific amount of a commodity for a predetermined delivery date some months hence.

Futures trading takes place in 'lots' that represent a specific amount of pigmeat, and producers, marketeers, feed companies and processors usually get involved in such trading by 'hedging'. Its aim is to minimize the impact of price reductions, and involves obtaining some protection from adverse price movements and the facility to lock into advantageous peaks and troughs in prices. It works like this: when there is a surplus of pigmeat, the situation is described as 'long'; if there is a shortage it is known as 'short'. Arable farmers and grain merchants tend to be long on cereal stocks, whereas pig farmers tend to be short on feed but long on pigs, and hedging helps redress this balance. Identifying a dependable, knowledgeable broker and establishing a rapport is the first step towards hedging.

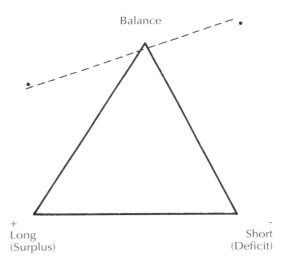

The concept of hedging.

SHOW TIME

Slick advertising campaigns from multinational pig breeding companies and sophisticated marketing programmes for finished pigs, bear little resemblance to how pigs used to be sold and how most people would still prefer to sell them. Traditionally, agricultural shows and the auction mart assumed the role of a diverse, well-stocked shop window. Pig farmers and butchers were attracted to the elite breedingstock which used to grace the show ring, and those that had grafted and schemed their way to the top of the pig breeding echelon enjoyed something approaching super-star status, albeit within the farming community.

Visually appraising pigs and the associated banter on the pig lines is a world away from computer tomography scanning. Despite the gargantuan changes within the pig industry, the thrill of raising pigs, preparing them for exhibition, and leading a treasured sow round a bustling show ring, is unsurpassed. The show ring remains a major source of trade for traditional pedigree breeders, and a place where the very best butchers still like to be seen and heard. It is a powerful, lasting symbol of the special link between people and pigs and, despite the preoccupation of the modern industry with technology, this fascination endures. The Rare Breeds Survival Trust, which has many attributes, plays a vital role as a safety net dedicated to ensuring that old genes do not become corrupted or extinct.

Showing pigs was always a popular spectator sport, and so it remains. It provides an opportunity for pig enthusiasts to get together, swap stories and do some useful trade, ranging from parochial bartering to enviable export deals. Such people prefer to buy pigs on their finely tuned instincts and the twitch of a nose, rather than via the frenzied manipulation of a computer keyboard. The pig lines and pig ring at a show ground have a subliminal magnetic effect on pig people, and remain a fascination to those who wonder what pigs are all about.

The National Federation of Young Farmers helps perpetuate the show culture, in that the stockpeople of the future are encouraged to develop a good eye for a good pig. Those wishing to get involved in showing will not find much help in the written word. The best strategy would be to talk to, and listen to, someone already established in this area, and to get involved at the 'sharp end'. Like creep feeding, pig showing is in a grey area, somewhere between art and science.

Disease restrictions and the need for movement licences has markedly reduced the number of live classes at agricultural shows. Furthermore, in this consumer-oriented society, carcase competitions have understandably assumed greater emphasis. The British Pig Association (BPA) oversees the best pig showing in the UK: it sets standards for the breeds and conditions of entry, it appoints judges and carries lists of approved judges, and it provides prizes. Every year it is involved with about fifteen major show events, as well as several regional show and sale days. For millions of urban dwellers – in other words, consumers of pigmeat – the show ring is the only opportunity they have to admire pigs. It always was an influential shop window, and in the future will still play a key role in promoting good pig public relations.

The sea-change in marketing may perhaps be summarized thus:

- Survival of the UK pig industry depends on implementing major changes in marketing strategies.
- Marketing organizations will compete less with each other and concentrate more on common objectives.
- Increased vertical integration will have a marked impact on pig production and marketing.
- Pig marketing will make more use of computer technology.
- Risk management will become an integral part of marketing strategies.
- The survival of traditionalists will depend on their enthusiasm, and their ability to supply specialist outlets.

Notes for Novices

- Be prepared for change, and remember ' you can't buck the market'.
- Keep 'on side' by participating in a 'quality assurance' scheme.
- Remember: what happens to a pig after it leaves the finishing pen can have a big impact on pigmeat quality.
- Sort out your market before embarking on a pig venture.
- Try to secure a special market outlet which pays a premium.
- Anticipate more vast short-term fluctuations in pig price because of globalization.
- Cost of production is crucial, particularly during lulls in market prices.

8 Pig Health Matters ————————

A veterinary surgeon with a special interest in pigs is the most appropriate person to entrust with the care of herd health. Veterinary expertise in pigs – or the lack of it – is difficult to define but easy to recognize. The density of pig farms in some areas of the UK is such that, by demand, some local veterinary surgeons have built up a specialist knowledge of pigs and their ailments. Elsewhere, practitioners necessarily restrict themselves to more routine pig health problems and work in conjunction with a consultant vet who visits the unit periodically. Many pig vets become members of the Pig Veterinary Society, an organization that holds conferences and workshops to help these specialists keep abreast of new developments within the pig industry. The unit veterinary surgeon must not be seen as a 'fire-fighting' service, but more of a strategist working in conjunction with the owner, manager and labour force on a particular pig unit.

Positive herd health management is the modern objective: consumers demand wholesome pigmeat, and have reservations concerning the routine use of medication. It is perhaps alarming that a report published by the Soil Association in 1999 entitled 'The Use and Misuse of Antibiotics' revealed that the consumption of antibiotics had increased by 1,500 per cent in thirty years: at the time of the survey, 1,225 tonnes of antibiotics were used within the UK every year, farm animals accounting for 37 per cent of the usage, pets 25 per cent and 38 per cent were consumed in medicines by humans. Society as a whole must take responsibility for this unsustainable strategy, due in large part to poorly designed buildings and badly managed pig performance, which can no longer be tolerated. 'Buying' pig performance via medication is expensive, besides which a much more sustain-

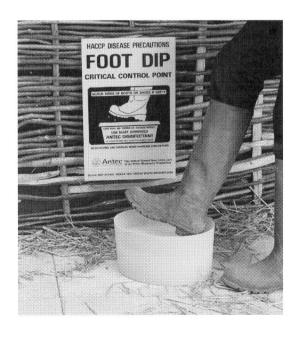

Boot hygiene helps reduce the risk of disease. (Antec International Ltd)

able, cost-effective approach to pig health, with better pig management and less medication, must be the objective of an enlightened pig industry.

PREVENTIVE MEDICINE

Keeping disease out of a pig unit is a priority measure, and remoteness from other pig units is a good starting point. If 'High Health Status' is required, the unit should be surrounded by a fence ideally 2.4m (7.8ft) high and extending to 500mm (20in) below ground to keep pigs in and any unwelcome mammals out. A car park should be located beyond the perimeter fence, and visitors should be directed to it – though such precautions become academic if visitors are not directed to a meeting point, or provided with a means of attracting the attention of staff. All visitors and staff must wear unit clothing and footwear, and respect boot-dipping requirements.

In drawing up a protocol for disease prevention, attention to detail is vital. The chances of achieving this objective are increased if all those involved with the unit are encouraged to understand and adopt a disease exclusion culture, and are kept informed by regular staff and management meetings.

MANAGING HERD HEALTH

If all involved with a pig unit strive to exclude disease from the farm, potentially everyone is a winner. The health of the pigs and their welfare improves, overall costs are therefore reduced, and inevitably this should bring about an increase in profitability. Furthermore, farm staff will be working in a healthier environment, their quality of work will be improved, and more time and effort can then be directed at achieving production targets.

Biosecurity contractors are widely used throughout the poultry industry. (Antec International Ltd)

Typical biosecurity standards on a broiler unit. (Antec International Ltd)

Staff training is an essential element in promoting this culture. Stock people must have basic training in key aspects of pig health, they must be kept abreast of new developments in management, vaccines and antibiotics, and they must always be on the lookout for new diseases. Unless the recommendations of the veterinary surgeon are implemented and monitored, the full benefits to herd health will not be realized. For instance, Humberside specialist pig vet John Carr advocates the routine monitoring of health indicators using a comprehensive checklist, an approach that nurtures a useful, on-going link between the veterinary surgeon and the pig unit staff, and which serves as a focus for discussion when the specialist veterinary surgeon visits the pig farm on a regular routine basis. Such visits also help to forge a link between the unit vet and the pig breeding company which stocks the unit. And at each routine veterinary visit, biosecurity should be moni-

Hygienic surfaces help reduce the incidence of disease. (SEGHERS genetics)

Manager's Daily/Weekly Report

Date: ....

AREA	3	2	1	AREA	3	2	1
Needle security				**2nd Stage Nursery**			
Drug storage				• Hygiene			
Foot bath hygiene				• Water			
Boot hygiene				• Feed			
Farrowing Area				• Floor			
• Hygiene				• Ventilation			
• Water				• Stock			
• Feed				**Grower House**			
• Floor				• Hygiene			
• Ventilation				• Water			
• Stock - sows				• Feed			
- piglets				• Floor			
Sow & Gilt House				• Ventilation			
• Hygiene				• Stock			
• Water				**Finisher House**			
• Feed				• Hygiene			
• Floor				• Water			
• Ventilation				• Feed			
• Stock - sows				• Floor			
- gilts				• Ventilation			
- boars				• Stock			
1st Stage Nursery				**Alarms checked**			
• Hygiene				**Gilt isolation**			
• Water				**AI Laboratory**			
• Feed				**Staff Canteen**			
• Floor							
• Ventilation				**External Appearance**			
• Stock							

Interpretation of scores:

3   Good

2   Attention to detail needed

1   Room for improvement

Signed.................................

Source: J. Carr, *Garth Stockmanship Standards*

Possible Sources of Disease on a Pig Unit

- Any pigs – especially sick pigs and dead pigs.
- Food containing pigmeat products. Staff sandwiches?
- Nearby pig units.
- Adjacent busy roads.
- Equipment borrowed from another pig unit.
- Second-hand equipment.
- New equipment.
- Clothing that has been worn on another pig unit.
- Staff who keep their own pigs, or visit other pig units or pig places.
- Birds, foxes, rodents, cats, dogs, flies.
- Semen and embryo transfer.
- All vehicles, especially pig lorries and feed lorries.
- Knackerman.
- Veterinary surgeon, sales representatives, etc.
- Deliverymen and tradesmen.
- Any unnecessary visitors.

USA a system known as the 'Isowean' system is practised on large units, and is now also influencing UK pig farms, some aspects of it being advocated by several well-travelled pig vets. The concept involves separating pigs of different ages, and moving them some distance away. The sow, in particular, is a major source of disease, and since weaner housing often adjoins the farrowing room, it can be difficult to break the disease spiral. Changing to all-in/all-out production and implementing some of the Isowean principles is now a feature of some of the larger, progressive UK pig units; indeed, as herd size increases, separating pigs into groups according to their age in weeks becomes more practical.

Safeguard your Pigs against the Introduction of Disease

- Thoroughly clean and disinfect all pig lorries and loading ramps.

- Visitors should park off site.

- Visitors should be 48-hour pig free.

- Visitors should wear coveralls and boots from the farm.

- Use, and regularly refresh, disinfectant foot dips.

- Only bring pigs and semen onto the unit from known UK sources.

- Outdoor pig units should put a fence 10m (30ft) outside the perimeter fence.

- Do not feed pigs with waste human food – The Diseases of Animals (Waste Food) Order 1973.

Source: The former British Pig Association

tored, and modified if it is found to be inadequate.

Of particular interest is the siting of the pig unit and any new buildings in relation to pig farms, roads, abattoirs and hauliers' lorries. Perimeter security must be checked, as well as the quality of management of isolation facilities. The arrangements for inward and outward transport of pigs will be discussed, along with feed and water supplies, feed storage and bedding facilities; for instance, if feed bins are sited carefully, feed lorries and their drivers need not enter the unit at all. Protocols for staff must also be approved, and strategies developed for keeping out birds and vermin.

In the past it was generally considered efficient to operate a compact pig unit on a self-contained site. However, in the

Pig Growth and Carcase Traits of Pigs (5.5 to 113kg) with Low and High Level of Immune System Activity

	Immune System Activity	
Pig Performance	Low	High
Feed intake (kg/lb day)	2.29 (5.05)	2.07 (4.56)
Days	129.5	149.5
Daily liveweight gain (g/oz)	850 (30)	690 (24)
Feed conversion efficiency	2.70:1	3.05:1
Carcase traits		
Carcase yield (%)	72.4	72.3
Backfat (mm/in)	27.6 (1.08)	31.4 (1.2)

Source: Iowa State University

Pig farmers are therefore being asked to look at their existing facilities to determine whether or not some minor adjustments could allow greater separation of age bands. In particular, outdoor producers have more opportunities to implement these ideas: thus, rather than rent a single block of 60 acres of light land, setting up ten separate blocks of 6 acres each could well be a better way of practising preventive medicine. However, practical considerations relating to the movement of both pigs and people often temper these strategies.

Slow Streamers

Researchers led by Dr Tim Stahly at Iowa State University studied two genetically similar groups of weaners, one with low immunity (i.e. from a 'clean' batch of pigs), the other with high immunity (i.e. they had been subjected to more disease challenge). They found that in the weaners with high immunity, substances called cytokines diverted nutrients away from growth in order to help fuel the protective immune system: consequently appetite was suppressed, the pigs spent more time sleeping, growth rate was slower, feed conversion efficiency worsened, and carcases became fatter.

The worst pig often gets the best pear.
(German proverb)

A follow-up trial at Iowa State University involving Williams *et al.* tested out this concept with pigs between 5.5 and 113kg (12lb and 249lb) liveweight. Again, low antigen exposure resulted in increased growth rates, leaner carcases and improved feed conversion efficiency. When immune activity was increased, particularly with genetically improved pigs, growth rate was suppressed.

This research highlights the need for nutritionists to formulate rations in rela-

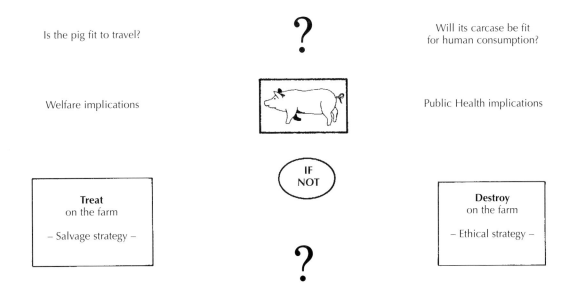

Is the pig fit to travel?

Will its carcase be fit
for human consumption?

Welfare implications

Public Health implications

IF NOT

Treat
on the farm

– Salvage strategy –

Destroy
on the farm

– Ethical strategy –

Questions for casualties.

tion to the health status of the pigs to be fed. It also strengthens the case for avoiding wasting high specification rations on disease-challenged pigs, and supports the practice of identifying and providing slow-stream pigs with specialist management. However, the key issue is that if the activity of the immune system is kept low, it appears that this is an efficient means of increasing appetite and lean-tissue growth rate.

Casualty Stock

Owners and those directly in charge of pigs have a joint responsibility for ensuring that casualty stock are disposed of appropriately and humanely. Again, prevention is the best policy. Thus sick or injured pigs with a realistic prospect of recovery should be identified at an early stage and isolated in a warm, draught-free, generously bedded environment. A plentiful supply of appetizing food and clean water must be readily available. In the event of the pig recovering, the statutory withdrawal time-interval following

medication must be observed before it is slaughtered or sold through a suitable outlet.

If a pig becomes lame, then its welfare must take precedence over the temptation to get the best price for it under difficult circumstances: loading a distressed pig onto a haulier's lorry and transporting it to a distant slaughterhouse would not be a responsible action. And when salvage is not an option, casualties should be killed on the farm. Understandably, slaughterhouses are reluctant to accept salvaged pigs that have been slaughtered on the farm; this reflects the great responsibilities involved in achieving the UK's coveted 'Mark of Distinction'. The general guideline is that if the pig is not fit to travel, it would not be fit for salvage.

The term 'casualty animal' is given legal definition under Regulation 19 of the Slaughter House (Hygiene) Regulations 1977. This states that a veterinary certificate must accompany any animal known to be, or suspected of being, diseased or injured if it is consigned to a slaughterhouse. During transport, the casualty pig

Legislation Regarding Pig Health and Welfare

Within the UK a whole raft of legislation applies to pig keeping. Summaries of some of the main requirements are set out below. They do not comprise an exhaustive list, and it is the responsibility of the individual to keep abreast of all current legislation.

The Agriculture (Miscellaneous Provisions) Act 1968 (1968 Ch 34)

The main purpose of part 1 of this Act is to give effect to the government's decisions on the report of the Brambell Committee in 1965 on animal welfare. It is an offence to cause or allow livestock on agricultural land to suffer unnecessary pain or unnecessary distress. Ministers are empowered, subject to parliamentary approval, to make mandatory regulations on welfare matters and to issue codes of recommendations for the welfare of livestock. They are also empowered to prohibit certain operations on animals with or with the use of anaesthetics.

The Welfare of Livestock Regulations 1994 (SI 1994 No 2126)

These regulations consolidate much of the legislation relating to the welfare of livestock on agricultural land. They contain separate schedules concerning laying hens in battery cages, calves, pigs and other livestock. Each schedule sets general requirements relating to such matters as prevention of injury, inspection, provision of feed and water, and the testing of alarms on automatic ventilation equipment. They also prohibit the electro-immobilization of livestock except as part of a licensed scientific procedure. Some of the other provisions of the schedules are explained below.

Schedule 3 – Pigs

This schedule prohibits the installation of new close-confinement stalls or tether systems, and bans the use of such existing systems from 1 January 1999. It prohibits a person from keeping a pig in a pen or stall unless the following requirements are met:

- the pig must be free to turn around without difficulty at all times;
- the area of the stall or pen is not less than the square of the length of the pig;
- none of the sides of the stall or pen has a length which is less than 75 per cent of the pig.

Limited exceptions, for acceptable management purposes, are set out in the schedule.

The Schedule also implements EC Directive 91/630 which lays down minimum standards for the protection of pigs. It prohibits the use of the 'sweat box' system from 1 July 1995, and for new or reconstructed accommodation, sets minimum space allowance for weaners and rearing pigs.

Schedule 4 – Livestock
The Welfare of Livestock (Prohibited Operations) (Amendment)
Regulations 1987 (SI 1987 No 114)
The Docking of Pigs (Use of Anaesthetics) Order 1974 (SI 1974 No 798)

This Order prohibits the docking of a tail of a pig more than seven days old without anaesthetic.

Although made under the 1968 Act, this Order relates to the use of anaesthetics as prescribed by the Protection of Animals (Anaesthetics) Acts 1956 and 1964.

The Welfare of Animals (Slaughter or Killing) Regulations 1995 (SI 1995 No 731)

For the purposes of these regulations, a 'slaughterhouse' is a place where commercial slaughter takes place for meat for human consumption Therefore, any slaughter on a farm where the meat is intended for sale makes that farm a slaughterhouse and the appropriate requirements of the regulations will apply.

The regulations also deal with culling of animals and birds on the farm, and slaughter or killing for private consumption. Specific provisions apply to slaughter or killing for disease control, the killing of fur-bearing animals and day-old chicks and the killing of embryos in hatchery wastes.

The Dogs Act 1906 – 1928 (6 Edw 7 Ch 32 18 – 19 Geo 5 Ch 21)

These Acts include provisions making it an offence for a person not to bury carcasses of livestock (cattle, horses, mules, asses, sheep, goats and swine only) belonging to him or under his control.

The Diseases of Animals (Waste Food) Order 1973

This Order defines waste food as:

(a) meat, bones, blood, offal or any other part of the carcase of any livestock or of any poultry or product derived therefrom or hatchery waste, or eggs or egg shells, or
(b) broken waste foodstuffs (including table or kitchen refuse, scraps or waste) which contain or have been in contact with any meat, bones, blood, offal or any other part of the carcase of any livestock or of any poultry.

Note: Meal manufactured from protein originating from livestock or poultry is, however, excluded from the definition of waste food.

The principal requirements of the Order are:

i. A prohibition of the possession of waste food which has not been processed as required by the Order on any premises for the purpose of feeding to livestock or poultry on these premises, unless a licence granted under Article 7 of the Order is held, or the feeding to livestock or poultry of waste food, or any feedingstuffs which have been in contact with waste food, unless waste food or such feedingstuffs have first been processed by means of plant and equipment operated under a licence granted under Article 7. (Article 3)
(These prohibitions do not, however, apply to the possession by any person of waste food originating from his own household, or to the use of such waste food provided it has first been processed as required by the Order.)
ii. A complete prohibition is imposed upon the feeding to any animal, poultry or other birds of any waste food brought into Great Britain as part of the stores on a ship, aircraft, etc. or of any other waste food which has been in contact with such imported stores. (Article 4)

The Movement and Sale of Pigs Order 1975

The basic requirements of this Order as applied to swill-fed pigs are that all pigs originating from a premises licensed to process swill must be moved under licence only to a slaughterhouse and to no other premises, except to similar premises owned by the same person.

When being transported to the slaughterhouse, swill-fed pigs must not be mixed with non-swill-fed pigs.

The Welfare of Livestock Regulations 1990

These regulations contain the following sections:

(a) Where the automatic equipment of an intensive unit includes a ventilation system, that system shall contain:

Legislation regarding Pig Health and Welfare *continued*

The Welfare of Livestock Regulations 1990 *continued*

 i. an alarm which will give adequate warning of the failure of that system to function properly (which alarm will operate even if the principal electricity supply to it has failed); and

 ii. additional equipment (whether automatic or not) which, in the event of such a failure of the ventilation system, will provide adequate ventilation so as to protect the livestock in the unit from suffering unnecessary pain or unnecessary distress as a result of the failure.

(b) The alarm mentioned in sub-paragraph (a) (i) above shall be tested and the additional equipment mentioned in sub-paragraph (a) (ii) above shall be thoroughly inspected, in each case, by a stock keeper or other competent person not less than once every seven days in order to check that there is no defect in it, and if any defect is found in such alarm or equipment (whether or not on it being tested or inspected in accordance with this paragraph), it shall be rectified forthwith.

The Animals and Fresh Meat (Examination for Residues) Regulations 1988

This requires pig farmers to keep records of animal medicines administered to their stock. The purpose of this record keeping is to ensure that withdrawal periods for animal medicines are observed.

Welfare of Animals during Transport Order 1992

This regulation revoked previous legislation on the transport of unfit animals. Paragraph (1), (2) and (3) or Article 3 of the Order, which are particularly relevant to the transport of casualty animals, are quoted in full below:

1. No person shall cause or permit an animal to be transported in a way which causes, or is likely to cause, injury or unnecessary suffering to the animal.

2. No person shall cause or permit the transport of an animal that is unfit by reason of it being in the state of being newborn, diseased, infirm, ill, injured or fatigued or having given birth within the preceding 48 hours or likely to give birth during transport or for any other reason.

3. Notwithstanding the provisions of paragraph (2) above, a bovine, ovine, caprine, porcine or equine animal may be transported to the nearest place for veterinary treatment or to the nearest available place of slaughter if the animal is not likely to be subject to unnecessary suffering by reason of its unfitness, but such an animal may not be dragged or pushed by any means, or lifted by a mechanical device, unless this is done in the presence of and under the supervision of a veterinary surgeon who is arranging for it to be transported with all practicable speed to a place for veterinary treatment.

---

should be penned separately from other pigs and be generously bedded. It must be taken to the nearest available abattoir, which must be given prior notification so that staff can receive it straightaway, thus avoiding any stressful delays on arrival. At weekends and over holidays when abattoirs are closed, sick or injured pigs must not be left suffering until the abattoir re-opens. The decision to kill the pig on the farm must be made at an early stage.

The prime responsibility of any veterinary surgeon is to safeguard the welfare of the pig, and he must therefore disregard commercial considerations when assessing 'fitness to travel'. This can be a contentious area, but his professional judgement must always be respected. Casualties are inevitable on any farm, and so too the need to make difficult decisions about them. Thus during his routine monitoring visits, in anticipation of such problems, vet and farmer must together discuss and review arrangements for casualties, and also work out a policy for the on-farm humane slaughter of doomed pigs.

Dead Pig Disposal

If you have livestock you will also have dead-stock.   (Anonymous)

Despite the commendably low levels of pig mortality achieved on UK pig units, the efficient disposal of dead pigs must be a high priority. Dead pigs have great potential for causing harm:

• The number of carcases for disposal increases as the unit size increases.
• They attract flies, vermin and dogs.
• Dead pigs are generally smelly and unpleasant.
• They could be a source of disease to pigs and people.
• Dead pigs detract from the amenity of the working environment.
• They tend to lower staff morale.
• Dead pigs can be a source of complaints

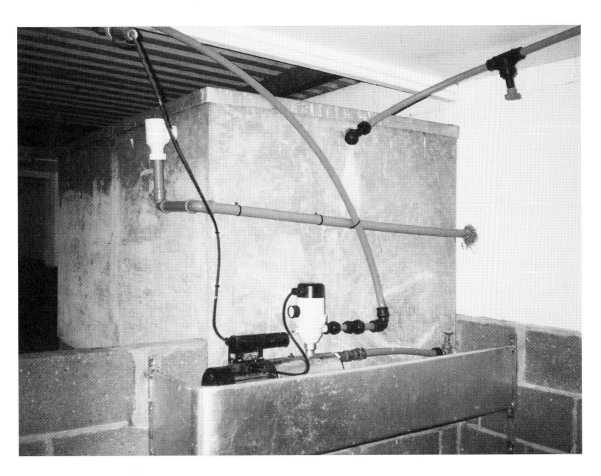

A 'proportioner' for supplying in-water medication. (PIGSPEC)

from neighbours and generate bad public relations.

Any sudden death should be regarded with suspicion, and anthrax considered as a possible cause, and this possibility should dictate the way in which such carcases are disposed of. In any event, units employing five or more people should provide in their health and safety manual a definite policy for the handling of dead pigs; inevitably this would recommend wearing rubber gloves to handle corpses, and the storing of dead pigs in a sealed container at some distance from the unit itself. The method of disposal is generally one of the following:

- collection from the site;
- prompt burial;
- below-ground digestion;
- incineration.

Since the demise of meat and bone meal there are fewer collection services, and these days you have to pay for them. Thus sometimes carcases remain on the farm for a few days until the knackerman was in the area, which could be a health risk, particularly in hot weather. Neither burial, nor placement in a below-ground tank, is an option near wells and aquifers. Carcase incineration is becoming more popular, particularly on large units; incinerators should be placed in a secure position with locked access.

Typically pig farmers may spend around £7,000 on a robust, refractory-lined incinerator. Money must also be spent on its installation, which invariably involves some wiring work, and the provision of a concrete apron and safety barriers. Incinerators are regulated under the all-embracing Environment Protection Act (1990), though if the burning rate is

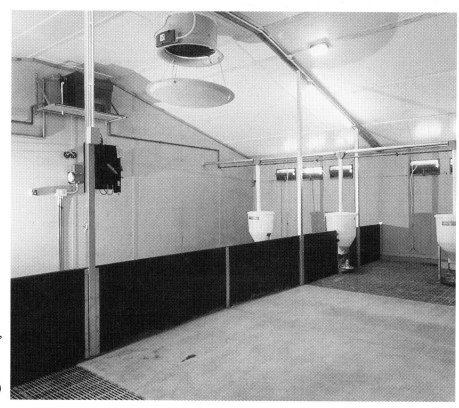

An immaculately cleaned 'Big Pen' for early weaned pigs. (Newsham Hybrid Pigs Ltd)

On-farm incineration of carcases is becoming more widespread. (William White Fabrications Ltd)

A purpose-built trolley for moving dead pigs prior to disposal. (Unitron (UK) Ltd)

173

After high temperature incineration, all that remains is the ash content of the carcase. (William White Fabrications Ltd)

under 50kg (110lb)/hour and is exclusively for the farm's use, the legislation is not quite so strict. However, there is talk of the need to conform to an EU Waste Incineration Directive which would 'gold-plate' existing regulations; this would necessitate the installation of expensive monitoring equipment and after-burners. A 600-sow unit producing 33 tonnes of dead matter per year would be well below the original 50kg/hour limit if in use for about seven hours, twice weekly. There are also EU proposals to ban the burying of farm livestock. No matter what the size of the unit, or whatever the legislation, the provision of efficient facilities for dead pig disposal will help to minimize the impact of this unpleasant reality.

Measures that might be employed to keep pigs healthier may perhaps be summarized thus:

- Use a specialist pig vet to develop an appropriate positive health management strategy.
- Increasingly regard antibiotics as a last-resort measure.
- Strive to keep up to date on pig health.
- Develop clear-cut policies for dealing with slow streamers, casualties and unexpected deaths.

MODERN PIG DISEASES

As pig herd size has increased globally, there has been a marked shift in herd disease patterns. However, their overall impact must be considered in relation to the high level of productivity on the average well managed pig unit. Even so, viruses that attack macrophages – and especially those found in the lung – have become more widespread, and since the macrophages are a key part of the body's defence mechanism, their demise leaves the pig open to many infections.

Porcine reproductive and respiratory syndrome (PRRS), sometimes known as 'blue ear disease', became widespread in the major pig-producing areas of the USA in the late 1980s. Ten years later it surfaced in Germany and Holland, and eventually found its way to the UK. This virus actually multiplies within the macrophages and eventually destroys them. Once the virus has entered the herd, it lingers, and tends to remain active indefinitely.

Then in 1991 in Saskatchewan, Canada, a new disease attacked weaners: growth rates in nursery pigs were retarded, they developed a characteristic pale skin, and suffered a high mortality rate. The disease was named 'post-weaning multisystemic wasting syndrome'

(PMWS). In 1999, veterinary scientists became aware that porcine circovirus (PCV) could be involved, and it may be that PCV type 2 (PCV 2) is implicated. By then the disease was widespread in Europe; in some outbreaks, diarrhoea was apparent, with reports of gastric ulceration in the absence of any wasting symptoms. Veterinary surgeons report minimal response to antibiotic treatment. The disease is particularly prevalent in pigs aged between eight and twelve weeks of age. If it is diagnosed early and the pigs hospitalized, about half of them will survive, whilst a quarter will probably eventually make a full recovery.

Another 'new' disease is 'porcine dermatitis nephropathy syndrome' (PDNS): in the UK it was first recorded in Scotland in 1993, although it had previously caused problems in other countries. It attacks twelve- to fourteen-week-old pigs and finishers: they become pale, suffer from diarrhoea, and some exhibit flat blue/red patches on their skin. Its mode of transfer is not known – there might be a link with PMWS, and even *Pasturella* bacteria – but as yet, management is the only weapon against it.

GLOSSARY OF PIG DISEASES

This list is by no means exhaustive, and simply aims to promote an awareness of some of the more common and important pig diseases. More detailed specialist textbooks are a useful source of further information on pig disease.

Gastric/Intestinal

Many gastric and/or intestinal diseases arise because of low standards of hygiene, or other management shortcomings. There is every likelihood that all-in/all-out production will become increasingly important in their treatment.

Clostridial Diseases
Caused by bacteria in the large intestine. There are several strains which multiply rapidly, producing lethal toxins. *Clostridium nouyi* can be a major problem in outdoor herds. *Clostridium perfringens* types A, B and C sometimes cause high mortality in piglets following diarrhoea.

Coccidiosis
Caused by small parasites in the alimentary canal. There are three types: *Eimeria*, *Isopora* and *Cryptosporidia*. Diarrhoea in suckling pigs is a typical symptom, but older weaners are also susceptible.

Diarrhoea
The most common and important disease in suckling pigs. Stresses such as chilling lead to *E. coli* diarrhoea which can be a widespread problem, particularly in pigs less than five days old in indoor units.

Notes for Novices

- Don't see your vet just as a 'fire fighter'.
- Ask around and find a vet who understands pigs.
- Never 'buy performance' by hiding poor management with antibiotics.
- Make your own luck – draw up a strategy for herd health promotion.
- Look to the poultry industry to learn about health management protocols.
- Think deeply about pig health before siting pig buildings.
- Remember, a pig's worst enemy is another pig.
- Farmers with no pigs and vast acres of light land make good neighbours.
- Identify 'slow streamers' and do something about them.
- Enrol yourself on a course about pig health.

Shortly after birth *E. coli* and *Clostridium perfringens* tend to colonize the gut.

Gastric Ulcers
Sows and growing pigs sometimes suffer erosion of the stomach near the point where the oesophagus enters it. Intermittent bleeding is a typical symptom. Causes are multifactorial, often involving feed and general management.

Rectal Prolapse
Mainly arises in sows and finishers, and can result in tissue damage, cannibalism and haemorrhage. Constipation can be a cause because of low fibre levels in the diet. Another cause is penetration of the rectum at mating. Allowing sows to lie on a steep slope is also a predisposing factor.

Salmonellosis
Salmonella bacteria are present in mammalian populations. Multiplication arises within the gut of growing pigs and sometimes in sows. Faeces often contain *Salmonella* when there is no trace of the disease. Improved slaughtering techniques aim to reduce carcase contamination by *Salmonella* and so minimize the risk of *Salmonella* entering the food chain.

Swine Dysentery (SD)
A nasty disease caused by the bacterium *Brachyspira hyodysenteriae*. Victims suffer inflammation of the large intestine and produce blood-stained, mucus-laden diarrhoea. SD can affect all pigs, and carrier pigs are often responsible for its spread.

Swine Fevers
African Swine Fever (ASF) or Classical Swine Fever (CSF) sometimes known as Hog Cholera (HC).

A virus disease which is notifiable in most countries; the two types are very similar. It is spread via nasal discharge, through the mouth, urine and faeces. It can enter herds via infected meat and is very contagious. The pig is the only natural host for this virus.

A new strain of Classical Swine Fever struck East Anglia in August 2000. Illegally imported pigmeat from Asia was thought to be the source. The disease was controlled by movement restrictions and a selective slaughter policy.

Transmissible Gastro-Enteritis (TGE)
There is no specific treatment for this disease, which is caused by a coronavirus. It is very contagious, and is extremely severe in suckling piglets. The main symptom is a watery diarrhoea, and if contracted within seven days of birth, most piglets die. Poor hygiene is implicated. The disease is susceptible to several disinfectants and is destroyed by sunlight. The development of sow immunity is of paramount importance. All-in/all-out management helps to minimize its incidence.

Disorders affecting the External Body

Abscesses
Sometimes arise in piglets following an injection or the removal of a tooth, perhaps the result of poor technique. They can also develop following injury to the feet, knees and tail. Abscesses in older pigs usually result from fighting, or as a result of some form of physical damage: for example, sharp edges or worn concrete penetrate the skin and abscesses develop on or near the site of injury. Tail biting is a frequent cause of abscesses in older pigs.

Erysipelas
Infectious bacterial disease, characterized by diamond-shaped marks on the skin. There are three recognized forms: acute,

sub-acute and chronic. Outbreaks are usually associated with fever, reproductive problems, arthritis and heart disease. In its acute form, sudden death can result.

Greasy Pig Disease (Exudative Epidermitis)
The bacterium *Staphylococcus hyicus* normally lives on the surface of the skin without any problems but, for reasons unknown, it sometimes flares up and causes a dermatitis which oozes a slippery fluid. It is most common in suckling pigs, weaners and gilts. Sows rarely suffer from this disease. Skin abrasions caused by injury or fighting, and lesions caused by mange appear to be pre-disposing factors.

Haematoma
Injury to blood vessels beneath the skin or in muscle tissue causes blood to leak out and pond up, causing an unsightly swelling. Sows in particular may develop a haematoma if they repeatedly rub or shake their ears following fighting or because of mange. Sometimes haematomas develop into abscesses which need early treatment.

Mange
Parasitic disease of the skin caused by either *Sarcoptes scabiei* or *Demodex phylloides*. The sarcoptic form is the most common and can be very irritating, and the pig reacts by rubbing the skin which becomes unsightly. Newly purchased pigs can be a source of mange. Any treatment must include the boar and his pen, since direct skin contact with breeding females is a recognized cause of spread. Some herds claim mange-free status.

Sunburn
This can be the scourge of outdoor pig units in summer. Skin damage is an obvious symptom, but sunburn can also cause reproductive failure and involve the resorption of embryos. The provision of shade helps reduce the risk of sunburn, and well-managed wallows are also helpful, although these tend to be used less where shade is available.

Teat necrosis
Teats fail to develop, or may disappear altogether. The condition is generally precipitated within a few days of birth: the tip of the teat is rubbed, and it subsequently dies and is sloughed off; rough floors are often the cause. The problem can be set in motion within minutes of piglets being born. This condition is particularly unwelcome on pig units where gilts are reared as replacement breeding stock.

Genetic/Congenital Disorders

Artesia Ani
Describes piglets born without an anus or rectum. Surgical intervention is never usually successful, and the best control measure is euthanasia. This condition is most prevalent in young herds, and is often linked to a particular boar. However, although it can be passed from one generation to the next, its heritability is low.

Hernia
Both umbilical and scrotal (inguinal) ruptures are genetic abnormalities of low heritability. Excessive stretching of the umbilicus at farrowing can give rise to umbilical hernias. Sometimes hernias occur just after a change of housing and reflect a defect in the new environment.

Pityriasis Rosea
Sometimes known as 'belly rash': rings of spots resembling burn marks develop over the surface of the belly; they spread, and after a few weeks may meet each other. The condition is not infectious, just looks

unsightly; however, it does not seem to be an irritant. It is congenital, and tends to break out after certain matings.

Splay Legs

A problem most commonly found in the back legs, particularly in piglets from Landrace gilts; characteristically piglets will assume a dog-sitting posture. It arises because of a weakness in muscle fibre in the hind legs. Splay legs impair mobility and its victims often fail to thrive because they cannot reach the teat to suckle. Smooth and/or wet, slippery floors exacerbate the condition.

Shaking Piglets

A viral disease commonly referred to as 'congenital tremor' (CT); it usually arises in first-litter newborn piglets, though its effects diminish as they get older. However, some piglets are so badly affected that they fail to suckle, and consequently starve to death. Ensuring that piglets receive colostrum at birth helps to minimize its impact. Sow immunity quickly develops.

Musculo-Skeletal Disorders

Bursitis

Can affect all ages: where the skin overlies bone and there is repeated pressure or trauma, a soft lump develops. Concrete floors and slats with wide slots between them are pre-disposing factors, particularly with weaners. Provided the lumps do not become infected the commercial significance of this condition is not great. However, the unsightly lumps would not be acceptable on stock retained for breeding.

Laminitis

Inflammation of the soft and sensitive vascular tissue that connects the bone within the hoof to the outer wall. Not a problem in piglets, but affected sows may need to be destroyed. Characteristically they will take to walking on their knees. The cause of laminitis in pigs is unknown.

Muscle Tearing

Most common in sows, which characteristically assume a sitting position like a dog because they cannot stand. Muscle tearing often follows splay legs; sometimes weak bones are implicated. Affected sows should be taken off slats and housed on a well bedded floor. Wet, slippery concrete floors must be avoided.

Osteochordrosis dessicans (OCD)

Similar to muscle tearing, but mainly affects older finishers and young replacement gilts. Gilts may be crampy in their gait or lame, or they may assume a sitting position. The cartilage covering the joints wears thin and becomes painful.

Reproductive/Urinogenital Disorders

Cystitis and Pyelonephritis

Cystitis describes an inflammation of the bladder, pyelonephritis of the kidneys. Cystitis is caused mainly by *Eubacterium suis*, occasionally by *E. coli*; it is confined to sows, which respond poorly to treatment. Eradication of the bacteria causing the disease is impossible, since faecal contamination of the vulva helps to proliferate them.

Prolapse

Prolapse of the uterus involves complete inversion of both horns of the womb: it turns itself inside out, usually as a result of prolonged straining by the sow. Older sows are prone to the condition, which usually arises within a few hours of farrowing, though sometimes not until the day after parturition. Sows with a prolapsed uterus must very often be slaughtered on site.

Prolapse of the vagina and cervix also

sometimes occurs, particularly in the immediate pre-farrowing period. Again it is more common in older sows. A starch-rich diet can be the cause, the fermentation of ingested foods giving rise to excess gas which results in abdominal pressure. Sows with cervical or vaginal prolapses respond well to treatment.

Mastitis

Inflammation of the mammary glands, sometimes known as Agalactia. Coliform mastitis involves *E. coli* and *Klebsiella* and is severe; staphylococcal and streptococcal mastitis is generally less so. The disease starts around farrowing time and within twelve hours is clinically apparent. Bacteria are thought to enter the udder via the teat canal or through the bloodstream. Clinical and sub-clinical forms of the disease are likely. Overuse of farrowing accommodation and poor hygiene is often implicated.

Metritis

Inflammation of the womb, sometimes referred to as Endometritis. Lactating sows will show signs of inappetance, and piglets are starved because the milk supply becomes inadequate. After farrowing, as the uterus shrinks it is normal for a mucous discharge to be observed for about four days; however, a prolonged discharge of a white or brown fluid from the vulva accompanied by rejection of food could indicate metritis, perhaps bacterial in origin.

Porcine Parvovirus

An infectious virus which affects the contents of the womb; it occurs throughout the world. An estimated 90 per cent of UK breeding herds are infected, and once established in a herd it is difficult to eliminate. Replacement breeding stock are susceptible to the disease. It is most common in gilts but can occur at any age, and outbreaks can persist for up to six months. In recent years, however, vaccination has given good control.

Respiratory Diseases

Actinobacillus pleuropneumonia (App)

The bacterium is carried in the tonsils and in the upper respiratory tract; it can only survive outside a pig for a few days, but can be spread short distances in droplet form. Most prevalent in pigs from eight to sixteen weeks, but it can arise at any time between weaning and slaughter; occasionally in sows as a secondary infection. It is characterized by continual short spells of coughing. Incubation time can be as short as twelve hours. It is spread by contaminated or carrier breeding stock brought on to the unit. Severe breathing difficulties are typical, followed by sudden death.

Atrophic Rhinitis (AR) and Progressive Atrophic Rhinitis (PAR)

Inflammation of the nasal tissues is known as rhinitis, when the tissues within the nose actually shrink and become distorted. In its mild form the infection causes irritation over a two- to three-week period; sneezing and tear staining are common signs.

Progressive atrophic rhinitis (PAR) is much more serious, and the bacterium *Pasturella multocidia* type D (toxigenic strain) is involved. The disease is most prevalent in young herds. In the event of a severe outbreak the whole herd has to be vaccinated. The routine vaccination of breeding stock can lower its incidence.

Pneumonia

A chronic respiratory disease which arises mainly in growing and slaughter pigs. In a newly infected herd its incidence is insidious at first, but subsequently it can 'explode'. Coughing is widespread throughout infected herds and tends to be continuous. Blood tests and micro-biological assays will help to identify the causative strain.

Swine Influenza (SI)
Caused by a number of closely related 'influenza A' viruses. Incubation is between half a day and two days and can be transmitted between pigs, people and birds. Poorly designed ventilation systems exacerbate the condition. If contracted by sows it can result in infertility. Its spread is rapid, and it causes distress in growing and finishing pigs, particularly during winter; however, in spite of this, pigs usually recover. Antibiotics can be administered via the watering system to prevent secondary bacterial infections, and severely affected pigs can be injected.

In Summary

Strategies for treating and nursing sick or injured pigs must be developed in conjunction with the unit veterinary surgeon. Nowadays there are also courses that specialize in pig health specifically geared towards stockmen and managers: of relatively short duration, they provide practical help regarding pig health, and ensure that 'progressive' pig people keep abreast of new developments in disease incidence, and in the control and prevention of disease.

A package-deal building with good disease-prevention facilities.
(Pyramid Systems (Malton) Ltd)

9 The Way Forward –

It takes a fool or a naive economist to predict pig prices six months ahead, and those that dare predict the future shape of the pig industry live even more dangerously. Living with pigs, working with them, and eating the products derived from them, will increasingly become more of a commercial and cultural balancing act; already consumer perceptions within and between EU trading partners are poles apart. Moreover the demands of animal rights activists, the vegetarian lobby and NIMBY (Not In My Back Yard) environmentalists cannot be ignored. Nutritionists express concern about the obesity problem concomitant with affluence, whilst medical practitioners are dismayed by the younger generation's preoccupation with 'the lean, mean look', whatever its consequences.

Within the EU, consumers in some countries seem to be deeply concerned about animal welfare issues, whilst others fail to see the point. Consumers with the ability to pay, and with a penchant for green credentials at weekends, will doubtless continue to buy pigmeat on price and convenience during busy working weekdays, yet will demand wholesomeness on other occasions when they have time to reflect and verbalize.

How will pigmeat be produced in the future? Quite frankly it is unrealistic to believe that anything that is 'green', pigfriendly and extensive is *good*, and that anything intensively produced is *bad*. So what will be the optimum size for the pig unit of the future, both commercially, and also environmentally and culturally acceptable? What will it look like, and who will run it? And would a total ban on antibiotics be feasible, or is it just an idealist's pipedream?

Whatever develops, and no matter how diverse pig units become, the pig and its biological and psychological interactions with *Homo sapiens* will continue to figure to a considerable degree. Just because pig units become larger, they must not be allowed to become factories. Breeding sows are not machines. However, it is inevitable that future strategies will be related to demand, and that in satisfying this growing demand, closer links within efficient supply chains will have to be developed.

In the global mass market, in particular, there will be more dependence on production strategies such as are commonplace in industrial manufacturing operations – though having said that, the maximum output of any future pig unit, like those of yesteryear, will always depend on the inclination of people to 'get trained, get busy and keep motivated'. Nevertheless, pig buildings and pig systems are bound to become more closely linked with sales output schedules; and if antibiotics and other medicaments are to be reduced, the physical resources on the farm will have to be compatible with production schedules – the days of living with a 'bottleneck' will fast disappear.

SPECULATION ON STRUCTURE AND MARKETS

If the forecasted increase in global demand for pigmeat becomes a reality, it will have to be produced by someone, somewhere. As less-developed nations become more affluent and migrate to vast centres of population, they will increasingly meet their pigmeat needs from large, intensive pig production units. Many of these pig farms will be located in areas where land is readily available, pollution is not yet an issue, and where there is a marked absence of sensitivity to pig welfare. The more deprived societies carry different priorities to those that are affluent; furthermore, low-cost labour will continue to be available in these less-developed societies, and a key feature will be that their pig environments will be highly automated and sophisticated. To some extent computers will help to overcome any shortfalls in stockmanship, but a total commitment to 'virtual management' would be unlikely. This form of pro-duction will be highly acceptable to many who have just discovered the delights and health benefits of eating lean meat.

More discerning consumers, however, particularly in affluent countries, will find such methods of pig production wholly unacceptable. These people will demand wholesome meat reared on systems of which they approve. This cultural divide will be exaggerated by national legislation, and consequently methods of production will reflect these niche markets. Already within Britain there is evidence of imported pigmeat where the contracts have been set up to meet specific UK demands.

Given the high density of the human population within the UK, there will still be many consumers who will continue to demand low-cost pigmeat, and who will show little concern regarding the system of production or the country of origin: their main preoccupation will continue to be price and convenience. And those pig producers in the UK who wish to supply this mass market will only survive if their efficiency equates with, or exceeds, that of

---

Farmers World Network, Farmers Link and the Agricultural Fellowship Submission to House of Commons Agricultural Select Committee on the Likely Effects of Globalization on UK Farming (2000)

Recent farm experience in the US

Pig production has moved away from farms to massive 'confinements', in spite of resultant welfare and environmental problems. Like other industrial activity, they can be moved around the world to exploit the advantage of cheap labour, lax environmental regulation or exchange rates. It is unlikely that pig production of this type would be tolerated in the UK. Farming incomes in the USA are again at rock bottom.

Public requirements

As already earmarked in reference to pig 'confinements', a number of very 'competitive' types of farming are quite unacceptable in this country for reasons of landscape, neighbourly relations, environment or animal welfare. This might be turned into a saving grace for British agriculture. However, current experience with pigs suggests that although public opinion may require high standards in the UK, it may not be able or willing to protect UK producers from competitors with lower standards. If such protection involved 'green box' payments, help might be even less likely.

182

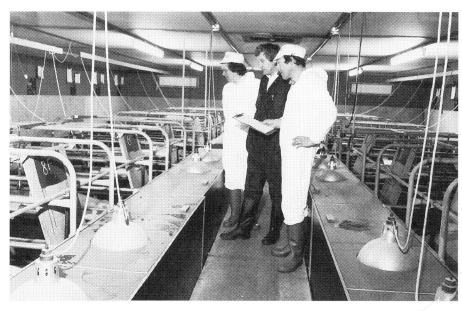

Well trained, motivated people will play key roles on future pig units. (TXU Europe (formerly Eastern Group))

overseas competitors. There is some credibility in the argument that if other countries could provide us with such pigmeat as a low-cost commodity, they should be encouraged to get on with it: UK farmers would then be less in the firing line regarding pollution and animal welfare, and many politicians would be 'let off the hook' – but it goes against our farming instincts.

Commodity markets are notoriously volatile, and with an increasingly global economy those depending solely on such a market could be very vulnerable. Fortunately the UK pig industry has made significant advances in producing wholesome, value-added pigmeat products, but the stark reality is that it must do this even more so in the future. Unless these valuable markets are nurtured, there is a danger that the UK industry as we know it, will be decimated.

There are also indications that some consumers associate wholesomeness with smaller pig units in which there is system transparency and reassuring traceability;

In some countries, large-scale industrialized pig units will help feed vast urban populations. (SEGHERS genetics)

the current vogue for farmers' markets adds weight to this argument. Elsewhere, people in less-developed countries living in rural areas will continue to depend on small pig units for their subsistence. Hence sophisticated big pig units and 'not so big' pig units should both feature in systems of the future.

FEWER ANTIBIOTICS

By whatever means, in the future there will be less reliance on pharmaceuticals and more emphasis on sound husbandry to maintain good health in pigs. Already an industry group called 'RUMA' (the Responsible Use of Medicines in Agriculture Alliance) has been set up to promote animal health through husbandry rather than medication. This group acknowledges the major contribution that antibiotics have made to animal health and welfare, but it urges farmers to 'establish strategies so they have less need for their use'. Scandinavian countries have led the way in discouraging the routine use of antibiotics as growth promoters. A voluntary ban on their use in finishing rations in Denmark had a positive impact on consumers and a variable impact on pigs; in particular, farmers reported an increased incidence of non-specific colitis.

Farming without antibiotics will necessitate changes in management strategies. When growth promoters were first excluded, Danish farmers observed that pigs tended to scour more because of the change in intestinal flora; then after about a month, the gut flora generally stabilized and the problem either disappeared or diminished. In an effort to achieve their goal, the Danes have implemented changes in ration formulation. Nutrient density has been reduced, and ingredients which are not easily digested have been replaced. New strategies have

been developed involving the addition of organic acids to dry feed: once the pH falls below 4.5, harmful bacteria, and particularly coliforms, are killed. Soaking rations for up to eight hours promotes fermentation which has the same effect. The next objective of the Danes is to eliminate antibiotic growth promoters from weaner pigs.

Probiotics have been around since Roman times, if not earlier, but their potential benefit to pigs has only been commercially exploited to any degree since the early 1980s. For example, the use of *lactobacilli* to eliminate coliforms from the gut of the pig has apparently worked wonders – *sometimes*. Recent work at Scotland's Rowett Research Institute has helped to unravel the mystery as to why probiotics have a variable response (in this instance, science followed the art), and there is now every likelihood that a more consistent, positive outcome will result from probiotic use as their mode of operation becomes better understood.

New thinking inevitably presents commercial opportunities directed with enthusiasm to a beleaguered pig industry already punch-drunk from 'flavour of the month' products, many of which disappear without trace within a few weeks of their launch. Products pioneered at some obscure university, allegedly achieving excellent results when fed to pigs in distant lands, tend to be associated with a lack of credible data and an excess of marketing hype. Nevertheless, enlightened farmers and their veterinary surgeons are extending the range of products used to fight disease, and are increasingly using these to complement new management strategies. Most producers know someone who seems to have gained market advantage by giving pigs acidified drinking water, by manipulating bacteria populations, using probiotics, or minerals such as copper sulphate and zinc oxide at levels which markedly suppress microbes. The problem is finding a way to quantify the perceived improvement.

Complex sugars already used in human nutrition to promote good health are now being included in pig rations to combat disease. How or why they work is largely unexplained, but results indicate an encouraging degree of success in lessening the impact of pathogens. Mannan oligo-saccharides are one such substance, with a metabolic pathway as tortuous as the product name. These are complex carbohydrates prepared from the yeast cell wall of *Saccharomyces cerevisiae*, its main components being mannan (30 per cent), glucan (30 per cent) and protein ($12^1/_2$ per cent); the cell wall has powerful antigenic stimulating properties, and this is attributed to the mannan content. The reason why yeast is biologically widespread throughout many animal species is because of its ability to resist degradation by acids. This characteristic could be useful in combating disease in pigs.

There is now evidence emerging that if mannans are added to feed, they can be identified by harmful bacteria and these then 'lock on' to these pathogens rather than the gut wall. The clever bit is that the mannans pass directly through the gut and are not broken down. Imagine them therefore as a Red Cross convoy, given a free passage in their task of removing 'nasties' from the gut. This new thinking could form a key role in fighting pig disease in the future.

IN-FEED ENZYMES AND LOWERED NUTRIENT DENSITY

Throughout the world, the efficacy of in-feed enzymes when added to both wheat- and barley-based broiler diets is well documented. It seems that in-feed enzymes are involved with the digestion of insoluble fibres known as arabinoxylans and betaglucans; these combine with other biochemicals, and tend to encapsulate cereal grains. Unfortunately when enzymes have been added to pig diets, responses have been less favourable than with poultry. However, recent research indicates that in-feed enzymes could in the future have a more beneficial impact on the pig industry: trials indicate that the added enzymes must be species specific, since transit time through the gut of a pig is up to ten times longer than in poultry.

Fibrous foods stimulate the secretion of natural enzymes, which in turn bring about an increased level of cell wall turnover. The fibre presents such a challenge to the gut that compared to the substrate on offer, excessive levels of enzymes are secreted. This is 'expensive' in terms

Enzymes added to finishing rations have been shown to keep pigs cleaner. (ABN Ltd)

*Eastbrook Farms
have pioneered
organic pigmeat
production.
(Eastbrook
Farms)*

of energy and protein breakdown, and much protein is lost directly into the gut. However, recent trials have shown that when weaners were offered barley-based diets with added betaglucanase, there was a reduction in this endogenous enzyme production.

It is likely that in the future the pig industry will see more benefit from in-feed enzymes, these benefits taking the form of increased growth rates and improved feed conversion. Furthermore, the ability of in-feed enzymes to 'lift' the digestibility of cereals should help to make raw materials less variable. Pigs fed rations with in-feed enzymes tend to be cleaner and, because of improved digestibility, nitrate and phosphate levels in muck and slurry are reduced. In other words, biotechnology will be used to improve the welfare of the pig, reduce pollution of the environment, and boost profits for the commercial producer.

If there is going to be less dependence on antibiotic growth promoters, it is likely that the specification of pig rations will also be lowered. Research has indicated that diets containing 15 to 16 per cent crude protein can be fed to growers without impairing growth rate or feed efficiency as long as the optimum balance of amino acids is supplied. Again, following the poultry industry, there is every likelihood that more synthetic amino acids will be fed to pigs; thus more use of pure lysine, threonine and methionine may be anticipated in the future. A spin-off from this will be less excretion of nitrogen in both urine and faeces, and a less offensive odour when it is spread on fields.

As agriculture becomes 'greener' there will be more uptake of 'environmentally friendly' forms of production. Furthermore, on 7 December 1999, the UK Agriculture Minister announced plans for 'a major switch of farm spending, from production aids to support for the broader rural economy': in fact a total of £106 billion was made available for 'green farming and rural development' over the following seven years.

ORGANIC PIGS

Surely organic pig farming will have an impact on this greening process. Particularly within the UK, the present

186

demand for organic pigmeat exceeds the current capacity of pig farmers to produce it. This is not a comfortable situation for profit-motivated supermarket buyers who are calling for more home-based production. The costs of running an organic pig farming system are much higher than those associated with a conventional system, and the selling price of the end product must reflect this. How long will a worthwhile premium last? There are reports from Scandinavia that the organic market is of a finite size, restricted by the fact that only a certain number of consumers are willing to pay extra for the product. A survey from Danske Slagterier suggests that pricing organic pigmeat at a premium of 30 per cent would result in a paltry 4 to 7 per cent increase in the market share over the next five years. If, however, the price premium were restricted to 20 per cent, the projected growth in Denmark would be 19 per cent.

> A sow doth sooner than a cow bring an oxen to
> the plough.   (Gloucestershire proverb)

Anyone intending to set up an organic pig unit must appreciate that the pig venture would have to fit into an overall commitment to organic practices on the farmland. In many instances arable and pig farmers have worked well together for their mutual benefit on conventional outdoor pig ventures: the organic option demands an even closer integration. The basic standards for organic farming production, processing, control and inspection are governed by EEC Regulation 2092/91. The UK Register of Organic Food Standards (UKROFS) regulates the certifying bodies in Britain, the main one being the Soil Association. Basically, unless produce conforms to specified standards, it is illegal to label and market it as 'organic'. Details of the requirements for organic pig production are published by the Soil Association: 'Organic farming

---

Statutory Requirements of Organic Farming Systems

- Two-year conversion period before full organic status is achieved (a progressive conversion of the farm is allowed).

- Adequate physical and financial separation of organic and non-organic units under the same management.

- Application to, inspection by, and certification with, an approved inspection body, such as Soil Association Certification Ltd.

- Adequate records must be kept to demonstrate compliance with the standards.

- Annual monitoring and inspection by the approved certification body.

- Strict requirements for labelling and for the use of additives and processing aids.

- Imported organic foods must have been produced and inspected to an equivalent standard.

Source: The Soil Association

---

means safe, GMO-free, nutritious, delicious food, a cleaner environment, biodiversity, superb animal welfare, more skilled jobs on farms, lower fossil fuel usage ... the list of benefits goes on and on ...' (Helen Browning OBE, Eastbrook Farms).

During 1998–99, UK sales from organic food topped £390 million and, to date, the UK organic market is growing at 40 per cent; moreover, in Europe the organic market has grown over a ten-year period by 25 per cent per annum and there is talk of up to a third of EU agriculture being organic by 2010. However, despite this tidal wave of innovation, developments within organic pig production have been relatively slow. When a three-year

The Principles of Organic Farming International Federation of Organic Agriculture Movements

- To work with natural systems rather than seeking to dominate them.
- To encourage and enhance biological cycles within the farming system, involving micro-organisms, soil flora and fauna, plants and animals.
- To maintain and increase the long-term fertility of soils.
- To use as far as possible renewable resources in locally organized agricultural systems.
- To work as much as possible within a closed system with regard to organic matter and nutrient elements.
- To give all livestock conditions of life that allow them to perform all aspects of their innate behaviour.
- To avoid all forms of pollution that may arise from agricultural techniques.
- To maintain the genetic diversity of the agricultural system and its surroundings, including the protection of plant and wildlife habitats.
- To allow agricultural producers an adequate return and satisfaction from their work including a safe working environment.
- To consider the wider social and ecological impact of the farming system.
- To produce food of high nutritional quality in sufficient quantity.

The Soil Association Certification Process for Organic Farming

- Submit your application for initial screening (application form, licensing fee and map).
- Inspector contacts you to arrange an inspection date.
- Inspection of operation – inspector completes report and discusses any action required.
- Producer certification team reviews inspector's report and recommendations (some reports may be referred to the Certification Committee for a final decision).
- Compliance form with details of the certification decision and any specific actions required is sent to you.
- Sign compliance form to indicate you can comply with the requirements (full requirements for certification detailed in the Standards for Organic Food and Farming).
- Certificate of Registration issued, valid for one year. NOTE: This certificate will only enable you to market your product as organic when the necessary conversion periods have been completed.

study was set up in May 1999 by the Centre for Organic Agriculture at Aberdeen University and ADAS Consulting Ltd, they discovered that there were only thirty-eight organic pig farms in the UK, representing a total of only 1,181 sows. This important study aims to monitor production and define best practice.

A challenge for organic pig production is to find ways of lessening feed costs. Ideally all feed given to organic pigs must be grown from organic sources, though at present, in practice it is possible to use up to 20 per cent of the daily dry matter intake from non-organic sources. There is, however, one feed company known as 'The Organic Feed Company' that specializes in producing natural, wholesome organic feed at an affordable cost. Several other innovators have also grasped the organic opportunity: for instance Sainsbury's are reputed to be the first UK supermarket to produce 'own label' organic pork sausages: they have developed a co-operative venture with East Brook Farms, Wiltshire, the pioneers of organic pig production in Britain.

To predict that organic pig production will expand substantially in the UK looks a safe bet. Quantifying the degree of this predicted expansion is the greater challenge.

IMPROVED PIG ENVIRONMENTS

The need for 'greener' production and the quest for better environments for farm workers will motivate the development of new concepts in pig buildings. The working environment will become less dusty and not quite so smelly. Increasingly pigs will be accommodated in large, labour-efficient, well-planned yards with finely tuned ventilation systems; such housing will become a more important component of differentiated end products. Already new concepts such as 'The Big Pen' layout have been adapted from the broiler industry: these systems allow good observation

of pigs, and call for less expenditure on gating and pen divisions. The practice of ad lib feeding means there is no need for a feed passage, and much of this extra space will be made available to the pigs. Such developments will help to complement the effort being made to cut down on antibiotic use.

IDENTIFICATION, HANDLING AND TRANSPORT

EU Council Directive 64/432 called for, amongst other things, the indelible marking of pigs so that their holdings of origin could be traced. This edict, and the need to develop novel feeding systems, should help to advance the electronic identification of pigs. The technology is already available to identify, track and monitor any valuable asset, and undoubtedly it will be used increasingly for the benefit of the pig industry.

Pig farmers of the future will make increasing use of 'radio frequency identifi-

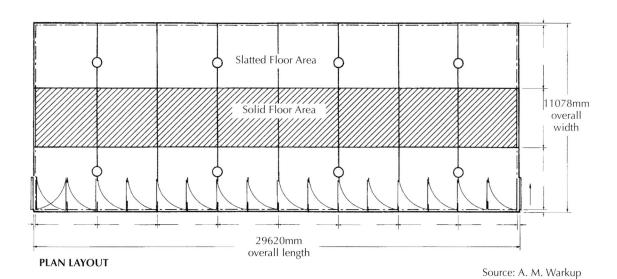

PLAN LAYOUT

Source: A. M. Warkup

Part-slatted Big Pen finishing house.

Well planned, finely tuned, pig-friendly systems will be developed. (Newsham Hybrid Pigs Ltd)

Early weaned pigs on a part-slatted, environment-controlled, 'Big Pen' system. (Newsham Hybrid Pigs Ltd)

Finishing pigs in a 'Big Pen' layout with push-through mucking out. (Newsham Hybrid Pigs Ltd)

cation' (RFID), commonly known as 'electronic identification' (EID). Identification and management will be eased by the use of electronic tags which will be read by hand-held computers (HHC), hand-held readers, and on large pig farms and at abattoirs, via static readers. Hand-held data loggers will become the working tools of the stockman of tomorrow. They will facilitate the harnessing of the power of the office computer, such that individual pig identification will be available within the pig pen or weigh passage. At a glance, the life history of individual pigs will become available, and pen-side electronic input of diary data will become a routine procedure.

Initially, compact, durable electronic ear tags will be the vehicle for this technology; eventually, lifetime identification via injectable subcutaneous devices will become a widespread practice. The relaxation of rabies regulations and the trend towards electronic tagging of companion animals will help drive this development.

Weighing pigs never was a pleasant chore, but improved technology is likely to make it into a pig-friendly automatic process. How useful it would be if a ten-week-old weaner could be weighed, and

from a single reading its slaughterweight accurately predicted! But in fact, workers at Silsoe Research Institute have brought this dream near to becoming a reality for commercial pig farmers of the future. The technique involves using a camera to capture a plan view of a pig when visiting a

Electronic knowhow has enabled group-housed sows to be identified individually. (Rattlerow Farms Ltd)

feeder station. The scientists have then refined this technique, known as 'visual image analysis' (VIA), such that its accuracy may be comparable with conventional weighing: they have developed a pig growth model, and calibrated it, using trial results, and have recorded an impressive fit between the actual weight and the weight predicted from visual image analysis. Already at Silsoe, VIA has been used to fine-tune phase feeding, and this has resulted in a saving of £3 a pig in trial work. Considering the widespread use of security cameras in both public and domestic locations, it seems highly likely that VIA could become widely available in pig farms of the future.

Given the abolition of border controls within the EU, attention is bound to be increasingly focused on avoiding the spread of disease by sick pigs in transit. This will be a commercial necessity: the 1993 importation of pigs infected with classical swine fever cost the Belgian economy around 75 million ECU. Computers will therefore soon be used to monitor pigs in transit, not only to pinpoint their geographical position, but more important, to monitor their welfare

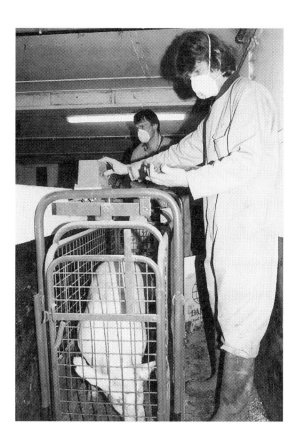

Weighing pigs never was a pleasant chore. (ABN Ltd)

– indeed, work at Belgium's University of Leuven is well on its way to making this a reality. Information will be transmitted from the deck of the haulier's lorry to a computer screen in an abattoir or vigilant veterinary centre, and on receipt of this the movement of any diseased pigs could be curtailed. Inevitably such systems would also be used to monitor the condition of pigs in transit, and those known to be stressed would be given extra lairage time at the abattoir. Furthermore, as traffic density increases on Europe's crowded roads, stressed pigs stuck in traffic would be re-directed to a more accessible abattoir. Quite apart from the welfare implications, this will also influence the efficiency of throughput in lairages and abattoirs, and this in turn

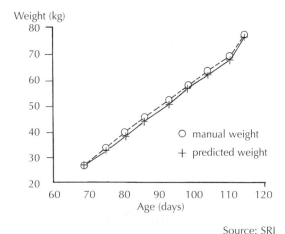

Source: SRI

Change with age of manual weight and predicted weight.

Visual image analysis (VIA) could make conventional pig weighing obsolete. (Silsoe Research Institute)

will reduce the likelihood of any drop in pigmeat quality, since quality is directly related to stress.

A SHARPER FOCUS

During a horrendously difficult time for the pig industry, the British Pig Industry Support Group (BPISG) emerged at grass-roots level and its unbridled enthusiasm took the industry by storm. It aimed to give pig people a greater say in their own destiny, and its explosive emergence shook existing organizations who were caught in an accident of history. It unashamedly forced changes of both structure and attitude within pig politics.

A positive outcome was the establishment of the British Pig Executive (BPEX) which was set up to give the pig industry a sharper focus. Generic promotion of meat has been, and will always be, important, and it is also vital that those who best understand both the potential and the actual problems of the modern pig industry, and are committed to it, should have more say in their own affairs. This is starting to happen. BPEX now decides on the strategic priorities for pig research and development and other pig activities, and these are managed by the Meat and Livestock Commission. Agreed technical strategic objectives are:

- To generate, through research and development, a flow of new products, processes and technologies that will create a competitive advantage for the British pig industry.
- To provide clear technical advice and services to help the British pig industry develop a competitive advantage, and to reassure consumers about the benefits of eating meat.
- To improve the level of training, technical expertise and qualifications in the meat industry.

Research, development and technology interaction activities include:

- Re-engineering of the cost base to improve the competitive position of the British pigmeat industry.
- Segmentation and differentiation of British pigmeat.

Another BPEX objective is to make pig producers aware of lost opportunities because of lack of uptake of commercially relevant research. The industry has repeatedly called for a more pro-active approach to the marketing of pigmeat. More aggressive advertising campaigns have already been launched and will no doubt be a feature of future marketing policy if this approach bears fruit.

Globally there are great opportunities for the pig industry, and BPEX will strive to ensure that the UK sector receives a worthwhile slice of the action. It will not

be a job for the faint-hearted. The future industry will be steered by people with marketing flair and a sound grasp of pig science and technology. New developments will not eliminate pig problems, but simply change their nature. Whatever complexities future production entails, the end product will only be delivered so long as the industry continues to attract people who 'just like pigs'.

Future trends in the pigmeat industry may perhaps be summarized thus:

- Pig welfare will be a key issue to some consumers, but not to others.
- This differentiation will define systems of production and market outlets.
- Biotechnology will be used judiciously for the benefit of consumers.
- Developments in electronics will have a major impact on systems of production and work quality.
- Organic production will increase.
- A much more focused pig industry will develop.

Electronics will be used to identify pigs and record data. (Oxley Systems)

Further Information —

USEFUL CONTACTS

ABN Ltd
ABN House, PO Box 250, Oundle Road,
Peterborough, Cambridgeshire, PE2 9QF
Tel: 01733 422744,
Fax: 01733 422843,
Mobile: 0802 596729,
E-mail: smcgarve@britishsugar.co.uk
Pig feed company

Alltech (UK) Ltd
Alltech House, Ryhall Road,
Stamford, Lincolnshire PE9 1TZ
Tel: 01780 764512,
Fax: 01780 764506,
E-mail: tarcher@alltech-bio.com
Web: www.alltech-bio.com
Suppliers of biotech products

Anglia Quality Meat Association Ltd
8 The Lanterns, Royston,
Hertfordshire, SG8 7UU
Tel: 01763 241222,
Fax: 01763 248923
Livestock marketing co-operative

Antec International Ltd
Windham Road,
Chilton Industrial Estate,
Sudbury, Suffolk, CO10 2XD
Tel: 01787 377305,
Fax: 01787 310846,
E-mail:
        antecinternational@compuserve.com
Web: www.antecint.com
*Manufacturers and suppliers of
biosecurity products*

AOT Proterma
Amsterdam,
Holland
Tel: +3120 626 3620
Fax: +3120 624 7620
Pigs futures market

Arato Pig Drinkers
Willow Farm, Mill Lane, Weeley Heath,
Clacton-on-Sea, Essex, CO16 9BZ
Tel: 01255 830288,
Fax: 01255 831532,
Mobile: 0468 154001,
E-mail: arato-uk@freeuk.com
Suppliers of pig drinkers and plumbing

Assured British Pigs
PO Box 68, Stourport-on-Severn,
Worcestershire, DY13 8ZD
Tel: 01299 829000,
Fax: 01299 829111,
Mobile: 07801 859428,
E-mail: marcusw@abm.org.uk
*The National Quality Assurance
scheme for pig farms*

G. E. Baker (UK) Ltd (Quality
Equipment)
Heath Road, Woolpit, Bury St Edmunds,
Suffolk, IP30 9RN
Tel: 01359 240529,
Fax: 01359 242086,
E-mail: baker@quality-equipment.co.uk
Web: www.quality-equipment.co.uk
Pig equipment specialists

Berkshire College of Agriculture
Hall Place, Burchetts Green,
Maidenhead, Berkshire, SL6 6QR
Tel: 01628 824444,
Fax: 01628 824695,
E-mail: enquiries@bca.rmplc.co.uk
Web: www.berks-coll-ag.ac.uk
*Training and education in pig
management*

BOCM Pauls Ltd
PO Box 39, 47 Key Street,
Ipswich, Suffolk, IP4 1BX
Tel: 01473 232222,
Fax: 01473 230509,
E-mail:
  marketing.pig.poultry@bocmpauls.co.uk
Web: www.bocmpauls.co.uk
Pig feed company

British Pig Association
Scotsbridge House,
Scots Hill, Rickmansworth,
Hertfordshire, WD3 3BB
Tel: 01923 695295,
Fax: 01923 695347,
Mobile: 0421 070434,
E-mail: bpa@farmline.com
Web: www.britishpigs.org
Promotion of pedigree pigs

British Society of Animal Science
PO Box 3, Penicuik,
Midlothian, EH26 0RZ
Tel: 0131 445 4508
Fax: 0131 535 3120
E-mail: BSAS@ed.sac.ac.uk
Web: www.bsas.org.uk
An association of animal scientists

Cambac JMA Research
Manor Farm,
Draycot Cerne,
Chippenham,
Wiltshire, SN15 5LD
Tel: 01249 758868, Fax: 01249 750143,
E-mail: lemanoir@aol.com
Pig research company

E. Collinson & Co Ltd
Riverside Industrial Park,
Catterall,
Preston, Lancashire, PR3 0HP
Tel: 01995 606451,
Fax: 01995 605503,
E-mail: info@collinson.co.uk
Web: www.collinson.co.uk
Pig feed equipment manufacturers

Comfoot Flooring
Walnut Tree,
Redgrave Road, South Lopham,
Diss, Norfolk
Tel: 01379 687641,
Fax: 01379 688015
Pig floor specialists

Cosikennels (J. A. & P. E. Wright)
Brettenham Manor,
Thetford, Norfolk, IP24 2RP
Tel: 01842 754061,
Fax: 01842 764143,
E-mail: jandpwright@farmline.com
Outdoor pig equipment manufacturers

Cotswold Pig Development Co Ltd
Rothwell,
Market Rasen, LN7 6BJ
Tel: 01472 371591,
Fax: 01472 371445
Pig breeding company and AI

Cover-All UK Ltd
White Rails Farm, Great Melton,
Norwich, Norfolk, NR9 3BX
Tel: 01603 810261,
Fax: 01603 811708,
E-mail: coverall@paston.co.uk
'Duraweave' mobile pig buildings

Danske Slagterier
Axelborg, Axeltoru 3,
1609 Copenhagen V,
Denmark
Tel: +33 116050,
Fax: +33 116814
Danish Slaughter Houses Association

Easton College
Easton, Norwich, Norfolk, NR9 5DX
Tel: 01603 731200,
Fax: 01603 741438,
E-mail: staff@easton-college.ac.uk
Training/education in pig management

EFOP: Eastbrook Farm Organic Pigs
36 Station Road,
Framlingham, Woodbridge,
Suffolk, IP12 4AU
Tel: 01728 723170,
Fax: 01728 621160
*A joint venture between organic pioneers,
Eastbrook Farms Organic Meat and
vertical integrator*

Euro Tier (DLG)
Eschborner Landster 122
60489
Frankfurt
Germany
Tel: +4969 247 88254
Fax: +4969 247 88113
German Pig Fair

Farm Animal Welfare Council
1a Page Street,
London, SW1P 4PQ
Tel: 020 7904 6531,
Fax: 020 7904 6533,
E-mail: s.wilson@aw.maff.gov.uk
Web:
www.gov.uk/animalh/welfare/default.htm
*Independent welfare advisers to
government*

Farm Energy Centre
National Agricultural Centre,
Stoneleigh Park,
Kenilworth,
Warwickshire, CV8 2LS
Tel: 024 7669 6512,
Fax: 024 7669 6360,
E-mail: info@farmenergy.com
Web: www.farmenergy.com
Advisers on efficient use of electricity

Farmex Ltd
Pingewood Business Estate,
Pingewood, Reading,
Berkshire, RG30 3UR
Tel: 0118 986 7532,
Fax: 0118 931 4432,
Mobile: 0831 402470
E-mail: hugh@farmex.co.uk,
Web: www.farmex.com
Environment control specialists

Forum Products Ltd
41–51 Brighton Road,
Redhill,
Surrey, RM1 6YS
Tel: 01737 773711,
Fax: 01737 770053,
Web: www.forum.co.uk
Suppliers of enzymes etc.

Freedom Food Ltd
The Manor House,
Causeway,
Horsham, West Sussex, RH12 1HG
Tel: 01403 223154,
Fax: 01403 211514,
E-mail: freedom-food@rspca.org.uk
Web: www.rspca/org.uk
*The RSPCA's farm animal welfare
labelling scheme*

Garth & Integra Veterinary Group
Garth House,
Straight Lane, Beeford,
 Driffield, East Yorkshire, YO25 8BE
Tel: 01262 488323,
Fax: 01262 488770,
E-mail: garth@garth.demon.co.uk
Web: www.garth.demon.co.uk
Specialists in pig health

Harper Adams University College
Edgmond, Newport,
Shropshire, TF10 8NB
Tel: 01952 820280,
Fax: 01952 814783,
E-mail: gscott@harper-adams.ac.uk
Training/education in pig management

J. Harvey Engineering
Parham Airfield, Framlingham,
Woodbridge, Suffolk, IP13 9AF
Tel: 01728 723083,
Fax: 01728 621071,
E-mail: harv@jharveyeng.freeserve.co.uk
*Manufacturers of outdoor pig keeping
equipment*

Health and Safety Executive
National Agricultural Centre,
Stoneleigh Park, Warwickshire, CV8 2LZ
Tel: 024 7669 6518,
Fax: 024 7669 6542,
Web: www.open.gov.uk/hse
Health and safety inspectors

JSR Healthbred
Northern SDS Centre,
Thorpe Willoughby,
Selby,
North Yorks, YO8 9NL
Southern SDS Centre,
Hilperton,
Wiltshire, BA14 7RN
Freephone: 0800 97 98 99,
E-mail: jsr.healthbred@farmline.com
AI

JSR Healthbred Ltd
Southburn, Driffield,
East Yorkshire, YO25 9ED
Tel: 01377 229264,
Fax: 01377 229403,
E-mail: jsr.healthbred@farmline.com
Web: www.jsr.co.uk
Pig breeding company

Meat and Livestock Commission
PO Box 44,
Winterhill House,
Snowdon Drive, Milton Keynes,
Buckinghamshire, MK6 1AX
Tel: 01908 677577,
Fax: 01908 671722
*Technical information/pigmeat
promotion*

Ministry of Agriculture, Fisheries and Food
Nobel House,
17 Smith Square,
London, SW1P 3JR
Tel: 0645 335577,
Fax: 0207 270 8419,
E-mail: helpline@inf.maff.gov.uk
Web: www.maff.gov.uk
Animal health and welfare information

National Centre for Pig Industry Training
Bishop Burton College,
Bishop Burton,
Beverley, East Yorkshire, HU17 8QG
Tel: 01964 553076,
Fax: 01964 553101,
Mobile: 0589 050401,
E-mail: philipsa@bishopb-college.ac.uk,
Web: www.bishopb-college.ac.uk/ncpit
Training/education in pig management

National Pig Association
PO Box 29072, London, WC2H 8QS
Tel: 020 7331 7650,
Fax: 020 7331 7630,
Mobile: 07715 174997,
E-mail: mike.sheldon@npanet.org.uk,
Web: www.npa-uk.net
*The 'single voice' representing the UK pig
industry*

National Pork Producers Council
P. O. Box 10383
Des Moines
IA 50306-0383
USA
Pig promotion/lobby group

Newsham Hybrid Pigs Ltd
Malton, North Yorkshire, YO17 6TD
Tel: 01653 697977,
Fax: 01653 694475,
E-mail: sales@newsham.co.uk,
Web: www.newsham.co.uk
Pig breeding company/AI

The Organic Feed Company
Allen & Page,
Norfolk Mill.
Shipdham,
Thetford, Norfolk, IP25 7SD
Tel: 01362 822900,
Fax: 01362 822910,
E-mail: allenandpage@dial.pipex.com
Organic pig feed specialists

PIC UK
Fyfield Wick,
Abingdon,
Oxfordshire, OX13 5NA
Tel: 01865 822200,
Fax: 01865 820187,
E-mail: ukinfo@pic.com
Web: www.pic.com
Pig breeding company and AI

PIGSPEC
The Garden House,
East Avenue,
Brundall, Norwich,
Norfolk, NR13 5PB
Tel: 01603 713073,
Fax: 01603 713073,
E-mail: pigspec@btinternet.com
Web: www.freeform.co.uk/pigspec
Independent pig consultancy

Porcofram Marketing
Olympia Mills,
Barlby Road,
Selby, Yorkshire, YO8 5AF
Tel: 01757 244055,
Fax: 01757 244066
Pig marketing specialists

Premier Genetics (a division of UPB Ltd)
Maitland Road,
Lion Business Park,
Needham Market, Ipswich,
Suffolk, IP6 8NW
Tel: 01449 722700,
Fax: 01449 722026,
E-mail: www.upb-porcofram.com
Pig breeding company

Premier Genetics AI Centre
Welborne Common,
East Dereham, Norfolk, NR20 3LD
Tel: 01362 858032,
Fax: 01362 858036
AI specialists

Pyramid Systems (Malton) Ltd
Showfield Lane,
Malton,
North Yorks, YO17 6BT
Tel: 01653 694994,
Fax: 01653 696685,
Mobile: 0802 490072,
E-mail: pyramidsys@farming.co.uk
Pig building manufacturers

Rare Breeds Survival Trust
National Agricultural Centre,
Stoneleigh Park,
Warwickshire, CV8 2LG
Tel: 01203 696551,
Fax: 01203 696551,
E-mail: rbst@demon.co.uk
Web: www.countrylife.org.uk/rbst
        or www.farmshop.net
Conservers of rare breeds

Rattlerow Farms Ltd
Hill House Farm, Stradbroke,
Suffolk, IP21 5NB
Tel: 01379 384304,
Fax: 01379 388272,
E-mail: k.poulson@farming.co.uk
Pig breeding company

SAC
West Mains Road,
Edinburgh, Midlothian, EH9 3JG
Tel: 0131 535 4000,
Fax: 0131 667 2601,
E-mail: b.sheppard@ed.sac.ac.uk
Web: www.sac.ac.uk
Pig research, education and advice

SEGHERS genetics Ltd
Grosvenor Mansions, Queen Street,
Deal, Kent, CT14 6ET
Tel: 01304 363363,
Fax: 01304 380795,
E-mail: uk-genetics@bettersciences.com
Pig breeding company

Silsoe Research Institute
Wrest Park, Silsoe,
Bedford, MK45 4HS
Tel: 01525 860000,
Fax: 01525 860156,
E-mail: sri.pr@bbsrc.ac.uk
Web: www.sri.bbsrc.ac.uk
Agricultural engineering researchers

Soil Association
Bristol House, 40-56 Victoria Street,
Bristol, BS1 6BY
Tel: 0117 929 0661,
Fax: 0117 925 0661,
E-mail: info@soilassociation.org
Web: www.soil-association.org
*Organic farming certification/general
information*

Rod Tuck Consultancy T/a Tuck Box Ltd
The Brambles, Burston, Diss,
Norfolk, IP22 3TH
Tel: 01379 741458,
Fax: 01379 741495,
E-mail: tuckbox98@aol.com
Web: www.tuckbox.co.uk
Creep feed specialists

United Kingdom Register of Organic
Food Standards (UKROFS)
301-344 Market Towers,
New Covent Garden, London, SW8 5NQ
Tel: 0207 7202144
Organic food registration authority

United Pig Marketing
Riverside House, Warlock Road,
Carlisle, Cumbria, CA1 2BJ
Tel: 01228 541566
Co-ordinator of marketing organizations

Unitron (UK) Ltd
Clay Cottage,
Clay Street,
Walsham Le Willows,
Bury St Edmunds, Suffolk, IP31 3BH
Tel: 01359 259452,
Fax: 01359 259452,
Mobile: 07771 923354
E-mail: unicamp@tesco.net
*Specialist supplier of AI and other pig
equipment*

A. M. Warkup
Aerodrome Works,
Lissett, Driffield,
East Yorkshire, YO25 8PT
Tel: 01262 468666,
Fax: 01262 468656,
Mobile: 0836 713727
E-mail: amwarkup@amwarkup.co.uk,
Web: www.amwarkup.co.uk
Pig building manufacturers

William White Fabrications Ltd
Blyth Road Industrial Estate,
Bramfield Road,
Halesworth,
Suffolk, IP19 8EN
Tel: 01986 874311,
Fax: 01986 845515,
Mobile: 07986 161881
E-mail: sales@wwf.demon.co.uk
Pig equipment specialists

WEBSITES

Antec International:
www.antecint.com

Elanco:
www.elanco.com

5M Enterprises Ltd 2000:
www.thepigsite.com

Farmers Weekly Interactive:
www.fwi.co.uk

Ministry of Agriculture
Animal Health & Veterinary Group:
www.maff.gsi.gov.uk

Ministry of Agriculture Fisheries & Food:
www.maff.gov.uk/maffhome.htm

National Farmers Union:
www.nfu.net.org.uk

National Pig Association:
www.npa-uk.net

Pig Disease Information Centre
www.pighealth.com

PIGSPEC:
www.freeform.co.uk/pigspec

Pigs UK:
www.pigsuk.com

Pig World:
www.pigworld.org

Tribune:
www.weekly-tribune.co.uk

Whole Hog:
www.wholehog.org

FURTHER READING

Books

ADAS *Building and Equipment Directory 2000* (ADAS Consulting Ltd 2000).

Carr, J. *Garth Pig Stockmanship Standards* (5M Enterprises Ltd 1998).

Caygill, J. C. and Mueller-Harvey, I. *Secondary Plant Production — Anti-Nutritional and Beneficial Actions in Animal Feeding* (Nottingham University Press 1999).

Close, W. H. and Cole, D. J. A. *Nutrition of Sows and Boars* (Nottingham University Press 2000).

D'Mello, J. P. F. (Ed) *Farm Animal Metabolism and Nutrition* (CABI Publishing 2000).

Done, S. (Ed) *Proceedings of the Fifteenth International Pig Veterinary Society Congress* (Nottingham University Press, July 1998).

English, P. R., Burgess, G., Cochran, R. S. and Dunne, J. *Stockmanship: Improving the Care of the Pig and other Livestock* (ISBN 0 85236 236 6 (1992)).

English, P. R., Fowler, V. R., Baxter, S. H. and Smith W. J. *The Growing and Finishing Pig* (Farming Press 1996).

Ewing, W. N. *The Feeds Directory* (Context Publishing 1997).

Gordon, I. *Controlled Reproduction in Pigs* (CABI Publishing 1999).

Gregory, N. G. *Animal Welfare and Meat Science* (CABInternational Publishing 1998).

Hemsworth, P. H. and Coleman, G. J. *Human – Livestock Interactions – The Stockperson and Productivity and Welfare of Intensively Farmed Animals* (CAB International Publishing 1998).

Muirhead, M. R. and Alexander, T. J. L. *A Pocket Guide to Recognising and Treating Pig Diseases* (5M Enterprises Ltd 1998).

National Research Council, USA *The Use of Drugs in Food Animals — Benefits and Risks* (CABI Publishing/National Academy Press 1999).

Smith, W. J. Taylor, D. J. and Penny, R. H. C. *A Colour Atlas of Diseases and Disorders of the Pig* (Wolfe Publications 1990).

Stark, B. A. Machin, D. H. and Wilkinson, M. J. (Ed). *Outdoor Pigs: Principles and Practice* (Chalcombe Publications 1995).

Stewart, C. S. and Flint, H. J. (Ed) *Escherichia coli 0157 in Farm Animals* (CABI Publishing 1999).

Taylor, D. J. *Pig Diseases* (Farming Press 1995).

Thornton, K. *Outdoor Pig Production* (Farming Press 1990).

Underwood, E. J. and Suttle, N F. *The Mineral Nutrition of Livestock* (CABI Publishing 1999).

Warriss, P. D. *Meat Science — An Introductory Text* (CABI Publishing 2000).

Wiseman, J., Varley, M. A., and Chadwick, J. B. (Ed). *Progress in Pig Science* (Nottingham University Press 1998).

Periodicals

International Pig Topics
Positive Action Publications
PO Box 4
Driffield
East Yorkshire
YO25 9DJ
Tel: 01377 241724

Pig Farming
Miller Freeman
Miller Freeman House
Sovereign Way
Tonbridge
Kent
TN9 1RW

Pig International
Watt Publishing Co
18 Chapel Street
Petersfield
Hanpshire
GU32 3DZ
Tel: 01730 261951

Pig Progress
Elsevier International
PO Box 4
7000 BA
Doetinchem
Netherlands
Fax: + 31 314 340515

Pig World
Arnford Publications
PO Box 100
Benniworth, Market Rasen
Lincolnshire
LN8 6LE
Tel: 01507 313798

Tribune
(British Pig & European Pig Markets)
Maycroft House
Toothill Road, Ongar
Essex
CM5 9LH
Tel/Fax: 01379 643961

Whole Hog
Arnford Publications
PO Box 100
Benniworth
Market Rasen
Lincolnshire
LN8 6LE
Tel: 01507 313798

Glossary

***ad libitum* (ad lib) feeding** The unrestricted supply of feed, day and night, usually in a dry form.

AI Artificial insemination.

amino acids There are estimated to be twenty-three individual amino acids in pigmeat protein. Eleven of these are so-called essential AAs.

anoestrus Failure to breed.

bacon The brine-cured meat from a pig carcase between 60 and 82kg (132 and 181lb).

baconer (UK) A class of finishing pig destined for bacon curing between 60 and 82kg (132 and 181lb) carcase weight.

back fat The layer of fat usually related to that covering the loin area of the pig's back.

Big Pen A housing system based on large groups of pigs and no feed passage.

biosecurity The strategy for keeping disease out of the herd.

Blue pig The cross of pig resulting from, for example, a British Saddleback and a Landrace.

boar Any uncastrated male pig, normally kept for breeding purposes.

breeding herd The total inventory of gilts, sows, boars and suckling piglets.

breeding pyramid The mechanism for providing commercial herds with superior genes.

carcase The remains of a pig once the gut, pluck and so on are removed, leaving the head, trunk, backbone, feet and kidneys. The tongue is usually included but an EU regulation governs the weight adjustment if it is excluded.

casualty An emergency slaughter pig.

clean pigs Slaughter pigs that exclude entire males and mated or breeding females.

condition score A five- or ten-point scale designed to measure the degree of fat/body reserve in breeding females.

COSHH Regulations 'Control of substances hazardous to health' regulations.

creep An area within the farrowing accommodation away from the sow, constructed to provide warmth, protection and sometimes creep feed and/or milk substitute for piglets.

creep feed Feed designed to be fed to suckling piglets in the creep area.

CT Computer tomography: a body scanning technique.

cycle A term used instead of 'parity' as a measure of a sow, based on the number of completed reproductive cycles. In some computer-recording schemes the gilt remains in the parity 0 until mated to produce her second litter.

Dam The maternal parent, as used in pedigree records.

DIY AI AI administered after collection and processing on the home farm.

Doppler The principle of ultrasound used in Doppler pregnancy testers.

dressed caracase weight The deadweight as a percentage of liveweight.

EHO Environmental health officer.

empty days The number of days between weaning and effective service.

ESF Electronic sow feeding.

F1 hybrid A first cross between two distinct breeds.

farrowing The birth of a litter of one or more live or dead pigs, normally occurring after the 111th day and before the 120th day after mating.

farrowing ark A special outdoor pig hut designed for one sow or gilt to farrow and raise her litter in, with reduced risk of crushing.

farrowing crate Specialized accommodation for the farrowing sow, designed to prevent crushing of piglets.

farrowing index The average number of farrowings per sow per year in a herd.

farrowing interval The time, in days, between two consecutive farrowings for an individual sow.

farrowing nest A free-access nest constructed of wood which provides protection to the piglets and reduces the likelihood of crushing.

farrowing rate The percentage of sows that farrow to service.

FCE Feed conversion efficiency.

FCR Feed conversion ratio: The number of kilograms of feed required to increase liveweight by 1kg.

feeder (UK) Any pig from weaning to slaughter age.

finishing pig Any pig from weaning to slaughter age.

flat deck A form of nursery for weaner pigs based on fully slatted flooring and supplementary heating.

full feeding Feeding pigs a given number of feeds a day, but attempting to satisfy their appetite on each occasion; also known as feeding to appetite.

gestation The period of pregnancy measured in days between effective service and farrowing.

gilt Female pig that has not yet farrowed and reared her first litter.

gilt pool A group of gilts awaiting service, to be used to replace culled sows.

HC boar A boar selected for its conformation attributes.

heavy hogs A class of slaughter pig usually weighing around 110 to 120kg (242 to 265lb) live when sent to the abattoir.

hectare A unit of land measurement (2.47 acres approx.).

heritability The amount of a performance measure that is passed on from one generation to the next; backfat and carcase characteristics are highly heritable, whilst reproductive ones (litter size and so on) are not.

hog Castrated male pig.

hybrid vigour The superior performance of the offspring as compared to the average performance of both parents. In pigs, the increase in numbers born is usually around 10 per cent.

K.O% Killing out percentage. The ratio of a pig's deadweight:liveweight multiplied by one hundred.

lactation The period of time during which a sow produces milk, starting at farrowing and normally ending with weaning.

lairage The pens where pigs are kept prior to slaughter.

litter scatter The percentage of litters with more than, or alternatively less than, a specified number of live piglets (used in computer-based analysis).

liveweight gain The increase in weight between two weighings.

maiden gilt A young female pig, not yet mated for the first time.

maintenance The nutrient requirement of animals for the continuity of the vital body processes.

multiplier breeder A pig keeper who increases or multiplies hybrid or purebred breeding stock for sale to commercial pig producers.

mummified piglets Dead piglets which are born in a discoloured or shrivelled state, because death occurred some time before farrowing.

nucleus breeder The pure-bred herd at the apex of a breeding pyramid which attempts to improve the genetic merit, and passes this on to the commercial producer directly or via a multiplier.

nursery Any specialized housing for the newly weaned pig, including bungalows, veranda units, flat decks and weaner kennels.

NVQ National Vocational Qualification.

oestrus The heat behaviour of females, during which the sow or gilts are receptive to mating by the boar.

oxytocin A hormone released from the pituitary gland at the base of the brain in response to stimulation of the udder, clitoris or cervix. It produces the milk let-down response and assists in contractions of the uterus and related muscles during birth and possibly mating; it is available for injection.

parity The number of times the sow has farrowed, including the expected farrowing. Cycle is often used instead as it is more accurate.

parturition The act of farrowing.

peptide Linked amino acid.

porcine parvovirus A virus affecting fertility that causes the SMEDI syndrome, and found in over 50 per cent of the national herd.

pork Fresh pigmeat.

porker A class of pig being finished for uncured pigmeat at relatively light weights.

probiotics These are feed additives or oral products based on materials of microbial origin which promote health and performance in animals. They are thought to do so by ensuring the most beneficial populations of bacteria in the digestive tract, and are a mixture of various organisms.

progeny testing Now almost universally replaced by performance testing. Involves testing the progeny of one sire and comparing their performance against the average of contemporary sires.

prolapse Either of the womb or rectum – they come outside the body due to weakened muscles or straining. They are both serious conditions.

prostaglandin One of several indictable products available to induce sows to farrow. This hormone switches off the progesterone-producing yellow bodies and triggers birth within twenty-five to thirty-five hours.

PVS Pig Veterinary Society.

return to service A sow showing signs of willingness to mate, usually around eighteen to twenty-four days from the last service.

runt Small, poorly developed pig(s) which can either be born small or get left behind due to inadequate nutrition.

rupture A weakness which allows part of the intestine to be forced either into the scrotum or from the navel (hernia).

scale feeding Feeding to a strict level which is below appetite – usually 75 to 85 per cent of ad lib.

service A single act of mating or copulation – it may be double or triple.

sire A male or paternal father.

sow stall A restrictive form of individual penning, now illegal in the UK.

suckler A piglet between birth and weaning.

suckling pig A piglet between birth and weaning.

weaner A pig which is permanently removed from the sow.

Index